BRITAIN'S
20 WORST
MILITARY
DISASTERS

BRITAIN'S 20 WORST MILITARY DISASTERS

FROM THE ROMAN CONQUEST TO THE FALL OF SINGAPORE

John Withington

First published 2011

Spellmount, an imprint of
The History Press
The Mill, Brimscombe Port
Stroud, Gloucestershire, GL5 2QG
www.thehistorypress.co.uk

British Library Cataloguing in Publication Data.
A catalogue record for this book is available from the British Library.

ISBN 978 0 7524 6197 7

Typesetting and origination by The History Press
Printed in the EU for The History Press.

Contents

Introduction

When I was a boy of eight or nine, I used to stand up in front of morning assembly at my primary school and recite Alfred, Lord Tennyson's 'The Charge of the Light Brigade'. That, I think, was my first encounter with military disasters. Of all the fifty-five lines in the poem, the one that struck me most was: 'Some one had blunder'd', perhaps because it was such a succinct explanation of what had gone wrong in this tragic, heroic episode. The story of the charge is featured in this book, as are plenty of other blunders – arising from bad planning, inadequate intelligence, confused objectives, or plain misjudgement.

But not all military disasters are down to blunders. In fact, they come in many shapes and sizes. Sometimes our forces were simply outclassed by a better-trained and better-organised foe – like the Ancient Britons when confronted by the Romans. Another common failing is underestimation of the enemy. This happened particularly in the colonial era, whether the foe were Afghans, Americans or Zulus. On other occasions, we see basic bad luck and things just going wrong in the fog of war.

Some disasters, like Hastings, were big and bloody battles, and marked a real turning point. Others, such as Yorktown, involved relatively little loss of life, but also had momentous consequences, while episodes like the burning of the fleet in the Medway in 1667 did not have notable long-term effects, but were nonetheless national humiliations. Perhaps it is not surprising that while the names of victories like Agincourt, Trafalgar and Waterloo have resounded down the ages, those of such major reverses as Castillon and Cartagena de Indias are very far from being household names, at least in Britain. Occasionally, a 'victory' might also be a disaster, like the Battle of the Somme, which caused almost unimaginable casualties.

A word about definitions. I have taken British military disasters to mean those suffered by Britain, or part of Britain, at the hands of an enemy from outside Britain, so English defeats at the hands of the Irish, Scots or Welsh, or vice versa, do not qualify.

Finally, a word of thanks to my wife for her unfailing patience, support and encouragement.

1

The Battle of the Medway, AD 43

We do not know exactly where the Battle of the Medway took place, but it was probably one of the biggest ever fought on British soil. It resulted in a decisive defeat for the ancient Britons and was the turning point in the Roman campaign to conquer Britain.

The emperor Caligula was a busy man, if the stories the Romans told about him are to be believed: what with turning his palace into a brothel in which respectable Roman women were forced to serve, throwing spectators to the wild animals in the arena, trying to have his horse made a consul and so on. So perhaps it is not surprising that he called off an invasion of Britain that he had planned for AD 40. Actually at least three other planned expeditions had been called off since Julius Caesar's second incursion nearly a century before, in 54 BC, when the great general stayed for three months and penetrated as far as the Thames Valley, winning victories over British tribes and seizing treasure and hostages.

When Caligula was murdered by his own bodyguards in AD 41, the new emperor, his uncle Claudius, quickly dusted off the invasion plan. Claudius had been surprised, and terrified, when he was chosen to succeed his nephew. Saddled with a reputation as the buffoon of the imperial family, attacking Britain seemed to offer him a couple of opportunities. First – a chance to rapidly establish his authority and prestige, and second – money, which Claudius needed to buy the loyalty of the army. The great Roman historian Tacitus said Britain was then reputed to be a rich country. The land was fertile, yielding produce 'abundantly', and there was 'gold and silver and other metals', while an invasion could also deliver booty and slaves.

Claudius may also have had another motive: the need to put the ancient Britons in their place. In the years since the birth of Christ, the Catuvellauni, who inhabited Hertfordshire, had been extending their lands under their formidable leader, Cunobelinus – Shakespeare's Cymbeline. One tribe who suffered from their ambitions were the Atrebates, who were friendly to Rome. One of Cunobelinus's sons, Adminius, was also pro-Roman, but when the king died in AD 42, his other two sons, Caratacus and Togodumnus, both anti-Roman, took power, and Adminius fled to Rome. Soon he was followed by Verica, the king of the Atrebates. According to the Roman historian Dio Cassius, writing about a century and a half later, it was Verica who persuaded Claudius to intervene. Apart from resenting the dents that the Catuvellauni had put in their prestige, the Romans were also afraid that the Britons might start destabilising the Roman province of Gaul, just across the English Channel.

Rome was confident. The Britons were divided: 'torn apart by the warring parties of different leaders', in Tacitus's words. 'It is very rare that two or more British tribes will come together to repel a common danger' he added. 'They fight separately and separately are defeated.' In AD 43 at Boulogne, Claudius assembled a force of about 20,000 legionaries, who had been serving on the Rhine frontier and in Pannonia (which straddles parts of a number of modern-day countries including Hungary, Austria and Serbia), as well as about 20,000 auxiliaries, recruited from tribes and nations allied to Rome. The expedition was to be led by Aulus Plautius, the governor of Pannonia. Tacitus says he was 'eminent for military abilities', and we know that he had helped suppress a revolt by slaves in Puglia. Beneath him, he had some talented commanders including the future emperor, Vespasian.

There was a problem however. The soldiers would not embark. Roman geographers had shown the known world as being surrounded by water. So what was this 'Britain' place across that great sea? Part of some other world? What would they find there? It did not help that some Roman sailors who had been shipwrecked on the remote island came back with stories, said Tacitus, 'of monsters of the sea, of forms half-human, half beast-like, things they had really seen or in their terror believed.' For up to two months, there was a standoff until Claudius's personal envoy arrived and persuaded the men to get into the ships. The expedition's leaders must have been concerned about how late in the campaigning season it was getting, but the delay may have been a blessing in disguise. The Britons seem to have concluded that the reports they had heard of a great Roman army about to embark must be mistaken. Their enemy would never leave their invasion this late, so the British militia was allowed to go home to get in the harvest.

Dio Cassius says the invasion force crossed the Channel in three groups, and landed unopposed, because the Britons 'had not expected that they would come'. Some at least of the Roman fleet is believed to have come ashore at the natural harbour of Richborough on the east coast of Kent. Once the Romans had arrived, however, the Britons were in no hurry to fight. Instead they drew the invaders on, trying to make them exhaust their supplies; in Dio Cassius's words, taking 'refuge in the swamps and the forests, hoping to wear out the invaders in fruitless effort, so that, just as in the days of Julius Caesar, they should sail back with nothing accomplished.'

The Romans did manage to track down two separate forces led by Caratacus and Togodumnus, and defeat them in skirmishes. Or perhaps the Britons picked a confrontation to test the invaders' strength. As the Romans continued their advance, one of the Catuvellauni's subject tribes surrendered, but by now the British militia had been reassembled and was gathering on the far bank of the Medway. It is not certain exactly where, but many modern historians think it was near Rochester, close to where the M2 bridge now crosses the river. According to some estimates, the Britons' army numbered up to 80,000, which would have meant that they outnumbered the Romans about two to one. If these figures are correct, this would have been the biggest battle ever fought on British soil except perhaps for the Battle of Watling Street (see chapter two).

The Britons had a small nucleus of professional, aristocratic warriors, but the majority of the army were workers on the land. They had some light chariots of a kind long regarded as obsolete on the Continent, but Caesar recognised that during his campaigns, their very unfamiliarity caused some confusion in the Roman ranks. He wrote that the Britons used them for 'driving all over the field hurling javelins' with the idea of generating 'terror inspired by the horses and the noise of the wheels', but they were not sufficiently heavy or armoured to break through determined infantry. Few of the Britons wore armour; they carried only small shields, and used long swords which needed a lot of room to swing, making concerted action difficult and meaning they were less effective at very close quarters. They had plenty of experience of war, but not of confronting a foe like the Romans – the first professional army ever to fight in Britain. The legionaries were heavy infantry, trained to close with the enemy and fight in packed ranks. Each one wore flexible strip armour, which protected the upper body but allowed freedom of movement. The head was protected by a bronze helmet, and they carried wooden shields big enough to screen most of the body. When combined in formation, these created a kind of mobile barricade. Each man carried two javelins and a short double-edged sword. The Romans also had an assortment of catapults and other missile-throwing artillery, but perhaps the greatest difference was that they were well trained and could execute pre-arranged manoeuvres on a signal. They could be detached and sent off to different parts of the field, and could operate en masse or as resourceful individuals. This gave them an operational flexibility the Britons simply could not match. The auxiliaries often added other specialist military skills – serving as cavalry, archers or light infantry – while sometimes they were used as expendable shock troops.

Waiting on the banks of the Medway, the Britons seem to have believed the heavily armed Romans would be unable to cross the river, so, according to Dio Cassius, they 'bivouacked in rather careless fashion'. In fact, among the Roman auxiliaries were men 'accustomed to swim easily in full armour across the most turbulent streams.' Some of these soldiers crossed and landed on the British right flank, taking the enemy completely by surprise, but rather than falling on them, this detachment concentrated on attacking the horses to disable the British chariots. Taking advantage of the chaos that this caused, Plautius then sent over a force of legionaries under Vespasian on the British left, which killed 'many of the foe'. Shaken though they were, the Britons rallied and fought doggedly, so the first day ended without a firm conclusion, which was extremely unusual for a battle of this era, and perhaps evidence that a very large number of men were involved. With the bridgehead on the British left still holding, the Romans used boats, and perhaps even a pontoon bridge, to send over more men to reinforce it, but the next morning, the Britons launched a determined counter-attack. For a time it seemed as though they might win, as they captured a number of leading Roman officers. Then came the crucial moment of the battle, as the commander of the bridgehead, Gnaeus Hosidius Geta, narrowly evaded the Britons and then retaliated so effectively that they were 'soundly' defeated.

It proved to be not just the turning point of the battle, but of the whole campaign, something the Romans recognised by awarding Geta a triumphal procession, a rare honour for someone who had not held the rank of consul. The British survivors managed to retreat and cross the Thames into Essex, seeking to cut off the Roman advance towards the Catuvellauni capital of Colchester. Once again, the Britons tried to take a stand somewhere on the river's banks, and once again Roman auxiliaries swam across, while other soldiers, wrote Dio Cassius, 'got over by a bridge' – possibly a temporary one. This enabled them to attack the enemy from 'several sides at once and cut down many of them'. Soon after – we do not know how – Togodumnus was killed and the emperor Claudius came over to put the finishing touches to the conquest.

Claudius spent sixteen days in Britain, and Dio Cassius says he won a battle himself, though not all historians are convinced that this is true. One of the triumphal arches voted by the senate to celebrate the conquest speaks of eleven British kings surrendering to him. Once he had gone back to Italy, the legions began gradually extending Roman power northwards and westwards. Caratacus, though, escaped and carried on a guerrilla war in the Welsh mountains. In AD 51, he was finally defeated. He sought refuge with the Brigantes tribe in the north of England, but their queen put him in chains and handed him over to the Romans. By then, says Tacitus, his fame had spread to Rome itself, where 'all were eager to see the great man, who for so many years had defied our power.' Claudius had him paraded through the streets with his family, but Caratacus spoke up defiantly, demanding: 'If you Romans choose to lord it over the world, does it follow that the world is to accept slavery?' Then, more subtly, he suggested that if the Romans killed him, he would quickly be forgotten, while if they spared him, he would be 'an everlasting memorial' to Rome's mercy. It did the trick. Caratacus and his family were pardoned, and did homage to the emperor.

2

The Battle of Watling Street, AD 60 or 61

Less than twenty years after the great Roman victory on the Medway, Queen Boudicca of the ancient British Iceni tribe was driven into revolt by the brutal, high-handed treatment she and her people suffered at the hands of the conquerors. Boudicca remains an iconic figure in British history, but her rebellion ended in comprehensive defeat at what may have been the biggest battle ever fought in Britain.

After the victories of AD 43 (see chapter one), the Romans gradually extended the area they governed and, according to Tacitus, 'the nearest part of Britain was reduced into the form of a province'. The Romans' diplomatic and political talents, however, did not match their military skills. In AD 47, tribes from outside the area under Roman control launched an attack. The Romans soon beat them off, but then responded by disarming tribes within their domain, who had been allowed to keep their weapons until then. The Iceni, who lived in Norfolk and the north of Suffolk, were incensed because they had not been conquered but had chosen to become allies of Rome. They rose in revolt, along with other British tribes, but were soon crushed.

History had not heard the last of the Iceni however. In around AD 58, Gaius Suetonius Paulinus became the Roman governor of Britain. Not a great deal is known about what he did before he arrived in Britain, except that he had put down a rebellion by the Moors in North Africa. By around

AD 60, he was in North Wales with the XIVth legion trying to extend Roman rule into Anglesey. Tacitus says he not only had to fight a 'dense array of warriors', but was also confronted by women 'in black attire like the Furies, with hair dishevelled', while the Druids lifted their hands to heaven and poured forth 'dreadful imprecations'. If that was not bad enough, Suetonius received news that the Iceni were in revolt again.

After the little falling out of AD 47, the Iceni's king, Prasutagus – 'famed for his wealth' according to Tacitus – had tried to remain friends with the Romans. He died in AD 59 or 60 (historians cannot agree) and left his estate to be shared between his two teenage daughters and the emperor Nero, who had succeeded Claudius in AD 54, 'under the impression that this token of submission would put his kingdom and his house out of the reach of wrong.' Indeed, leaving part of their estates to the emperor was a device sometimes used by wealthy Romans to try to ensure that the terms of their wills were carried out. The kind of special relationship that Prasutagus had constructed with the Romans, though, often did not survive beyond the death of the individual concerned, and now the empire's top financial officer in Britain, the procurator Decianus Catus, treated the whole of the king's lands as though they belonged to Rome.

Romans helped themselves to the possessions of the Iceni nobility 'as if they were the spoils of war', while relatives of the king were treated like slaves. Prasutagus' widow, Boudicca ('Boadicea', the name by which she used to be more commonly known, seems to have come from a miscopying of Tacitus) was then probably in her thirties and acting as regent. She appears to have protested, and for her pains she was flogged, while her daughters were raped. Not surprisingly, this drove her into revolt. Boudicca, Dio Cassius tells us, was formidable: 'she was very tall, in appearance most terrifying, in the glance of her eye most fierce, and her voice was harsh; a great mass of the tawniest hair fell to her hips.' Besides this, he continues, she was 'possessed of greater intelligence than often belongs to women.'

It was not just the Iceni who were treated in this way. The Romans had also performed the considerable feat of alienating the Trinovantes. Before the conquest, this tribe from southern Suffolk and Essex had fought a long, unsuccessful war with the Catuvellauni (see chapter one), and had seen their lands and their capital, Colchester, taken over. So when the Romans appeared and took the Trinovantes' oppressors down a peg or two, they had a chance to win them over. Instead, they turned Colchester into their first *colonia* in Britain – a place where veterans were given land when they retired from the army. The veterans, though, grabbed more than they were supposed to, and: 'drove people out of their houses, ejected them from their farms, called them captives and slaves.' The Romans also put up a temple to the emperor Claudius, made a god after his death, and those Britons unfortunate enough to be chosen as priests for the cult were forced to 'squander their whole fortunes'. So now the Trinovantes made common cause with the Iceni, as did other tribes 'not yet cowed by slavery'.

When the rebel army had gathered, according to Dio Cassius, Boudicca ascended a mound of earth to address it. She wore her usual outfit – a gold necklace around her neck and a tunic of 'divers' colours' beneath a thick mantle fastened with a brooch. She also held a spear 'to aid her in terrifying all beholders'. In the past, she told them, they may have been deceived by the Romans' 'alluring promises', but now they had learned the difference between freedom and slavery the hard way, and 'how much better is poverty with no master than wealth with slavery.' They had been taxed to the hilt, robbed of their possessions, 'stripped and despoiled'. Would it not be better to be dead? The Britons should have expelled these Romans just as they once beat off Julius Caesar. She continued: '… let us, my countrymen and friends and kinsmen – for I consider you all kinsmen, seeing that you inhabit a single island and are called by one common name – let us, I say, do our duty while we still remember what freedom is, that we may leave to our children not only its name but also its reality. For, if we utterly forget the happy state in which we were born and bred, what, pray, will they do, reared in bondage?'

They should not fear the Romans who were less numerous than them, and less brave, 'and here is the proof: they have protected themselves with helmets and breastplates and greaves'. Not only that but they skulked behind fortifications. What a contrast to the 'rough and ready action' that the Britons preferred. That was not the rebels' only advantage however: if necessary, they could escape to swamps and mountains where their enemies could not find them, they could endure 'hunger, thirst, cold, or heat' far better than the Romans, who needed constant supplies of 'bread and wine and oil' and when they could not get them, they died. For the Britons, on the other hand: 'any grass or root serves as bread, the juice of any plant as oil, any water as wine'. She concluded: 'Let us, therefore, go against them trusting boldly to good fortune. Let us show them that they are hares and foxes trying to rule over dogs and wolves.'

Colchester was first in line for destruction. The city was not fortified, and the rebels overran and razed it almost immediately, massacring the veterans and their families. Next they set off for London, a busy trading centre first established by the Romans shortly after the conquest. A small force from the IXth legion tried to intercept Boudicca's rebels, but she ambushed them and cut the infantry to pieces, while the cavalry fled. At this point, Decianus Catus, 'alarmed by this disaster and by the fury of the province which he had goaded into war by his rapacity', ran off to Gaul. Suetonius had raced back from Anglesey so quickly that he reached London before Boudicca, but came to the conclusion that he did not have enough men to take on her army. So, as Tacitus put it: 'he resolved to save the province at the cost of a single town.' Unimpressed by the 'tears and weeping of the people, as they implored his aid', he took with him only the ones who could keep up with his army. Those 'chained to the spot by the weakness of their sex, or the infirmity of age, or the attractions of the place' were abandoned to be massacred by the rebels while London was completely destroyed for the only time in its history. Nor was that the end of the devastation. A month later, St Albans went the same way. By this point Dio Cassius reckons that Boudicca's host had killed 80,000, and recounts some particularly revolting ways in which victims were alleged to have been put to death. The figure probably represents a huge exaggeration, but the slaughter was plainly terrible.

Meanwhile, Suetonius had managed to scratch together a force of about 10,000 drawn from the XIVth and XXth legions supplemented by auxiliaries from nearby garrisons, though another Roman commander, Poenius Postumus, refused to bring his troops from Exeter for reasons that are not known. According to Dio Cassius, the governor was at first reluctant to take on Boudicca's host, which was now said to number up to 230,000, and preferred to wait until 'a more convenient season'. Perhaps he hoped the tribal coalition would fall apart, but soon he was running short of food, and 'the barbarians pressed relentlessly upon him'. So, probably as Boudicca advanced along Watling Street, now the A5, he decided he had to stand and fight.

We do not know exactly where Suetonius confronted the foe, though many historians now favour a site at Mancetter, to the south-east of Atherstone in Warwickshire. Stories that the action happened at Battle Bridge near King's Cross in London, and that Boudicca's body is buried under one of the station platforms, tend to be dismissed. Wherever the exact site, Suetonius chose his ground with great care, selecting a narrow gorge with a forest behind him and a wide plain sloping away at the front. He packed his legionaries tightly in the centre, flanked by the more lightly armed auxiliaries, with the cavalry on the wings. The Britons were 'confidently exulting, a vaster host than ever had assembled'. They felt so sure of success they had even brought their wives with them to watch the defeat and massacre of the hated Romans from their wagons, which were arranged rather like a grandstand on the edge of the plain. Tacitus says Boudicca rode with her daughters in a chariot, and approached 'tribe after tribe'. She claimed it was 'usual for Britons to fight under the leadership of women', but on this occasion, she told them she was not fighting as a queen, but as 'one of the people'. Her mission was to avenge her lost freedom, her scourged body and the outraged chastity of her daughters. 'Heaven', she declared, 'is on the side of a righteous vengeance' and reminded them that they had already wiped out the only Roman force that had dared to confront them. As for the one they were about to face, it would be overwhelmed by the 'din and the shout of so many thousands' not to mention their charge and the blows they would inflict. Her resolve, as a woman, was to 'conquer or die'. If any men did not want to join her, 'they may live and be slaves'.

Nor were the Romans going to get away with going into battle without a long speech beforehand. First Suetonius drew attention to the fact that the Britons were accompanied by their families. He told his men: 'you see more women than warriors.' Because the Romans were so heavily outnumbered, it would add to the glory of their victory. He told them to close up their ranks, fling their javelins, and then attack with swords. They must forget about plunder until the day was theirs, then 'once the victory has been won, everything will be in your power.' According to Dio Cassius, Suetonius declared that the enemy's boldness was in reality 'nothing more than headlong rashness unaided by arms or training.' The Romans had been 'wronged' by the rebels, and now it was time for Boudicca's army to pay the price. If his force won the day, 'no one else will any longer withstand us' and Roman soldiers everywhere would look up to them. He added that the Britons had committed numerous atrocities: did they wish to meet the same fate, or did they want to avenge those who had died and 'at the same time furnish to the rest of mankind an example, not only of benevolent clemency toward the obedient, but also of inevitable severity toward the rebellious'? The gods were on their side, and the foe they were about to meet were their 'slaves, whom we conquered even when they were free and independent'. But he added, just suppose they were to lose, it would be better 'to fall fighting bravely than to be captured and impaled, to look upon our own entrails cut from our bodies, to be spitted on red-hot skewers, to perish by being melted in boiling water' – the dreadful fates that might await them if they fell into the hands of the Britons. For the Romans too, it was conquer or die.

Then the governor gave the signal for battle. While the Britons advanced 'with much shouting mingled with menacing battle-songs', the Romans remained silent. The field narrowed as Boudicca's host approached the Roman lines, forcing them into a temptingly tight mass. As soon as they were within range, each Roman soldier threw his two javelins 'with unerring aim'. Then, on a signal, the legionaries advanced in their famous v-shaped wedge formation behind a wall of shields that bristled with swords. Precisely what ensued is not clear, but Dio Cassius speaks of a long, hard battle. The Romans' initial charge 'easily broke through' the Britons, but then Suetonius' men found themselves 'surrounded by the great numbers of the enemy, they had to be fighting everywhere at once.' Horsemen cut down infantry, infantry cut down horsemen. The Britons would attack in their chariots, knocking the Romans 'helter-skelter', but then, because they had no armour, they would be driven back by Roman arrows. Both sides were 'animated by the same zeal and daring', and it was not until 'late in the day' that the Romans finally prevailed. They slew many and took many captives. According to Tacitus, who was writing closer to the event and whose father-in-law was with Suetonius that day, it was a much more one-sided affair. He says the legionaries' wedge-formation attack, backed up by auxiliaries and cavalry 'broke through all who offered a strong resistance'. Many Britons 'turned their back in flight', but they could not get away because the wagons blocked their retreat. The Romans killed not just British soldiers, but also women, and 'the very beasts of burden', creating a huge mound of bodies. Suetonius' army had 'great glory', and 'some' claimed that 80,000 Britons had been killed, for the loss of only 400 Romans.

Dio Cassius says 'not a few' rebels made their escape 'and were preparing to fight again', but that Boudicca 'fell sick and died'. The survivors gave her a 'costly burial', then scattered to their homes. Tacitus agrees that the Romans were unable to capture the queen, though he says she poisoned herself. In the West Country, Poenius Postumus, who had refused to bring his troops to join Suetonius, fell on his sword. Whatever the differences in the accounts they give of the Battle of Watling Street, Tacitus and Dio Cassius both agree that it ended in complete defeat for the Britons. It is hard to believe Boudicca's army really did number almost a quarter of a million, but even if it had been only half that size, it would make this the biggest battle ever fought in Britain.

For the Britons, the military disaster would bring a terrible aftermath. With the help of reinforcements sent from Germany, Suetonius ravaged 'hostile' tribes 'with fire and sword'. Even those who had merely 'wavered' in their loyalty to Rome might expect the same fate, and the Britons also started to perish from starvation. Because they had expected to be able to seize supplies from Roman granaries, they had neglected to sow their fields, but they eventually got a helping hand from an unexpected quarter. The emperor Nero was so alarmed at reports of the devastation, and the impact it might have on tax receipts from Britain, that he sent a special envoy to investigate, and soon Suetonius was replaced as governor, though he was received with honour on his return to Rome. A new governor, Petronius Turpilianus, arrived with a policy of conciliation and mending fences instead of scorched earth.

Boudicca became an iconic figure in British history. A statue of her imposing figure in a chariot stands close to the Houses of Parliament, and lines from William Cowper's ode to the rebel queen adorn it:

Regions Caesar never knew
Thy posterity shall sway.

Her defeat, though, had been comprehensive. The cities she destroyed were re-built and restored to prosperity, and the failure of her rebellion brought an end to serious resistance to the Romans in the south of England.

3

The Battle of Mons Graupius, AD 83 or 84

We tend to think of Roman rule in Britain as extending only as far north as Hadrian's Wall, but the Scottish Highland tribes suffered a comprehensive defeat at the hands of the Romans in AD 83 or 84 perhaps as far north as Aberdeenshire. They are said to have lost 10,000 killed, to the Romans' 360.

'History will be kind to me' said Winston Churchill, 'for I intend to write it.' Gnaeus Julius Agricola, the Roman governor of Britain in the late AD 70s and early AD 80s, had perhaps the next best thing. His son-in-law was the great Roman historian Tacitus, and virtually everything we know about the Battle of Mons Graupius comes from his account. Agricola was a Gaul, born in modern-day Provence in AD 40. His father, a magistrate, was put to death by Caligula for refusing to pursue a judicial vendetta against a senator to whom the emperor had taken a dislike. Agricola came to Britain while still a very young man, and served on Suetonius's staff during Boudicca's rebellion (see chapter two). In the early AD 70s, he helped to extend Rome's dominance into the north of England, and by AD 78 he was governor. Next he concentrated on subduing Wales, before advancing into Scotland with the IXth and XXth legions. All the way up to the Tay, he built forts and won victories over 'tribes hitherto unknown'. Then he advanced further north into the territory of the Caledonians, but found it difficult to bring them to battle.

Their mysterious land must have seemed a very strange place to most of Agricola's soldiers. Tacitus wrote that normally in Britain, the sky was 'obscured by continual rain and cloud' while in the north of Scotland, the summer nights were bright and very short so that, on those occasions when there were no clouds, 'the splendour of the sun can be seen throughout the night.' In addition to his operations by land, Agricola also used his fleet to harry and terrorise coastal villages, in an effort to cause 'widespread alarm'. His force, according to Tacitus, included some Britons 'of remarkable bravery', and unsure where he might meet the enemy, he divided it into three divisions. One night, the Caledonians fell on the IXth legion in a surprise attack, and might have inflicted serious damage if Agricola's scouts had not alerted him to the danger, enabling him to arrive with reinforcements in the nick of time, and drive the enemy off. This escape, wrote Tacitus, inspired the Romans to try to 'penetrate the recesses of Caledonia' and 'discover the furthest limits of Britain'. The tribesmen, though, were also encouraged. They sent their wives and children to safe havens, picked up their weapons and gathered to confront the foe, having 'made up their minds to be either avenged or enslaved'.

Tacitus says the Caledonians had 'ruddy hair and large limbs' and were armed with 'huge swords and small shields'. Now Agricola was about to face around 30,000 of them, drawn from various Highland clans, and their ranks probably also included some fugitives from the south of Scotland. The exact date of the battle – historians argue about whether it was in AD 83 or 84 – is unknown, as is its location. Tacitus says it happened at Mons Graupius, which some modern historians believe was in the Bennachie range, about 20 miles north-west of Aberdeen. Tacitus writes that the Caldeonians had many leaders, but there was one, 'superior to the rest in valour and in birth', named Calgacus. It is not certain whether he is Tacitus' invention, useful as a mouth in which to put the sentiments of the Caledonians, or a real person, for he is mentioned by no one else, and his name appears to be derived from a Celtic word for 'swordsman', but if he did exist, he is the first inhabitant of Scotland whose name has come down to us.

Tacitus loved to report speeches of those about to lead their men into battle, and this time he really went to town. He has Calgacus saying he was confident the day would see 'the beginning of freedom for the whole of Britain'. To the Caledonians, slavery was 'a thing unknown'. They had thought their remoteness 'on the uttermost confines of the earth' would save them from being 'polluted' by it. There were 'no tribes beyond us, nothing indeed but waves and rocks' but the Romans were even more terrible than those rocks. It was no use seeking to escape their oppression by 'obedience and submission'. The Romans were the 'robbers of the world', whose lust for booty had 'exhausted the land'. He continued: 'If the enemy be rich, they are rapacious; if he be poor, they lust for dominion; neither the east nor the west has been able to satisfy them… To robbery, slaughter, plunder, they give the lying name of empire; they make a desert and call it peace.'

The Romans would take their enemies' children and kin as slaves, steal their wealth, grab their harvests for their granaries. The Caledonians could expect no quarter from this dreadful foe, but they should not be afraid, as Rome owed its conquests to the disunity of those who should have stood together against it; now it was the Roman Army that would fall apart. Composed 'of every variety of nations… Gauls and Germans, and, I blush to say, numerous Britons', it was 'held together by success and will be broken up by disaster.' The Romans had 'no wives to kindle their courage; no parents to taunt them with flight'. Their homes were far away and here they were 'hemmed in' by 'a sky, a sea, and forests which are all unfamiliar to them … the gods have delivered them into our hands.' Once the action started, the Britons would recognise their true interests, the Gauls would 'remember past freedom', and both would desert the Roman cause. When the Caledonians had defeated this army, there was 'nothing to dread'. Roman forts were ungarrisoned, the people in their towns were disaffected. So was it to be liberty or slavery? 'This field', concluded Calgacus 'is to decide'. His men showed their enthusiasm, notes Tacitus, 'as is usual among barbarians, with songs, shouts and discordant cries.' Then the 'boldest warriors' stepped forward.

The Romans were just as keen to get on with it, and Agricola had trouble holding them back, but he managed it for long enough to deliver a speech of his own. He praised his troops for their achievements: they had advanced 'beyond the limits reached by former armies' until they occupied 'the last confines of Britain'. He reminded them that on their march, they had sometimes felt wearied by the 'morasses, mountains, and rivers' they had had to traverse, and that they had often cried impatiently: 'When shall we have the enemy before us? When shall we fight?' Well, now here he was, 'driven from his lair'. Now they must remember that 'everything favours the conqueror, everything is adverse to the vanquished.' Safety lay in fighting and winning, but danger in retreat. They would lack supplies and 'knowledge of the country' and if the day should go against them, an 'honourable death' was better than 'a life of shame… And it would be no inglorious end to perish on the extreme confines of earth and of nature.'

Agricola recalled that when the Caledonians had been attacking the IXth legion, the freshly arrived Roman reinforcements sent them packing 'by a shout'. Of all the Britons, these were 'the most confirmed runaways', and indeed running was the only way they had been able to survive: 'Just as when the huntsman penetrates the forest and the thicket, all the most courageous animals rush out upon him, while the timid and feeble are scared away by the very sound of his approach, so the bravest of the Britons have long since fallen; and the rest are a mere crowd of spiritless cowards.' They were going to fight now not because they wanted to, but because the enemy had cornered them. 'Extreme terror' had rooted the Caledonians to the spot so that the Romans could achieve 'a splendid and memorable victory'.

Agricola's speech too was greeted with 'a great outburst of enthusiasm', though not presumably the 'songs, shouts and discordant cries' that could be expected from barbarians. Estimates of his strength vary from 17,000 to the 30,000 that would have given him parity with the Caledonian side. In the centre, he placed his 8,000 auxiliary infantry, with 3,000 cavalry on the wings. His legions he held back, because 'his victory would be vastly more glorious if won without the loss of Roman blood', but, of course, they could be thrown in should things go wrong.

The Caledonians had the advantage of high ground, but Calgacus had posted his vanguard on the plain, while the rest rose 'arch-like' up the slope of Mons Graupius. Soon the plain 'resounded with noise and with the rapid movements of chariots and cavalry'. Afraid that the enemy might attack him on the flanks as well as frontally, Agricola widened his battle line, against the advice of some senior officers who also urged him to bring up his legions. The general not only rejected their suggestions, but also sent his horse away so he could lead his men on foot. The battle began with an exchange of missiles, which both sides withstood with 'steadiness and skill'. Then Agricola ordered his auxiliaries from the Low Countries to close with the enemy, believing that the Caledonians would be hampered by their 'small bucklers and unwieldy weapons'. Their huge swords were not pointed, which made it difficult for them in packed, close combat. For Agricola's veterans, on the other hand, such engagements were meat and drink, and now they began to 'close with the enemy, to strike them with their shields, to disfigure their faces'. They broke through the force on the plain, and then started to advance up the hill, as other auxiliaries joined in and began cutting down the Caledonians.

By now, the Caledonian cavalry had fled, and their charioteers could make no impression on the packed Roman infantry. It was a scene of great confusion, with chariots 'destitute of guidance' and riderless horses dashing wherever 'panic urged them'. Then the Caledonians on top of the hill began moving down to try to help their beleaguered comrades. Fearing they might attack his troops in the rear, Agricola sent in his cavalry, and the Caledonians' 'repulse and rout was as severe as their onset had been furious', while 'the open plain presented an awful and hideous spectacle.' The Romans pursued, wounded, captured, and slaughtered the enemy, who were fleeing 'in whole battalions'. Some even rushed to the Romans unarmed, and 'gave themselves up to death'. The field was covered with 'scattered arms, corpses, and mangled limbs, and the earth reeked with blood.' As they entered a forest, some of the fleeing Caledonians rallied and ambushed their pursuers, until Agricola, 'who was present everywhere' sent cavalry and light infantry to search the tribesmen out 'like a party of huntsmen'. Then it became every Caledonian for himself, with each man seeking safety as best he could in the 'distant and pathless wilds'. Only 'night and weariness of bloodshed' ended the Roman pursuit. Tacitus says 10,000 Caledonians were killed, against 360 on the Roman side. We hear nothing of the fate of Calgacus. What role did he play in the fighting? Was he killed? Did he escape? After delivering that rousing speech, he disappears back into the silence from which he momentarily emerged. When the action was over, 'elated by their victory and their booty, the conquerors passed a night of merriment.' Meanwhile, 'amidst the mingled wailings of men and women', the Caledonians tried to remove their wounded from the field. Then they fled from their homes, sometimes setting fire to them. The next morning revealed 'the extent of the calamity'. Everything was now silent: 'the hills were forsaken, houses were smoking in the distance, and no one was seen by the scouts' sent off in all directions. The battle had happened right at the end of summer, and Agricola could advance no further, but had to lead his army back south, deliberately taking his time in order to 'overawe' the Scottish tribes.

So the Caledonians had been heavily defeated without Agricola ever having to commit his legionaries to the fight, but Mons Graupius was not a knockout blow in the way that Watling Street had been. Tacitus estimated that two thirds of the tribal army had been able to melt away from the killing grounds. Back in Rome, according to Tacitus, the emperor Domitian learned of Agricola's victory with 'joy in his face but anxiety in his heart', fearing that the governor's popularity and his evident military prowess might turn him into a dangerous rival. Agricola was awarded the 'usual triumphal decorations', but soon afterwards he was recalled from Britain, though by then he had served an unusually long stint as governor. Dio Cassius claims that Domitian had him murdered nine years later, but there is no evidence for this.

Disastrous as it must have seemed to the Caldeonians at the time, Mons Graupius would actually represent the high watermark of Roman power in Scotland. Tacitus complains that his father-in-law had 'completely conquered' Britain, and that his successors 'let it go'. Agricola had built a major base at Inchtuthil, north of Perth on the river Tay, which could have been a springboard for further expeditions, but Rome began having to remove troops from Scotland to defend the empire's Danube frontier, and in AD 87 Inchtuthil was abandoned. In AD 122, the emperor Hadrian began building his famous wall, which set a clear northern frontier for the province of Britain stretching from Bowness on the Solway Firth to Wallsend on the Tyne, and separated 'the Romans from the barbarians', as his biographer put it. Twenty years later, the emperor Antoninus Pius tried to push the frontier back 100 miles to the north by building a wall along the 36-mile gap between the Clyde and the Firth of Forth, but within two decades this Antonine Wall had to be abandoned in the face of continuous attacks. The Romans withdrew once again to Hadrian's Wall and, in spite of a number of further attempts, they were never able to absorb Scotland into the empire.

4

The Anglo-Saxon Conquest: Crecganford, AD 457 and Dyrham, AD 577

During the Anglo-Saxon Conquest, which took place over a century and a half, the Britons would suffer many defeats, but among the most disastrous were Crecganford, possibly modern Crayford, in AD 457 where 4,000 Britons were slain, and Dyrham 120 years later when the Saxons killed three British kings.

After nearly four centuries in Britain, the Romans began to leave as their empire started to fall apart. The *Anglo-Saxon Chronicle*, which was compiled in the ninth century from earlier materials, recorded that in AD 409: 'the Goths took the city of Rome by storm, and never afterwards did the Romans rule in Britain.' But long before then, indeed by the end of the third century, Saxon raiders from modern-day Germany were already making life a misery for many people in the south and east of England, and some may well have settled in East Anglia, Essex, Kent, Sussex and the Isle of Wight. Unlike the Romans, the Saxons were not a disciplined professional army, but separate bands of adventurers hungry for land and plunder. Meanwhile, by the middle of the fourth century, the Picts and Scots were also mounting troublesome raids on Britain from Scotland. Before the Romans left, they had put in place a programme of improvements to coastal defences, but once they had gone, the Britons looked pretty helpless.

Gildas, a sixth-century British monk who specialised in doom and gloom, said they were 'utterly ignorant ... of the art of war', dismissing them as 'timorous chickens'. Their Germanic foes, on the other hand, resembled 'hungry and ravening wolves' with 'greedy jaws', who 'spread slaughter on every side'. Their depredations left Britain 'entirely destitute of provisions' while the people were butchered 'like sheep'.

According to Gildas, around the middle of the fifth century the British notables had held a crisis meeting at which, a 'proud tyrant' named Vortigern, who seems to have been some kind of military overlord, had the bright idea of hiring the pagan Saxons as mercenaries to fight the Picts and Scots. The Romans had often used this kind of arrangement themselves, but Gildas considered it an extraordinary decision, like inviting 'wolves into the sheep-fold'. The Saxons were 'fierce and impious ... a race hateful both to God and men'. The chronicler lamented: 'Nothing was ever so pernicious to our country, nothing was ever so unlucky.... Those very people whom, when absent, they dreaded more than death itself, were invited to reside, as one may say, under the selfsame roof.' The *Anglo-Saxon Chronicle* says that in AD 449, at Vortigern's invitation, two brothers named Hengest and Horsa arrived in Britain, possibly at Ebbsfleet in Kent. Whether they were real people or mythical heroes is not clear; their names mean 'stallion' and 'horse' in Old English. The *Historia Brittonum*, a chronicle written in Wales in the ninth century, says they brought three ships full of men. At first, hiring Hengest and Horsa must have seemed like a good move, because the *Anglo-Saxon Chronicle* records that Vortigern 'ordered them to fight against the Picts, and so they did, and had victory wherever they came.'

The Saxons sent word back to Germany of the 'worthlessness of the Britons and of the excellence of the land', and men from other tribes such as the Angles and the Jutes began to arrive in England, though all of them tended to be described as 'Saxon'. According to Gildas, disaster should have been foreseen: 'Their mother-land, finding her first brood thus successful, sends forth a larger company of her wolfish offspring, which sailing over, join themselves to their bastard-born comrades. From that time the germ of iniquity and the root of contention planted their poison amongst us, as we deserved, and it shot forth into leaves and branches.' At first, he said, the Britons provided their mercenaries with provisions, which 'being plentifully bestowed, stopped their doggish mouths.' Soon, though, the Saxons began to complain that these were 'not furnished in sufficient abundance'. They 'industriously aggravated each occasion of quarrel' and threatened to apply their 'sharp talons' to despoil the whole island unless they were better rewarded.

The *Historia Brittonum* tells it slightly differently: Vortigern promised to supply the Saxons with clothing and provisions so long as they fought for him, but as more and more 'barbarians' arrived, the Britons could no longer afford to continue with this arrangement, so he said: 'Your number is increased; your assistance is now unnecessary; you may, therefore, return home, for we can no longer support you.' Hengest might have been a barbarian, but he was endowed with 'craft and penetration'. He sent home for support, and sixteen vessels appeared, bringing not only 'warlike troops' but also his beautiful daughter. The Saxons then invited Vortigern to an 'entertainment', at which he ordered his daughter to ensure that the British king was well plied with wine and ale, so that he 'might soon become intoxicated'. The plan worked so well that Vortigern 'at the instigation of the devil' fell madly in love with her and asked for her hand, promising her father anything he wished in return. Hengest said: 'I'll take Kent', or words to that effect. It was duly handed over, while 'the maid was delivered up to the king, who slept with her, and loved her exceedingly.' Hengest, for his part, ordered another forty ships' worth of men and attacked the Picts again. Then Vortigern is supposed to have started going badly off the rails, marrying his own daughter, and having a son by her.

By 455 the Britons and Saxons were at war, and Hengest and Horsa fought Vortigern at Agaeles threp – perhaps Aylesford in Kent. Horsa was killed, as possibly was one of Vortigern's sons, but 'Hengest succeeded to the kingdom and Aesc, his son.' Despite all these ups and downs, according to the *Historia Brittonum*, Vortigern remained besotted by his beautiful Saxon wife and her kinsmen continued to run rings around him, offering 'peace and perpetual friendship' which he, 'unsuspicious of treachery', swallowed whole, while in reality the incomers were plotting the takeover of southern and eastern England. Not all the Britons were as compliant as Vortigern though, and the battle of 455 would be just the first encounter of a long war that lasted over a century and a half.

The main Saxon weapon was the spear, though those of noble blood and a few others would also use a double-edged sword, about 2 feet 6 inches long. Some soldiers carried a circular shield of leather and wood, but body armour and helmets were rare, and usually worn only by those of the highest rank. Tactics were not sophisticated, and most battles turned into grim hand-to-hand melees. As we have seen, though, Hengest was cunning.

According to the *Historia Brittonum* he invited the top British soldiers and nobility to a feast, got them drunk, and then murdered 300 of them, insisting that Vortigern be spared so that he could be ransomed. The price of his liberty was Essex, Sussex and Middlesex, plus 'other districts'. Not long after, the British king died in a fire or was swallowed up by the earth.

This being the Dark Ages, there is a great deal we do not know about the struggle between the Britons and the Saxons. It is clear however that fortunes ebbed back and forth. In one encounter, the Britons are said to have scored a notable victory by getting St Germanus to lead them. He taught the army to shout 'hallelujah' and this was enough to put the enemy to flight. However, they appear to have suffered a fairly decisive defeat in 457 at Crecganford, which some historians think may have been Crayford. There, says the *Anglo-Saxon Chronicle*, Hengest and Aesc 'slew 4,000', suggesting this was one of the biggest battles of the conflict. The Britons then 'forsook Kent and fled to London in great terror.' This is the last reference in the *Chronicle* to London as a Romano-British city.

The Britons seem to have been gradually driven to the west. In 465, in one of a series of victories over the 'Welsh', the Saxons slew a dozen nobles. In 491, the South Saxons took Pevensey, perhaps the last British stronghold along the south coast, and killed all the inhabitants, who may have included many refugees from other places, so that 'there was not even one Briton left there' and seventeen years later, they killed a Welsh king and 5,000 men. By 519, they had taken Wessex, by 530 the Isle of Wight, and by the next decade, they were in control of Northumbria. For a time in the late fifth or early sixth century, according to Gildas, the Britons enjoyed better fortune, winning a number of significant victories. The *Historia Brittonum* credits some of them to 'the magnanimous Arthur', though he is never mentioned by Gildas. The *Historia* says he was commander in a dozen battles, and 'in all these engagements the Britons were successful.' Unfortunately for the Britons though, 'the more the Saxons were vanquished, the more they sought for new supplies of Saxons from Germany.'

The year 577 saw another decisive battle and this time we can be fairly sure of the location. It happened close to the village of Dyrham, about 7 miles from Bath. Some historians are prepared to be even more precise, and say the exact location was a hill fort about a mile to the north of the village. The Saxons had been expanding north-westwards from Hampshire, and if they reached the river Severn, they would cut the Britons of south-west England off from those in Wales. Three British kings, Coinmail, Condidan, and Farinmail – perhaps the rulers of Bath, Cirencester and Gloucester – confronted the Saxons, led by Ceawlin, the king of the West Saxons and Cuthwine. One theory is that the Saxons charged down from the hill at dawn, taking the Britons by surprise and sweeping through them. Certainly it appears that they were decisively defeated and their three kings were slain. Following the battle, the Saxons took Bath, Cirencester and Gloucester.

After this, there appear to have been no more notable victories for the Britons – something Gildas lamented as a disaster, but accepted as a just punishment for 'former crimes'. All over what had been Roman Britain, dreadful spectacles were to be seen:

> all the columns were levelled with the ground by the frequent strokes of the battering-ram, all the husbandmen routed, together with their bishops, priests, and people, whilst the sword gleamed, and the flames crackled around them on every side… in the midst of the streets lay the tops of lofty towers, tumbled to the ground, stones of high walls, holy altars, fragments of human bodies, covered with livid clots of coagulated blood.

The Britons could not even bury their dead, but left them to be consumed in the 'ravening bellies of wild beasts and birds'. Some fled across the seas, while others tried to escape to the mountains, but were 'murdered in great numbers'. Others still, threatened by famine, gave themselves up to be slaves to their conquerors. By AD 600, most of what had been Roman Britain, except for Wales, Devon and Cornwall, and parts of the Pennines and the North West, was in the hands of the Saxons. Gildas sometimes seems to be laying it on a bit thick, but modern genetic evidence confirms that the Britons' defeat was indeed comprehensive, with between 50 and 90 per cent of Romano-British males being killed or driven out and replaced by Anglo-Saxon immigrants.

5

The Battle of Hastings, 1066

Perhaps the most famous date in English history, and rightly so. The defeat of King Harold by William the Conqueror was a genuine turning point that saw the sweeping away of an entire ruling class, and the imposition of a new one brought in from the Continent. The battle itself however, like Waterloo, was a close-run thing that could easily have gone either way.

Being king of England in the eleventh century guaranteed neither long life nor job security. In 1013, Svein Haraldsson, the king of Denmark, invaded the country and forced King Ethelred the Unready to flee. The following year, Svein died and Ethelred returned. Two years later Ethelred himself died, naming his son, Edmund Ironside, as king; but by then Svein's son Cnut – the king formally known as Canute – had invaded and conquered most of England and in 1016 defeated Edmund in battle. The two men agreed to share the country between them, but Ironside died a month later. Cnut took over the whole of England until he died in 1035, when another power struggle erupted between Harold Harefoot, the son Cnut had with his English mistress, Aelfgifu, and Harthacnut, king of Denmark, one of the fruits of his marriage to Ethelred's widow, Emma. Things got even more complicated when Emma persuaded the two sons she had borne to Ethelred – Edward and Alfred – to come out of exile in Normandy and try to seize the crown. When they ran into opposition, Edward prudently headed back to the Continent, but Alfred was captured by the formidable Earl Godwin of Wessex, who handed him over to Harefoot's men. They blinded him so brutally that he died. Meanwhile Harthacnut was preparing to invade England, but, in 1040, before he could make his move, Harefoot died, allowing Harthacnut to succeed to the throne without a battle. Within two years he too was dead, and the crown passed to Emma's son Edward, whose attempted coup had failed seven years before.

Perhaps surprisingly after all this turmoil, Edward managed to rule for twenty-four years, never forgiving Godwin for his part in his brother's murder. In 1051, relations between them got so bad that the earl was driven out of England, but he was so powerful that the following year Edward had to allow him back. Because of his piety the king was dubbed 'the Confessor' and made a saint, but perhaps all that religion was a bit inhibiting when it came to producing an heir. His marriage to Earl Godwin's daughter Edith was childless, and on his deathbed on 5 January 1066, the king nominated as his successor Godwin's eldest son Harold, who was by then the most powerful nobleman in the realm, and had shown himself to be a formidable warrior. Harold Godwinson, though, was not the only claimant. Edward the Confessor's family had become closely entwined with the court of Normandy across the English Channel. Edward's mother, Emma, was the daughter of Duke Richard I of Normandy, and when she, Ethelred and their children had been forced to flee from Svein Haraldsson, it was in the duchy that they sought refuge. Edward had spent most of the next twenty-five years there, and after he became king, Norman influence would be strong, and often resented, at his court. There were Norman officials in his household, Norman priests in his chapel, and three Normans were made bishops. It is also possible that at the time of his feud with Godwin, he made a promise to name Duke William of Normandy as his successor, while in 1057, he also seems to have promised the throne to Edgar the Atheling, the grandson of Edmund Ironside.

Some, though not all, historians believe this tangled web had another thread. In 1064, according to some chroniclers, Harold made a journey to the Continent. Let us assume he did. Was he going, as Norman propaganda would later assert, at Edward's request to offer the throne to William or to confirm an offer that had already been made? Or was Harold travelling on his own account, planning to visit various European rulers to assess how they would react if he became king? Or was his errand simply to ransom some of his kinsmen who were being held hostage by Duke William? Whatever his purpose, the story goes that Harold was shipwrecked on the coast of Ponthieu in north-east France. Maybe it was no accident, and wreckers, for which the area was notorious, had lured his ships to disaster. Anyway, someone recognised him, and he quickly found himself in the custody of the local count, Guy, who clapped him in irons and began salivating over the ransom he might receive.

Guy, however, owed allegiance to William of Normandy, and had himself once been thrown in a dungeon when he got on the wrong side of the duke. So when William heard about Harold, the count quickly handed him over. The English earl was treated as an honoured guest. He even accompanied William on a campaign in Brittany, helped capture a castle, and rescued some Norman soldiers from quicksand. Being an honoured guest, though, did not mean Harold was free to leave, and the Normans would later claim that before he departed, he took an oath of allegiance to William, promising to promote his claim to the throne of England, and accept him as Edward's successor. In one version of the story, Harold swore his oath on a chest covered with a cloth, which was then revealed to hold holy relics.

Once Edward was dead, no time was wasted in getting Harold, now aged about forty-three, on the throne, and he was crowned the next day. When William heard the news, he quickly swung into action. The first step was to get his nobility to fall in behind a plan to invade England. Initially, there was a good deal of opposition, but gradually the doubters were browbeaten into acquiescence. Next, the duke sent envoys to England to press his claim. They came back with fleas in their ears, Harold curtly informing them that Edward had named him as his successor, that the entire English nobility had ratified his choice, and that was the end of it. None of this could have been a surprise to William, who was already ploughing other diplomatic furrows. The story of Harold's alleged oath helped to win over Pope Alexander II, though the Holy Father was in any case seen as a serial endorser of Norman aggression, and was keen to bring to heel northern European countries such as England that he regarded as grossly disrespectful of his authority.

Diplomacy marched hand-in-hand with preparation for war. An army and its horses had to be assembled, supplied and fed, and to get it across the Channel, William would need to build or commandeer hundreds, perhaps thousands, of boats. In England, Harold's brother Gyrth suggested mounting an invasion of Normandy to disrupt the build-up, but the king vetoed the idea. William meanwhile was stirring the pot in England. Harold had fallen out with his younger brother, Tostig, earl of Northumberland, the previous year, and Tostig and his family had gone into exile. In the spring of

1066, William encouraged the disgraced earl to mount raids on the south coast of England with a band of adventurers he had recruited.

To combat the threat, Harold brought his fleet around to the Isle of Wight and mobilised the fyrd – the Anglo-Saxon militia – calling up, according to the *Anglo-Saxon Chronicle*, 'greater naval and land hosts than any king had ever done in this country'. His army may have numbered tens of thousands. At the same time, William continued to gather his forces at the port of Dives-sur-Mer. Promising plunder, land and titles, he managed to attract nobles from other parts of France and from as far away as southern Italy. By the beginning of August, the duke had got together his whole task force of perhaps 14,000 men – 8,000 battle troops, another 2,000 for garrison duties, 4,000 sailors and other non-combatants – plus 3,000 horses. The Normans were descended from the fearsome Northmen – Viking warriors who had conquered northern France and southern Italy and frequently devastated Britain – while William was a star graduate from the school of hard knocks. His father, Duke Robert II of Normandy, had never got around to marrying his mother, and to everyone except the Normans, he was known as William the Bastard. Duke Robert died when his son was just eight. Two of his guardians were killed, and a courtier had his throat slit in William's bedchamber while the lad slept. At one time the boy was in so much danger he had to be hidden in a variety of peasant hovels. Shortly after he came of age, he faced a rebellion by his cousin, which he beat off only with the help of King Henri I of France, but it gave William his first experience of war. He then joined Henri on a series of other campaigns. The Normans always seemed to be fighting, and William quickly became a seasoned, and brutal, warrior. In 1052 for example, he captured Alençon, where some of the citizens had been rash enough to taunt him over his illegitimacy. William seized those he deemed responsible and had their hands and feet cut off.

The duke kept his army at Dives for a month until food and supplies were running short, and his horses had grazed every available blade of grass. It may be that he was prevented from mounting his invasion because the wind was never in the right direction, but it seems unlikely that these conditions would have lasted so long, so perhaps Dives was never intended to be the jumping-off point. Certainly, at the beginning of September, William transported his army further up the coast to Saint-Valéry in Ponthieu, where they were much closer to England. Meanwhile, Harold was having to let his huge host return home to get in the harvest. He had also allowed his fleet of 700 ships to return to London, and had lost some of them in a storm. Then, shortly after disbanding his army, he learned that King Harald Hardrada of Norway, along with Tostig, had landed in Yorkshire. The Norwegian also wished to grab Harold's crown. Harold mounted a forced march north, travelling, as the *Anglo-Saxon Chronicle* put it 'night and day as quickly as he could'. By the time he reached the north, the invaders had defeated the English at Fulford, near York, on 20 September, but just five days later, Harold fell on them at Stamford Bridge, winning a decisive victory in a bloody conflict which saw 'countless numbers' slain, including Hardrada and Tostig themselves.

At Saint-Valéry, William really was delayed by adverse winds, but two days after Stamford Bridge, their direction changed and he was able to set sail. It must have been a nerve-wracking journey. Most of his forces were travelling in open boats about 40 feet long with a single mast and sail, heavily laden with horses and men. The English fleet could have given them real problems, but they were nowhere to be seen. There was some alarm in the middle of the night when William's flagship lost touch with the rest of the vessels, perhaps because, unlike the others, it was not burdened down with horses, but the duke had instructed all his craft to carry lanterns, and soon others came into sight. On the morning of 28 September, he landed at Pevensey, having lost just two boats on the crossing. The port had strong fortifications and until Harold had had to go north to fight Hardrada, it had been well guarded, but now it was deserted and the Normans came ashore unopposed. Indeed, the only invaders who ran into trouble were a group who arrived at Romney by mistake and were attacked and probably killed.

There were English garrisons at Dover and Romney, but Harold had taken away the one at Hastings. Within twenty-four hours of arriving, William had successfully demanded the town's surrender, and got his hands on valuable supplies of food. When he landed, the duke would not have known whether he would have to fight Harold or Harald for the crown of England, but news of the English victory at Stamford Bridge would have reached him soon afterwards. Harold rested for two days at York, and then on the third he decided he must make another forced march, this time back south to deal with the other threat to his throne. Most of the army were in no fit state to fight again so soon, so Harold just took his professional crack troops – the housecarls. He asked two leading northern earls, Morcar and Edwin, to follow him as quickly as they could with their housecarls and militia, but their loyalty was suspect. They had dreams of independence for Northumbria, and thought a Norman victory might help that cause.

Travelling on horseback, Harold and his housecarls covered the 190 miles from York to London in just eight days. On the way, he learned that William was already ravaging Sussex. Having established his headquarters at Hastings, the duke controlled about 50 square miles, providing a haven for his fleet, food for his men and fodder for his horses. However, he must have realised that time was probably on Harold's side. He needed to draw the English king into battle quickly before he could gather his full strength. Savagely 'harrying' the local people, and burning down their houses was one way of achieving that, and the Normans were experts.

William also sent a monk as an ambassador to Harold, with a suggestion that an independent commission should assess their rival claims. William probably did not expect it to have any more success than his earlier overtures, and, indeed, Harold was furious, and was restrained with difficulty from killing the envoy on the spot. His brother Gyrth now urged caution. In just a few days, Harold would be able to raise many more men, and the corps of archers he had left behind in the north would join him. Why not wait before giving battle? Gyrth also suggested scorching the earth between Hastings and London, saying that William's horses would never make it through the wilderness, but Harold felt duty bound to help his people in Sussex as quickly as he could. He must also have felt that every home burned down by William was a dent in his prestige. The king was afraid that William too might have reinforcements arriving, though surely the English fleet could have made it very difficult for them. Anyway, a forced march followed by a surprise attack had seen off one invader, why should it not work on William too?

Gyrth tried another tack. Let him lead the force that confronted the Normans, then even if he should be defeated, Harold would be there to fight another day, and would easily be able to put another army in the field. After all, the victory at Stamford Bridge had followed a defeat five days earlier at which Harold was not present. It all fell on deaf ears, and on 11 October the king and his army set out to meet the invader. Harold insisted that his brothers Gyrth and Leofwine accompany him, along with all the leading nobility of Wessex and southern England, thus putting all his eggs in one basket. He would not even wait for the Home Counties militia. Instead he left word for them to join him at Hastings with all speed. A chronicler writing in the next century reckoned that Harold set out with, at most, half of his potential forces.

Over the next three days, his army covered nearly 60 miles so that by the time they reached Caldbec Hill, about 4 miles north of Hastings, late on the night of 13 October or maybe even early on 14 October, they must have been exhausted. Having picked up some additional support on the way, Harold's force probably numbered about 7,000. There was an elite nucleus of perhaps 2,000 housecarls plus some mercenaries, then there were the aristocrats – the thegns of the shires – and finally the fyrd, the peasant levies of varying quality. William's army was probably slightly smaller, but of higher all-round standard. Some were nobility, others were landless knights who had joined up for profit. They were disciplined, and had had plenty of experience of war. Unlike Harold, William could call on archers and cavalry.

The duke's scouts had told him of the approach of a great Saxon army, and William kept his soldiers on alert all night in case they attacked. It had been an impressive feat of organisation to keep the Norman Army together so long, and to get them to England with virtually no casualties, but now it was make or break. The Normans had to win, while a drawn battle would be enough for Harold, allowing him to keep William hemmed in with diminishing supplies while English reinforcements arrived. As day broke, William tried to grab the high ground astride the road to London at Battle Hill, but Harold's men got there first, and held the position in spite of a deadly fusillade from William's crossbowmen. This gave the English some advantage, as the land fell away in front of the position, though it was not a steep slope.

It may be that Harold had expected only to encounter William's foraging parties and not his army, and that this is why the *Anglo-Saxon Chronicle* records that:'William came upon him unexpectedly before his army was set in order.' Whatever the truth, it seems that after that first skirmish, both sides took a few hours to get organised for battle. The English line stretched for about half a mile along the crest of the ridge. All the horsemen dismounted to fight on foot. To try to stiffen the resolve of the fyrdmen, Harold had mixed them up with his housecarls, fighting in helmets and coats of mail; together they formed a redoubtable shield wall that protected the front of the army and its flanks. Harold instructed his men that whatever they did, they must not break ranks.

According to the chroniclers, William made clear to his soldiers that there was no alternative but victory. Retreat was impossible, and defeat would mean death – probably of some very unpleasant kind. He pointed to the banner the Pope had given him: God was on their side, the oath-breaker Harold would be punished, and to underline the point, about his neck he carried some of the holy relics on which the English king had allegedly sworn an oath. The duke vowed that if the Normans prevailed, he would build a church on the site of the battle. Then there was military pedigree: their forbears, the Norsemen, had never been defeated by the English in any of their battles. William went in the centre with the Normans. On the left, he put what he considered his weakest troops: the Bretons. They would attack Harold's right – regarded by William as the weaker side – while he placed his other French troops and foreign mercenaries on his own right. All of them were arranged with archers in the first rank, then infantry, and finally the cavalry in the rear.

For his first assault, William planned to use just infantry and archers, holding back his cavalry until the English had tired. The battle began with an exchange of missiles, and the Saxon javelins, hatchets and even stones attached to pieces of wood flung downhill were much more effective than the Norman arrows fired uphill. The English massed ranks appeared to offer a tempting target, but most arrows either struck the housecarls' shields or passed harmlessly overhead, and when the Normans closed in to attack with their swords, they were cut down in dozens. After about half an hour, the attack was petering out, and William was forced to send in his cavalry after all, but, having to charge uphill, it barely dented the shield wall, while the house-carls inflicted great damage with their fearsome two-handed axes which cut right through the Normans' chainmail armour and even their shields. The English had taken some casualties, but William's army many more.

At this point, the Bretons seem to have faltered and begun fleeing down the hill. The men of the fyrd lost their heads, and in spite of Harold's stern order not to break ranks, they charged off in pursuit of the enemy. When some got too far ahead of their comrades, a few of the Breton cavalry wheeled around and picked them off with ease. Harold now tried to take advantage of the confusion in the Norman ranks, and got the shield wall to advance in formation. At this point, William was knocked off his horse, and a rumour swept through his army that he was dead. The Normans were within an ace of defeat, and Eustace of Boulogne, one of the duke's commanders, argued for a general retreat, but William got a new horse, raised his helmet and showed himself to the troops. Then he grabbed a spear and started using it to whack some of those who were taking to their heels, shaming them into making a stand.

There followed the turning point of the engagement. As with a number of things to do with the Battle of Hastings, what exactly happened, and why, remains a mystery, but the Saxon advance halted. Perhaps this was the moment when Harold's brother, Leofwine, was killed, and some of the

Saxons suddenly found themselves leaderless. Anyway, as the English lost the initiative, William rallied his men and drove the enemy back with heavy losses, though they managed to reform their shield wall and a furious hand-to-hand fight followed, with the Normans gradually making inroads on the Saxon left. William lost a second horse, but the Saxons suffered a more grievous blow when Harold's other brother Gyrth was killed. By then it was about 2pm, and William knew that he was running out of time. If he failed to decisively defeat the Saxons over the next three hours or so, nightfall would rescue them, and who knows what reinforcements might arrive. William of Poitiers, Duke William's chaplain and his authorised biographer, described Hastings as a 'battle in which one side launched attacks and manoeuvres, the other stood like rocks fixed to the ground'. That became more and more true in these final stages. It really was Norman attack versus Saxon defence.

Earlier in the battle, the Bretons had extracted some success from failure when, after they had fled from the Saxon lines, they managed to turn and kill some of their pursuers. It appears that now some groups of Breton cavalry may have used feigned retreats to draw the fyrdsmen on the English right away from the outcrops of hill where they had been put to stop the shield wall being outflanked. One group of Saxons managed to lure dozens of the enemy into a wooded area, where they plunged into a hidden ravine, causing the deaths of many horses and riders, but their lack of discipline had weakened Harold's right, allowing the Normans to seize vantage points so that they would be able to attack the shield wall from there as well as from the front.

With about an hour of daylight left, some of the fyrdsmen seem to have started drifting away, as William's crossbowmen finally began inflicting serious damage. He had told his archers to try a new tactic – to fire their arrows in the air. This would enable them to inflict casualties on the Saxons' rear ranks and the housecarls would have to raise their shields to protect themselves, opening them to attack from the front. The fighting was still fierce, and William was knocked off his horse a third time, and almost killed before his men rescued him, but at last his cavalry broke though the shield wall, and increasingly reduced the Saxons to fighting back-to-back in small groups.

At this point, the Norman archers' new tactic may have claimed the life of the English king if the traditional story is true and Harold was felled by a chance arrow shot to his eye. Or maybe not. Some chroniclers tell another story: that William dispatched a specialist hit squad of four knights who killed Harold in spite of the fierce resistance of his housecarls fighting to the last man. As news of his death spread, no doubt more of the militia melted away. The isolated pockets of Saxons still fighting were no match for the Norman cavalry and were cut down. Just too late, English reinforcements began arriving, and there were enough of them to sufficiently alarm Eustace of Boulogne into telling William that a whole new Saxon army had come. He was wrong. Though the new arrivals did manage to secure one small, final success, by rallying some of their fleeing comrades by a wood where once again a hidden ravine claimed the lives of many Norman cavalrymen; by now the day belonged to William. Apart from those who had fled, the only English soldiers to escape were a small number of wounded who had been left for dead and managed to crawl away from the field under cover of darkness.

By the standards of the time, it had been an unusually long battle, and a bloody one. The Normans lost perhaps 2,500 dead and wounded, the English maybe 4,000, and most of the wounded from both sides could expect to die. The extent of the slaughter sent a shockwave across Europe, and William felt obliged to do penance for the number of deaths he had caused, as well as building a church – Battle Abbey – on the site as he had promised, its high altar supposedly at the spot where Harold fell. Harold's mother asked William for her son's body and offered a handsome payment in gold, but he had the last Anglo-Saxon king buried under a mound of stones beneath a cliff by the sea. Perhaps he hoped it would prevent a cult developing. It did not. England echoed with stories that Harold had got away from the battlefield and escaped to Germany, or that he was leading a band of guerrillas against the Normans, or that he had become a religious hermit.

The conqueror remained at Hastings for six days after the battle, waiting for the now leaderless English to submit to him. Instead, the Saxon nobles named as king sixteen-year-old Edgar the Atheling. So William reverted to his trusted technique of 'harrying'. He began with Romney, where local people were subjected to executions and maimings for their temerity in attacking the stray Norman invaders who had landed there. The news of these dreadful reprisals probably reached Dover, which gave in without a fight, though the Normans still looted it. Next was Winchester, the ancient capital of the Godwins' Wessex heartland, which surrendered to William's messengers. The fact that the Anglo-Saxons had not gone in for building castles made William's job much easier.

When he advanced on London at the end of November though, the Saxon defenders came out to fight, and after a short encounter, the duke withdrew, though not before he had put Southwark to the torch. So it was back to burning and pillaging, as his army looped away through Surrey, Hampshire and Berkshire, then back towards the capital via Hertfordshire, until at Berkhamsted, Edgar and the remaining English nobility begged him to accept the throne. He was crowned on Christmas Day, but this did not end English resistance. There were revolts in many parts of the country, but especially in the north of England in 1069. William put the insurrection down with great brutality in what became known as 'the harrying of the North'. It was said that between York and Durham he left no house standing, and no human being alive that his horsemen could run down, and eighteen years later the Domesday Book recorded that huge areas of northern England were still devastated. Even a Norman chronicler who otherwise admired William castigated it as 'brutal slaughter', adding 'God will punish him'.

By the end of his reign William had firmly established Norman rule in England. If those nobles who submitted to him at Berkhamsted believed that by so doing, they would be allowed to keep their lands, they were sorely disappointed. The stuff about God being on William's side, the Pope endorsing his expedition, and Harold being an oath-breaker was all very well, but most of the nobles who had joined up did so in pursuit of profit. They had delivered William victory, now he had to deliver them land and wealth. This meant not just a change of king, but a clean sweep of a whole Anglo-Saxon ruling class and its replacement with a new Norman nobility. The Domesday Book shows that by 1086, in the whole of England south of the Tees, only two Englishmen held baronial estates from the king. The castles that the Anglo-Saxon kings had neglected to build were now erected 'far and wide', and, said the *Anglo-Saxon Chronicle*, William imposed 'a very heavy tax … oppressing the unhappy people'.

So the Battle of Hastings on 14 October 1066 turned out to be one of the cleanest breaks in British history, and yet it could so easily have turned out differently. It is tempting to see the Norman victory as inevitable, as William and his men were clearly far more sophisticated in the arts of war. In fact, the conqueror was no military superman, and during a series of French wars over the last decade and a half of his life, he never won a decisive victory. Hastings was actually a very close-run thing. On the day, if William had failed to rally the Bretons, or if he had been killed, as he nearly was on at least one occasion, the Normans would almost certainly have lost. Even without William's death, it looked at one point as though the Saxons would win, and why the battle turned, we do not know. If Harold could have held out for just another hour, the campaign might have swung in his favour, with fresh troops arriving and his fleet perhaps being able to attack William's rear. Even if the Saxons had been defeated, but Harold had managed to escape death, the result would not have been decisive, and William would surely have had to face at least one more major battle. Harold had made a great miscalculation. He could not be faulted for energy, courage or daring, but by staking everything so dramatically on a single roll of the dice, fighting William with a depleted army and eliminating the possibility of a second chance, the last Saxon king himself turned Hastings into the decisive military disaster that it undoubtedly was.

6

The Battle of Castillon, 1453

When a war goes on for 116 years, you would expect to lose a battle or two. During the Hundred Years War with France, alongside great English victories like Crécy, Poitiers and Agincourt went defeats such as Orléans and Formigny, but it was at the relatively small engagement at Castillon that England finally lost the whole war.

The histories of England and France had been closely entwined ever since the Norman Conquest, with the English kings holding significant lands across the Channel. Edward III of England, who was king when the Hundred Years War began in 1337, was also duke of Guyenne in southwest France, and count of Ponthieu on the English Channel at the mouth of the river Somme. The incident that started the conflict was an attempt by the French king, Philip VI, to grab Guyenne. In retaliation, Edward claimed the crown of France on the grounds that his mother was the sister of the previous king, Charles IV, who had died without leaving a son. It is misleading, though, to see the war as a neat England v. France struggle, and many soldiers in the 'English' armies were drawn from what we would now call France. At the Black Prince's famous victory at Poitiers in 1356 for example, at least half of his troops came from Gascony.

The names of that and other great English triumphs, like Crécy and Agincourt, resonate through our history, but, of course, during a conflict as lengthy as this, fortunes ebbed back and forth. The high tide of English power came under the great warrior king, Henry V, who won the Battle of Agincourt. When he died, he left as his heir the infant Henry VI, who became king of England and France, and was crowned in Notre Dame when he was nine years old. Henry, though, was a shadow of his father, and the conflict began to swing in France's favour. In 1429, inspired by Joan of Arc, the French raised the siege of Orléans, and from then on, they were in the ascendancy. They began gradually conquering English-held territory until in 1450 a victory at Formigny gave them Normandy. The following year, Guyenne, also known as Aquitaine, was lost to the English crown after three centuries.

The French king who made these conquests, Charles VII, had come up the hard way. His father, Charles VI, was prone to periodic fits of insanity, during which France would often decline into disorder. (Charles VI, incidentally, was also the grandfather of Henry VI.) During one such episode when the young Charles was ten years old, rioters even broke into the palace. Four years later, Charles's mother ran off to join the Burgundians, the great rivals of the French royal family, who were often in alliance with the English. The following year, they took over Paris and the young prince had to flee, but he quickly garnered enough support to take over from his father as regent. In 1419, he had made peace with the Burgundians, and while he and his allies were holding a meeting with them, Charles's friends murdered the Burgundian duke. At the age of nineteen, Charles became king of France.

Three decades later, when Charles's forces entered Guyenne they were not welcomed with open arms, and they had to lay siege to a number of towns such as Bayonne, St Emilion, Bergerac and the capital, Bordeaux. Once the new administration was in place, the Guyennois found its approach to taxation far too efficient for their liking. Local people were also worried that the lucrative wine trade with England might be disrupted. So, in 1452, secret envoys travelled to the court of Henry VI with the message that if an English army was sent, Bordeaux would rise against the French. The power behind Henry VI's throne, the Lancastrian duke of Somerset, was delighted. Losing Guyenne had been a terrible humiliation, and had led to his great rival, the duke of York, marching on London with an army. It was only by the skin of his teeth that Somerset had held on to power.

The man he chose to lead the expedition was the doughty old warrior John Talbot, earl of Shrewsbury – 'the English Achilles'. Before he was twenty, Talbot had been fighting in the Welsh wars, and had gone on to be lord lieutenant of Ireland, where he mounted a series of devastating raids against local chieftains. He served Henry V in France, gaining a reputation as one of the most daring and ferocious captains of his age. A master of the surprise attack, he was nicknamed 'the Terror of the French' and it is said that French mothers would frighten naughty children by telling them that Talbot was coming. But the earl could also be rash. In 1429, his determination to take on a French army that outnumbered his forces by more than two to one led to defeat and capture. After he was taken prisoner, then released a second time in 1450, he promised never again to put on armour against the French. Talbot had thirty years' experience of fighting across the Channel, but by now he was well into his sixties.

In October 1452, he landed near Bordeaux with a force of about 3,000. Not a huge number, but Talbot probably believed that one Englishman was worth two French, and he had managed to pull off one of his surprises. Charles VII had been expecting the English to invade Normandy, and he had no proper army in Guyenne. Bordeaux was as good as its word, and the townspeople turned out the French garrison, and opened their gates to the English. Then all of western Guyenne rose, and the few towns and castles garrisoned by the French were quickly overrun.

Before the end of the year, Talbot was sent 3,000 more troops, led by his favourite son, Viscount Lisle. Charles VII bided his time, laying plans for an invasion, and in the spring of 1453, he sent three armies against Guyenne – one from the north-east, one from the east, and one from the south-east. Talbot decided he would engage each one separately. In July, the army advancing from the east laid siege to the town of Castillon on the Dordogne, about 30 miles from Bordeaux. At first, the English commander resolved to leave the townspeople to their fate so that he could confront the French closer to Bordeaux, but they sent messengers, who pleaded their case so eloquently that he finally agreed to come to Castillon's rescue. Talbot may also have been told that the French force had a confused and disunited chain of command.

What they also had, though, was a great pioneer of artillery, Maître Jean Bureau, a former lawyer, who had already played an important role in the conquest of Normandy. He was described by a contemporary chronicler as 'a man of humble origins and small stature, but of purpose and daring'. The same chronicler said Bureau had originally worked for the English. The technology of guns had advanced a great deal during the century of war since they were first used by the English at Crécy in 1346. The weapons themselves were more robust, thanks to advances in casting, but more importantly, powder had improved. It no longer had to be mixed on the battlefield, and it could propel missiles with much greater power. Reasonably effective handguns had also come into use. They had to be mounted on a rest and were too cumbersome to use in the field, but they could be effective in siege warfare. For all the advances, though, artillery of this era remained temperamental, with cannon still liable to explode, and Bureau was a brilliant technician who knew how to get the best out of it.

The French had plenty of respect for Talbot. Besides, they did not know how many Gascons might have flocked to his colours, so Bureau prepared their position at Castillon very carefully. Outside the town, 700 men were put to work building a fortified camp, consisting of a deep trench behind which was a wall of earth, strengthened by tree trunks. One side of the camp lay along the Lidoire River, and the other was a few hundred yards from the Dordogne, into which the Lidoire flowed. The land-side fortification, rather than being built in a straight line, had a series of bulges and indentations. It is not clear whether this was deliberate design or whether it simply followed the line of a dried-up stream, but either way, the effect was that any assaulting force would be vulnerable to attack on its flank. Bureau then mounted his guns on the wall. He was said to have 300, though it is not known how many of these were handguns. The total French strength was perhaps 10,000, including 1,000 Breton cavalry who were stationed about a mile from the camp.

Early on the morning of 16 July, Talbot set out from Bordeaux. His numbers might by now have been approaching 10,000. Over the next twenty-four hours, he covered nearly 30 miles. Not surprisingly, only his mounted troops, numbering about 1,300, had managed to keep up. His infantry and artillery fell well behind. The next day, as his men emerged from a wood near Castillon, they came upon a French detachment in a priory, and routed them, killing many and putting the rest to flight. By then, Talbot had heard about the fortified French camp, so he sent Sir Thomas Everingham to look it over while he refreshed his soldiers with a cask of wine and settled down to wait for the rest of his army to catch them up. Almost immediately, a messenger from Castillon rushed up to say they had seen clouds of dust rising from the direction of the French camp. The enemy was beating a hasty retreat!

The opportunity to turn a rushed withdrawal into a chaotic flight was a temptation too great for a commander as bold as Talbot to resist. He ordered his men to attack at once. Because of that promise never again to put on armour, the earl wore a crimson satin gown with a purple hat over his snow-white hair. He alone stayed mounted, while his men charged the ramparts on foot, led by Everingham, and shouting 'Talbot! St George!' They ran into a hail of shot as the French fired point-blank into their ranks. It is said that Sir Thomas managed to plant the standard in the wall, but he was killed soon after, and according to a contemporary account, each French cannon shot brought down five or six of the English. Talbot must have realised almost immediately that the dust cloud had not after all signalled a French retreat. In fact, the only people departing had been camp followers sent out of harm's way before the action began.

Some of Talbot's men managed to cross the ditch and scale the earthworks, and for an hour they put up a brave fight, tussling with the defenders hand-to-hand. By this time some of the troops who had fallen behind on the march were starting to arrive, taking the English strength up to perhaps 4,000, but the *coup de grâce* was not long in coming as the 1,000 Bretons rode up and crashed into the English right flank, trampling 'all their banners underfoot', as a contemporary account put it. The English broke and started to flee towards the Dordogne. Talbot and Lisle desperately tried to rally them, but the earl's horse was hit by a cannon ball and fell on top of him, pinning him to the ground. A French archer used his axe to finish off this most feared English captain, as he lay there helpless. Lisle was also killed, and the French pursued the defeated foe for miles through fields littered with English dead. A few managed to escape, but much of Talbot's army was effectively destroyed. French losses were estimated at as few as 100. Castillon was one of the first battles in history where the gun played a crucial role in deciding the outcome.

The town surrendered to the French the next day, and others followed suit as Bureau's artillery approached, until, by the end of September, only Bordeaux held out. The French laid siege to the city and blockaded the river Gironde, and on 19 October, it surrendered. The Hundred Years War was finally over. As a reward for his part in England's defeat, Charles VII made Jean Bureau mayor of Bordeaux for life. The only part of France that now lay in English hands was Calais and the area around it known as the Pale.

Talbot's body was recovered, trampled and disfigured, the day after the battle. The manner of his death meant that he passed into legend as a heroic veteran on a horse fighting in the old chivalric way against the cold, heartless new technology that would take over war. At first he was buried on the field at Castillon, but forty years later, his remains were brought back to England. Such was the respect in which he was held by his enemies that they raised a chapel to him on the site of his death, and a memorial stands there to this day. A French chronicler described him as the 'famous and renowned English leader who for so long had been one of the most formidable thorns in the side of the French, who regarded him with terror and dismay'. There cannot be many towns that have a main street named after a defeated enemy general, but Castillon is one, with its Avenue John Talbot.

The earl may have passed into legend, but the defeat had dire consequences for the English crown. The following month, Henry VI suffered some kind of seizure, which meant he had 'no natural sense nor reasoning power' for seventeen months. Was it brought on by the news from Castillon? Whether it was or not, the long war had bankrupted the country, and in 1455, England would fall into civil war as the Lancastrian and Yorkist factions fought over the throne for thirty years in the Wars of the Roses. Henry himself would be put to death in the Tower of London in 1471.

For a long time, the English dismissed Castillon as a temporary setback, believing that one day they would be back in Guyenne, and the French had to build citadels at Bordeaux and Bayonne to keep the local population in line. In 1457, Charles VII was still complaining that every day, he had to 'watch the coast'. Even in 1475, during the Wars of the Roses, Edward IV mounted an invasion of French territory from Calais, but agreed to withdraw in return for a payment from the French king, while Henry VII and Henry VIII both attacked their neighbour. England lost its last French possession, Calais, in 1558, but the dream died hard, and English monarchs still described themselves as kings or queens of France until 1802.

7

The Battle of the Medway, 1667

Perhaps Britain's greatest ever naval humiliation came in 1667 when a Dutch fleet sailed right up the Medway dispensing destruction in its wake. The Dutch destroyed a dozen ships and carried off the pride of the navy, HMS Royal Charles. *It is said that while this disaster unfolded, King Charles II was chasing a moth around his mistress's bedroom.*

The English and the Dutch fought three wars in twenty-five years during the second half of the seventeenth century, as the world's two greatest trading nations tried to establish commercial supremacy by other means. While England was briefly a republic under Oliver Cromwell, it got the better of the first conflict, which ended in 1654, but within a decade the two sides were fighting again. In 1664, England, now once again a monarchy ruled by Charles II, took New Amsterdam from the Dutch and renamed it New York. The following year, the war spread to Europe. It started well for the English with a victory over the Dutch fleet at Lowestoft in 1665. Then France and Denmark joined in on the side of the Dutch. At the same time, a series of misfortunes began to overtake King Charles's realm, and particularly London. In 1665, the Great Plague killed perhaps 100,000 people in the capital, one fifth of its population, and other cities such as Norwich and Southampton were also badly hit. For a time, all funding for the navy was cut off. In June 1666, having to split the fleet to combat its multiple foes, the Royal Navy suffered heavy losses at Dutch hands in the Four Days' Battle, after which the enemy blockaded the Thames. The following month the tables were turned, with England victorious in the St James's Day Fight, but then, at the beginning of September came another catastrophe, the Great Fire of London, which destroyed up to a third of all the houses in the city, as well as many important public buildings.

By now, the House of Commons was getting heartily sick of the Dutch War, and, especially, of paying for it, so in January 1667, Charles's government put out peace feelers via France. King Louis XIV was receptive, but it was much harder to draw the Dutch to the negotiating table. Finally, in March, they agreed to start talks at Breda, but there was plenty of intelligence to show that, for the moment, the enemy were planning to keep fighting. In fact, they had decided to fit out seventy-two men-of-war as well as a number of smaller ships. On 22 March, Samuel Pepys, then surveyor-general of victualling for the navy, wrote in his famous diary that the king's brother, Lord High Admiral the Duke of York, was 'going from port to port' inspecting fortifications, as it was feared the Dutch might launch an invasion. By 18 April, though, Pepys records that a more complacent attitude had set in, with a belief that the Dutch 'cannot send out a fleet this year'. In fact, by early May, their fleet was not only at sea, but had raided Burntisland in the Firth of Forth. Even so, less than three weeks later, King Charles was instructing his brother to pay off the crews of a number of ships, despite the fact that, according to Pepys, the Dutch negotiators at Breda were being 'very high and insolent, and do look upon us as come over only to beg a peace'. By the end of the month, many people in the government were convinced that the Dutch were going to attack again, but where? Ministers commissioned rapid work on fortifications at Bridlington, Portsmouth and Plymouth, sent a contingent of soldiers to the Isle of Wight, and ordered fireships to be prepared. They were right to be worried. On 30 May, the Dutch had resolved to do 'something notable'. Their plan was the brainchild of Johan De Witt, a dauntingly clever man who had been elected grand pensionary – effectively prime minister – of the Dutch Republic at the age of twenty-eight, was also a successful businessman and the author of one of the first textbooks on analytical geometry.

Four days later, news reached Pepys that the Dutch were out in force with eighty warships and twenty-five fireships 'while we have not a ship at sea to do them any hurt with'. He bemoaned Charles II's 'negligence'. On 7 June, as one of the English negotiators arrived back from Breda with initial peace proposals, Dutch ships were sighted off the Kent coast, and that night they anchored close to the mouth of the Thames. Unfortunately, England's sailors were seriously demotivated. Instead of being paid in cash, they were getting 'tickets' – IOUs that could supposedly be cashed at the navy treasury in London. During the winter some had rioted, and in March, Pepys had come upon 'a poor seaman, almost starved for want of food'. He sent him half a crown and ordered that his ticket be paid. In the first few days of June, he had noted that the crew of the *Happy Return* were refusing to put to sea until they had been paid, and another two or three ships were also 'in a mutiny'.

The Dutch fleet was under the command of Admiral Michiel De Ruyter, who had first gone to sea as a cabin boy at the age of nine. He fought the Barbary pirates and then the English in the First Dutch War, while in the Second Dutch War he had already won a victory in the Four Days' Battle. Also accompanying the fleet was Cornelius De Witt, the brother of Johan, and an important politician in his own right, who brought with him secret sealed orders. On the night of 7 June, he opened them. Some of the Dutch commanders were horrified when they heard that they were to sail up the Medway and strike at the heart of English power, considering the plan to be located somewhere between foolhardy and impossible. It meant they would have to overcome not just the enemy's defences but also some treacherous waters. De Witt, however, proved extremely persuasive. He had detailed soundings made of the river so the Dutch would know it like their home waters, and he timed the enterprise to take advantage of an exceptionally high tide. By now, Londoners were in a panic, fearing that the capital was the enemy's target. When Pepys went up to the office on 8 June, everyone was talking about how the Dutch guns could be heard quite clearly by people living to the east of the city, and Charles ordered the mobilisation of the Home Counties militia.

Meanwhile, De Ruyter split his fleet, keeping a strong squadron off the Thames as cover, and sending seventeen warships along with twenty-four auxiliaries and fireships up the Medway under the command of Admiral Willem van Ghent. This task force was accompanied by Cornelius De Witt. For a time, they were delayed by unfavourable winds, and on Sunday 9 June, the king sent off his illegitimate son, the duke of Monmouth, to help the local militia. Pepys noted acidly that Monmouth would be accompanied by 'a great many young hectors … but to little purpose, I fear, but to debauch the country women thereabouts.' The government had also ordered more fireships to hamper Dutch operations, while Sir Edward Spragge was put in charge of a squadron to harass them. He was rumoured to have spent some time in his youth as a slave trader in Algiers, and was said by Pepys to be 'a merry man that sang a pleasant song pleasantly', but he had also been knighted for his gallantry at the Battle of Lowestoft. Spragge stationed some ships at Gillingham to defend a chain that had been put across the Medway, and a Dutch attempt to land on the Isle of Thanet was beaten off.

Monday morning saw the duke of York dispatching men down to defend the crucial Royal Naval Dockyard at Chatham, while the government got more and more anxious about when the fireships being made at another naval dockyard at Deptford were going to be ready. Pepys and some colleagues tried to gee things up, but he was disturbed at the lack of progress: 'Lord! to see how backwardly things move at this pinch', while the enemy seemed to be getting closer by the hour! Another member of the navy board was sent off with money to pay the sailors who might be expected to face the Dutch at any moment, but Pepys feared it was too late, because so many had grown 'used to be deceived by us'. The diarist made a visit to Gravesend, where he heard the Dutch guns, while local people told him the enemy were at Sheerness. Already, some were moving out their possessions, and Pepys was warned that there were 'not twelve men to be got in the town to defend it'.

It was quite true that the Dutch were at Sheerness. Indeed, following a bombardment of an hour and a half, they had landed 800 troops and after three hours' fighting had taken the fort, raising their flag above it. They also captured fifteen cannon along with munitions and supplies. The next morning, Pepys was assailed with 'more letters still' asking where the fireships were, and a desperate message from Commissioner Peter Pett, who was in charge at Chatham, and was 'in a very fearful stink for fear of the Dutch, and desires help for God and the King and kingdom's sake'. Pett also confirmed that Sheerness had been lost, 'which is very sad'. As the day wore on, letters inquiring about the fireships began arriving 'every hour almost' from the duke of York's private secretary, Sir William Coventry, who had once been one of the most prominent advocates of pruning the navy's budget. The government had also made an order saying that it could seize 'any man's ship', and indeed Coventry believed the country now faced such a serious emergency that the king could 'by law, take any man's goods'. When Pepys got home, he had a long 'serious talk' with his wife 'about the sad state we are in'. That night, London echoed to the sound of drums calling up members of 'the trainbands [militia] upon pain of death to appear in arms to-morrow morning with bullet and powder, and money to supply themselves with victuals for a fortnight'.

Now King Charles called in the heavy mob. George Monck, duke of Albemarle, was given the job of organising the English defences. Albemarle had been a ferocious general for Oliver Cromwell, but he had turned Royalist to engineer the Restoration in 1660. Then in the two wars against the Dutch, he had proved himself an equally formidable marine commander, playing a crucial role in the victory on St James's Day. First he sent back good news: the chain across the Medway was in good order, and the great men-of-war, ships like the 82-gun *Royal Charles*, the vessel which had brought the king back from exile, were 'safe ... against any assault'. This put 'great joy' into Pepys's heart. In reality, the picture was less rosy. On his way to Chatham, Albemarle had looked in at Gravesend, and found there were hardly any guns there, nor on the opposite side of the Thames at Tilbury. Then he had rushed on to Chatham, and was soon tearing his hair. There was little ammunition, and he had to have a store broken into to get tools to work on the defences. Ships had been sunk to try to impede the enemy's progress, but in the wrong places.

Fortunately, the Dutch had been proceeding cautiously through the difficult waters after taking Sheerness. An advance task force was sent to reconnoitre, but De Ruyter ordered that there were to be no landings. The admiral followed with the rest of the ships, and when he had caught them up, he and De Witt got into a longboat to direct operations from the head of the fleet. They saw four blockships that the English had sunk, the fortifications of Upnor Castle, the chain across the river at Gillingham, and the great ships of the Royal Navy. Captain Jan van Braakel, who was under arrest for having disobeyed orders, asked for permission to force his way up the river. He burst through the sunken ships and then fired on and took over an English frigate. Two captured Dutch merchantmen were supposed to be protecting the chain, but a Dutch ship, commanded by Captain Jan van Rijn, set them on fire, along with the *Monmouth,* and broke the chain.

The English shore defences were now being exposed. There were not enough gunners, but worse, the oak planks that should have been put under the guns had been pilfered, so thinner wood had to be used, and when they ran back after firing, the guns went straight through the planking and sank into the ground. Not only that, but most of the powder was in too bad a state to use, while some of the cannon balls were too big. The defenders could not stop the Dutch reaching Gillingham Reach where the pride of the Royal Navy lay at anchor. Many ships had scarcely a man on board. The Dutch sent two fireships against the 76-gun *Royal Oak* without success, but a third then set it ablaze. The men on board quickly abandoned ship, except for a Scots army captain named Archibald Douglas who ignored all urgings to leave, replying that his family never left their place of duty. He perished in the flames. Back in London, Pepys had gone to see Sir William Coventry, and was told by his clerk that the Dutch had broken through the chain 'which struck me to the heart', but worse news would arrive later that day. The enemy had captured the *Royal Charles* and taken her off as a prize. It was a national scandal. Pepys smelt revolution in the air. Mindful, no doubt, that Charles II had been king for only seven years and that it was less than twenty since his father had been beheaded, the diarist feared 'that the whole kingdom is undone'. He also began wondering who would be blamed for the disaster. Might the king make him the scapegoat? Even though 'God knows! I have, in my own person, done my full duty.' He went to bed 'full of fear and fright' and hardly slept a wink.

The *Royal Charles*, though, was not the half of it. Dutch fireships had also set ablaze two other men-of-war: the *Royal James* with eighty-two guns, and the *Loyal London*, with ninety. As each ship fell to them, De Ruyter's men gave out a cheer. According to one observer, Albemarle's depleted batteries caused the enemy no more trouble than a fly. Only when they had used up all their fireships did De Ruyter retire, taking with him the *Unity* as well as the *Royal Charles*, which was removed, as Sir Edward Spragge said later by 'a sorry boat and six men'. The Dutch lost just fifty men. Sir Edward Gregory, an official at Chatham Dockyard, lamented: 'The destruction of these stately and glorious ships of ours was the most dismal spectacle my eyes ever beheld.'

Samuel Pepys was not the only famous diarist distraught at events. John Evelyn acknowledged that the Dutch fleet had carried out an 'audacious enterprise', but was in no doubt that for England, it constituted a 'disgrace', that had been brought about by 'unaccountable negligence'. He now feared that the enemy might 'venture up the Thames even to London', so he sent away his 'best goods, plate, etc'. Both 'country and city' were gripped by 'panic, fear and consternation, such as I hope as I shall never see more; everybody was flying, none knew why or whither'. As the full magnitude of the disaster began to be revealed, Pepys decided Commissioner Pett deserved 'to be hanged'. With no one knowing how much further the enemy might penetrate, from 4am on 13 June the king and the duke of York had been down at the Thames ordering ships to be sunk at Barking Creek and other places. Then Charles raced off to address the London militia. All this put

Pepys into 'such a fear' that he decided to send his father and his wife to the country, with £1,300 in gold. He also made himself a 'girdle' in which 'with some trouble' he carried around £300 in gold on his person, so that if things turned nasty, he would 'not be without something', recognising that 'in any nation but ours, people that appear (for we are not indeed so) so faulty as we, would have their throats cut'. Besieged 'every minute' by demands on all sides 'for this or that order', he grew increasingly concerned about the absence of any further news from Chatham, where the dockyard now seemed to lie at the mercy of the Dutch, 'so that we are wholly in the dark'. In London, people were 'dejected' and 'talking treason in the streets openly', saying the country had been betrayed by people close to the king, and that we were 'governed by Papists'. Many were moving their families and 'rich goods' out of town, afraid now that the French would invade. Pepys went home to make his will.

The next day, fresh details of England's humiliation reached the diarist. Eyewitnesses had heard English voices on those Dutch ships that had destroyed the pride of the Royal Navy; voices that shouted: 'We did heretofore fight for tickets; now we fight for dollars!' Some seamen now turned up at Pepys's office and told him they were prepared to go and fight the Dutch if their tickets were paid, and they got what they were owed, 'but otherwise they would not venture being killed', while in the streets of Wapping, women were shouting: 'This comes of your not paying our husbands.' In Westminster, people demanded the recall of Parliament, while ministers blamed each other for laying up the great ships and leaving the fleet defenceless. The Lord Chancellor, the earl of Clarendon, had his trees cut down, his windows broken, and a gibbet set up outside his house, while Pepys and his colleagues had to put a guard on the door of the office. Downriver, guns had been stationed at Woolwich and Deptford, and more ships sunk, though in the panic, said Pepys, some had been sent to the bottom packed with valuable stores. Now at last, word did arrive from Chatham, but it was not good news. Albemarle had ordered Coventry to stop paying wages to the men employed at the dockyard, because he had found that 'not above three of 1100 in pay there did attend to do any work' and there were other allegations of absenteeism on a heroic scale. The purser of the *Princess* admitted that although notionally he had 180 men on his books, 'there was not above five appeared to do the King any service'. It is hard not to sympathise, though, with the men from Deptford, cursed by Pepys as 'the most debauched, damning, swearing rogues that ever were in the Navy' who turned up at his office and said they would do no more work unless their tickets were paid, especially when there never seemed to be any shortage of money for Charles II's numerous mistresses, courtiers and other assorted hangers-on.

The next day Albemarle complained he could not call on any small boats at Chatham, because they were 'employed by the men of the Yard to carry away their goods'. Pepys's mind turned once again to the question of who would be blamed for the fiasco, and so on Sunday 16 June, he popped into the office 'to look out several of my old letters to Sir W. Coventry in order to the preparing for justifying this office in our frequent foretelling the want of money'. The next day, he got clerks to transcribe key passages of the relevant documents, while naval commanders kept besieging the office complaining that 'if they miss to pay their men a night, they run away'. The tension in London was given another twist on the night of 17 June as fire broke out at Deptford. Rumours quickly spread that the Dutch had arrived, and people rushed to grab any weapons they could, but in fact the blaze had broken out by accident as the yard worked on the order for fireships.

The disaster now claimed its first political victim, as Commissioner Pett was dragged off to the Tower. It put Pepys 'into a fright, lest they may do the same with us' and sure enough on 19 June, he was summoned to appear before a Privy Council committee with all his 'books and papers touching the Medway'. Pett was brought from his prison to explain why he had not moved the 'great ships' out of harm's way, and why the small boats had been used to carry away his own things. Pepys thought 'he answered very sillily, though his faults to me seem only great omissions', but Coventry and the earl of Arlington were 'very severe against him; the former saying that, if he was not guilty, the world would think them all guilty'. Pett replied that he did not use a boat until there was only one left, and that then he used it only to take away models of ships, which were 'of great value'. When some members of the council replied that they wished the enemy had taken the models instead of the ships themselves, Pett replied that 'the Dutch would have made more advantage of the models [on which the design of new ships would be based] than of the ships', but the council just laughed. To Pepys's great alarm, one of the clerks in the ticket office told him the next day that everyone was saying he was in the Tower with Pett.

The only bright spot was that Albemarle's hastily improvised defences seemed to have saved Chatham Dockyard from destruction, but dread about where the Dutch would strike next still gripped the nation. At Harwich and

Portsmouth, people were terrified, while Londoners fretted that the Dutch would sail up to Newcastle and burn the ships that kept the capital supplied with coal. With the Dutch fleet continuing to 'stop up the river', and with fuel already running short, the king asked John Evelyn to see 'whether there could be any peat or turf found fit for use'. Ominously for Charles, a story was doing the rounds that while the enemy had been burning the fleet, he was chasing a moth with his mistress, Lady Castlemaine. Pepys groaned that 'the King do follow the women as much as ever he did' so England has 'a lazy Prince, no Council, no money, no reputation at home or abroad'.

The diarist was getting desperate: 'all out of heart with stories of want of seamen, and seamen's running away, and their demanding a month's advance, and our being forced to give seamen 3s. a-day to go hence to work at Chatham'. He had reached the conclusion that 'the seamen of England ... would, if they could, go over and serve the King of France or Holland rather than us'. The previous day the navy board had sent money down to Chatham, but now Pepys discovered that some sailors had attacked the barge and carried off the payroll. On 27 June, the diarist was woken at 3am with the news that the Dutch were on the prowl again with eighty of their ships heading up the river, that more ships needed to be sunk, 'and I know not what'. Evelyn had seen their fleet at the mouth of the Thames and lamented how 'triumphantly' it sat – 'a dreadful spectacle as ever Englishmen saw, and a dishonour never to be wiped off!' Off Chatham lay the 'carcass' of the *Loyal London*, the *Royal Oak* and the *Royal James* 'still smoking'.

On 30 June, Pepys went to look at the new fortifications that had been put up around the Medway, noting that the chain was now 'very fast'. Local people told him how well those Dutch soldiers who had come ashore had behaved. They 'killed none of our people nor plundered their houses', in contrast with the king's own soldiers who 'plundered and took all away' and were 'far more terrible to those people of the country-towns than the Dutch'. De Ruyter was planning an attack up the Thames at the beginning of July, but was unable to get beyond Gravesend because of the blockships and fireships that were waiting for him. He also tried to land 1,500 men near Harwich, but was driven off, and the Dutch threatened Dartmouth and Plymouth too. It was only when the Treaty of Breda was signed at the end of July that the danger was finally removed. The agreement restored to each country the possessions they had held before the war began, except that England kept New York and New Jersey, while restrictions that we had imposed on Dutch merchant ships were lifted.

For the Dutch, the Battle of the Medway had been a great national triumph. Commemorative medals were struck, and the great Dutch poet, Joost van den Vondel, celebrated it in verse, describing how the English had tried to halt their fleet with a chain, but that the 'lion's roar' of the Dutch had torn it to 'rags'. The coat of arms from the stern of the *Royal Charles* can be seen in Amsterdam's Rijksmuseum to this day, along with many pictures of the engagement. In England, a Parliamentary Commission was set up to find out who was responsible for this great national humiliation. Pepys escaped condemnation, though the navy board was criticised for paying seamen by tickets. The main helping of opprobrium was reserved for Commissioner Pett. He was ideal material, being suspected of Nonconformist and republican sympathies, and he faced accusations of having failed to obey orders from the duke of York, Albemarle and the navy commissioners to moor the *Royal Charles* in a safe place, of omitting to see that the ships were properly manned, and of failing to block the channel by sinking a vessel inside the chain. At one point, Parliament began impeachment proceedings, but these were quietly dropped. Pett lost his job and died soon after in obscurity, though his cousin Phineas continued to work at Chatham as master shipwright. This convenient rush to lay all the blame at the commissioner's door was satirised by the great poet, Andrew Marvell:

> After this loss, to relish discontent,
> Someone must be accused by Parliament;
> All our miscarriages on Pett must fall,
> His name alone seems fit to answer all.

The main English political victim though, proved to be the earl of Clarendon, who had faithfully served Charles II and his father for decades through thick and an awful lot of thin. The earl had actually opposed the war, but he was isolated at court partly because of his disapproval of its spectacular immorality, and he was also unpopular in Parliament. When the mob began baying for his blood, Charles, ever the pragmatist, cut him loose. The charges that MPs tried to lay against him did not stand up, but when they decided to put him on trial anyway, Clarendon fled abroad and died in exile seven years later.

Within five years of the Treaty of Breda, England and Holland were at war again, with France this time on Charles's side. It brought a sticky end for the De Witts. When France invaded the Netherlands in 1672, there were violent demonstrations against them, and demands that their sworn enemy, Charles's nephew, Prince William of Orange, should replace them. Cornelius De Witt was tortured and put on trial, and when his brother came to visit him, both were lynched by the mob. England made peace in 1674, but the French and Dutch fought on. De Ruyter again distinguished himself, but was mortally wounded in battle in 1676. In 1685, the duke of York went on to succeed his brother as King James II of England, but not for long. His espousal of Roman Catholicism, and his constant attempts to advance its cause, led to his being deposed after just three years by none other than William of Orange, who became King William III.

8

The Siege of Cartagena de Indias, 1741

You might call it 'the Defeat of the British Armada'. In 1741, a huge force of ships and men was sent against Spain's South American Empire, but, amid bitter inter-service rivalry, it suffered a humiliating defeat at the fortress of Cartagena in modern-day Colombia. The disaster helped bring down Britain's first prime minister.

If there was a prize for the most oddly named conflict in which Britain has ever been involved, the War of Jenkins' Ear would surely be a strong contender. In 1738, Captain Robert Jenkins told Parliament that seven years earlier, his merchant ship, the *Rebecca*, had been boarded by Spanish coast-guards off Havana. Claiming that he was carrying contraband goods, the Spaniards had tied him to the mast, cut off his ear, pillaged and damaged his ship, then set it adrift. Stale though it might be, Jenkins's story chimed in with other complaints about Spanish harassment of British ships, and with national ambitions to dominate trade with the New World. Sir Robert Walpole, Britain's first real prime minister, who had then been in power for seventeen years, was more cautious and tried to resist the increasingly belligerent mood, but in October 1739, he reluctantly declared war on Spain, remarking of the public mood: 'They now ring the bells, but they will soon wring their hands.' As war loomed, Edward Vernon, a veteran of earlier clashes with the Spaniards, offered his services to the Admiralty, and was promptly promoted to vice-admiral and given command of the West Indies squadron, a task no serving senior officer wished to take on. He arrived in the Caribbean just as the war began, and set out his plans for capturing Spanish colonies to the Secretary of State, the duke of Newcastle, who was as enthusiastic about the war as Walpole was lukewarm. Vernon advised laying 'aside all thoughts of … expensive land expeditions' and instead concentrating on exploiting Britain's naval strength. So although Havana, with its great dockyard, would be the most glittering prize, instead Vernon advocated an attack of the smaller port of Porto Bello, in what is now Panama, which was crucial to Spain's silver trade. With a force of six warships, he quickly captured it. The admiral became a national hero. Medals were struck in his honour, mugs were decorated with his face, and he was made a freeman of the City of London.

The government now threw caution to the winds, and decided to dispatch the biggest force ever sent to the West Indies – 10,000 men and more than twenty additional ships of the line. The idea of capturing Havana, 'the key to all America', was revived, but ministers decided to leave the final decision to Vernon and the army commander they had sent, Lord Cathcart. The best chance of success would have been to get the task force out quickly and catch Spain off balance, but more than a year would pass before Vernon's reinforcements reached him. While he was waiting, in March 1740, he bombarded the coastal city of Cartagena de Indias, but was not able to take it. He told Newcastle that if he had had 3,000 troops he probably could have captured it, and he decided that when the British Armada reached him, Cartagena should be its target, because he believed it would be possible to seize it quickly before disease took its inevitable toll. By the time the fleet reached Vernon in January 1741, 600 of the troops had already died of sickness, including Cathcart himself, and another 1,400 had fallen ill. The new commander was Major-General Sir Thomas Wentworth, regarded by his critics as inexperienced and lacking in imagination and initiative. Vernon and Wentworth were in joint command, but at first, the general bowed to the admiral's greater experience, and went along with the plan to target Cartagena.

The city was well fortified, and its 6,000 defenders used booms and warships to block its approaches. The Spanish commander was Admiral Blas de Lezo. Nicknamed 'Half-man' he had lost more parts of his anatomy in the service of Spain than Nelson would do defending Britain: an arm, a leg and an eye. A wily, tenacious and experienced campaigner, he had been fighting the British for nearly forty years. Vernon's fleet was off Cartagena by early March, and its ships began systematically destroying some of the smaller forts around it, allowing troops to land near the city on 10 March in exactly the kind of 'expensive land expedition' the admiral had earlier warned against. Sickness continued to take its toll, and Vernon had to raid the ranks of the soldiery to provide enough men to crew the ships. He had imagined that, once ashore, Wentworth would soon be on the attack, but instead the general proceeded cautiously, making his men build earthworks and batteries. Serving as a surgeon's mate on board one of the British men-of-war, the *Chichester*, was the novelist Tobias Smollett, who would write a vivid account of the campaign. He said erecting the earthworks was slow going, because the men were so 'relaxed by the heat of the climate, that they could not bear much fatigue'. Wentworth asked for another 1,600 men to be sent from the ships, but Vernon refused, believing there were quite enough soldiers for the job in hand. However, on 17 March he did put 300 sailors ashore. They destroyed a Spanish battery 'with great valour', but the defenders quickly rebuilt it, and did their work so effectively that a 60-gun ship was not able to demolish it. Five days later, Wentworth's land batteries began bombarding the fortifications of Cartagena's harbour at Boca Chica, but the Spaniards replied 'with great vigour'. Then six British ships joined in the firing, and the force was able to take Boca Chica, and demolish the boom across the mouth of the harbour: 'an extraordinary success', thought Smollett. Another important achievement came on 27 March when the British captured a spring, providing some relief for men 'sweating under the sun' who had been restricted to just a pint and a half of water a day. But it was not just the quantity of water that was a problem. Smollett records that it was stored in dirty vessels, and 'so little pains' had been taken to clean them that it 'was corrupted, and stunk so abominably, that a man was fain to stop his nose with one hand, while with the other he conveyed the can to his head'. As for the food, the staple diet was 'putrid beef, rusty pork and bread swarming with maggots'.

The British needed results fast. Before long the rainy season would begin and make conditions even more unhealthy, so on 30 March a council of war decided there should be a further landing of soldiers and guns with the aim of taking the fort of San Lazaro which stood on a hill above Cartagena. This would isolate the city completely. The Spaniards now abandoned two outer forts and the British moved in and took possession, while the enterprising Captain Renton in the *Experiment* managed to break through the blockships that Blas de Lezo had sunk, and fire his guns at the city, setting houses alight. On 5 April, Vernon dispatched George Washington's half-brother, Lawrence, with a force of Americans, to take the convent of La Popa above the city, allowing the invaders to site artillery there and inflict further damage. (Lawrence would name his Virginia estate 'Mount Vernon' in honour of the admiral.) By now Vernon was so confident that he sent a message to London saying Cartagena was about to fall. All this time, though, Blas de Lezo had had his men working feverishly, clearing lines of fire and building a trench around San Lazaro. At an army council of war the following day, British officers debated whether they should attack at once before the Spaniards had finished, but Wentworth said he needed to build batteries first, and with the men suffering 'greatly from the excessive heat', progress was again slow. When this news was delivered to Vernon, he reacted with 'great contempt' declaring that the delay was completely unnecessary.

By now, relations between the two commanders had deteriorated dramatically, with Smollett writing: 'It is a melancholy truth, which, however, ought to be told, that a low, ridiculous, and pernicious jealousy persisted between the land and sea officers.' It had got so bad that they took 'all opportunities of thwarting and manifesting their contempt for each other, at a time when the lives of so many brave fellow subjects were at stake.... Instead of conferring personally, and co-operating with vigour and cordiality, they began to hold separate councils, drew up acrimonious remonstrances, and sent irritating messages to each other.' Indeed, both seemed to be wishing for 'the miscarriage of the expedition, in the hope of seeing one another stigmatised with infamy and disgrace'. Vernon, he says, was a man of 'strong prejudices, boundless arrogance, and over-boiling passions' while Wentworth, 'though he had some parts, was wholly defective in point of experience, confidence, and resolution'. When the general asked Vernon to bombard the town from some of his ships 'which lay inactive', the admiral refused complaining the water was too shallow for them to get close enough in. Smollett believed this was untrue, and wrote that if four or five ships had been moored in a line with their guns blazing, 'in all probability, the town would have surrendered immediately; for it is well known that the inhabitants expected no other fate, and had by this time sent their wives and children, together with their most valuable effects, into the country'. By now, so many British soldiers were falling sick that there were barely enough to mount a proper guard, 'much less to cut down the wood and raise a battery, so as to attack San Lazaro'.

Against the advice of some of his commanders, Wentworth, under pressure from Vernon, finally agreed to attack the fort in the early hours of 8 April, but a guide took one group of men the wrong way as they searched in the dark for the trenches on which the enemy had been working so hard. When they finally found them, they ran into deadly musket fire and were 'slaughtered'. Colonel Grant and his men advanced on the left 'with great gallantry', but he was mortally wounded 'before any advantage could be taken of his success'. At the same time, their guide was killed, and they were able to make 'no further progress, but remained on the side of the hill, exposed to a severe fire from the castle and the town, which did great execution'. The Americans in the rear were supposed to carry scaling ladders and hand grenades, but they refused, though many of them joined in the fighting 'very bravely'. Indeed, overall, wrote Smollett: 'no officers or soldiers could act with more courage, alacrity, and perseverance than that which was manifested on this unhappy occasion'. As it grew light, Wentworth tried to press the assault 'but by this time the soldiers were disheartened', and the Spaniards were able to keep reinforcing their trenches so that in the end, the British were forced to retreat with the loss of 200 killed, and double that number wounded, of whom 'the majority did not recover'. A number of others were taken prisoner. Smollett acknowledged they were treated 'with great humanity' while their captors 'loudly extolled' their courage. The novelist put most of the blame for the troops' failure on Vernon, complaining that if he had sent a few ships to attack the town and create 'a diversion in their favour, the enemy would have been distracted, and their fire so divided, that neither the land forces nor the men of war could have suffered much damage, and in all probability, the city would have been surrendered'. Even if he had just sent a force of sailors, that might have been enough because 'the sailors, being more accustomed to climbing and boarding, might have applied the ladders, scaled the walls, and forced the gate'. As it was, Vernon would not even send ashore enough men to make up those the army had lost. Defenders of the admiral say he was afraid disease would rage through any who did land and that he would not then have enough to crew his ships.

On 14 April, the two services finally got together and held a council of war on board Vernon's ship. They decided that as the troops were 'greatly diminished, weakened, and fatigued' and water was 'almost exhausted … the siege of such a strong place as Cartagena could not be attempted with any probability of success'. There was no alternative but retreat. Captain Charles Knowles kept on firing his mortars at San Lazaro, but he was too far away to do any damage and the enemy just laughed. Meanwhile, the British wounded were having a terrible time, languishing on hospital ships

'in want of every necessary comfort and accommodation. They were destitute of doctors, nurses, cooks, and proper provision ... they had not room
to sit upright; they wallowed in filth, myriad of maggots were hatched
in the putrefaction of their sores, which were not dressed.' Those strong
enough to raise themselves up and look out saw the bodies 'of their fellow
soldiers and comrades floating up and down the harbour, affording prey to
the carrion crows and sharks'. According to Smollett, 'every ship of war in
the fleet could have spared a couple of surgeons' to go and help, and many
surgeons begged their captains for permission, but it was invariably refused
because of the 'diabolical rancour' between Vernon and Wentworth.

The British Armada, the greatest fleet ever sent to the Caribbean, which
'might not have only ruined the Spanish settlements in America, but even
reduced the whole West Indies under the dominion of Great Britain'
would leave Cartagena 'in damage and disgrace'. Soldiers and sailors continued to die 'in great numbers, and universal dejection prevailed'. Of
the 10,000 who had set out from England, just 1,700 were still fit for
duty. The propaganda battle did not end, though, with Vernon sending
home dispatches and edited highlights of his correspondence designed
to show Wentworth in a bad light. The admiral took no responsibility for
the disaster, maintaining in a letter that he had destroyed the enemy's forts
and ships, and procured 'a safe landing for the army as near Cartagena as
they could desire, without their having so much as a single musket shot
fired at them; and to land all their artillery, and whatever they desired
afterwards. And when they had stayed as long as they cared for, I took
the same care of their re-embarkation, without their having a musket
shot fired at them.' Their subsequent failure was their own affair, and he
was 'heartily sick of conjunct expeditions with the army'. Soon after, a
pamphlet appeared attacking the army's performance that was believed to
have been written by Captain Knowles, one of Vernon's closest associates.
For the government, Cartagena was all the more embarrassing because,
when they received Vernon's premature claim of victory, they had ordered
special commemorative coins to be minted. As the truth about the disaster
became known, it helped bring down Walpole after twenty-one years in
power. When it had withdrawn from Cartagena, the task force attempted
attacks on Santiago in Cuba and Panama, but both failed amid continuing
acrimony, and in the autumn of 1742, Vernon was recalled to England.
To the public he remained a hero, but while Wentworth was immediately given a new command in Flanders, Vernon found himself kicking

his heels. In 1745, he was back in action and promoted to admiral, but the following year he was sacked over the publication of some of his private correspondence with the Admiralty. Five months after the British had withdrawn from Cartagena, Don Blas de Lezo died of wounds he had received in the siege. The defeat of the invasion force was seen as the greatest triumph of his career, and his statue, minus the appropriate body parts, stands to this day in the city.

9

Surrender at Yorktown, 1781

General Cornwallis's surrender at Yorktown came after a battle that had probably cost no more than 150 British lives, but it was one of the most important defeats in British history, for it meant the loss of the American colonies.

By the summer of 1781, the American War of Independence had been raging for six years, and the British did not have just the rebels to contend with, but also the French, the Spanish and the Dutch who had all pitched in on the side of their enemy. There were effectively two wars going on – one in the northern colonies centred on New York, where the commander-in-chief, the rather cautious Sir Henry Clinton, had his headquarters, and the other in the south, where Lord Cornwallis was in command. Clinton had shown himself a brave and knowledgeable officer during the Seven Years' War, but he was a shy and introspective man, and this grew worse after the death of the wife he adored. Cornwallis was, by his own description, 'corpulent'. Honest and decent, he was also devoted to his wife and his two children. He would have preferred to enjoy his country estate in Suffolk, but when the American rebellion broke out, he had felt it was his patriotic duty to offer his services. Communication between the two commanders was a major headache. It could take weeks to get a message from one to the other, but anyway Cornwallis did not have much time for Clinton, assuming that before long he would be replacing him, while Clinton was nervous about his position and reluctant to impose his will on Cornwallis, who he believed was held in higher regard by the government.

Cornwallis considered that a decisive victory in Virginia 'may give us America', but Clinton feared that he was about to come under attack from a joint French-American force much bigger than his own. This followed the commander-in-chief's capture of an enemy courier carrying a letter detailing plans for a major attack on New York, along with a hint that this would be the last campaign in which the French would be helping. Clinton concluded that it was now crucial to avoid 'all risks as much as possible', because then 'time alone would soon bring about every success we could wish'. The problem was that the British commander could not make his mind up about what exactly the American commander-in-chief, George Washington, was up to, admitting 'I cannot well understand Mr Washington's real intentions.' Washington had begun his military career fighting for the British against the French in America, but had failed to distinguish himself, and when his hopes of promotion were thwarted, he resigned his commission. Then he had become a leading light in the colonists' campaign against taxes imposed by London, and was appointed leader of the rebel forces in 1775. The puzzled Clinton now sent Cornwallis a series of missives, some of them contradictory, but they culminated in an instruction that he should fortify Old Comfort Point, near Portsmouth in Virginia, as a base for the Royal Navy. When Cornwallis examined the site, he thought it completely unsuitable. Instead, he decided that the mouth of the York River, about a mile wide, commanded on either side by Yorktown and Gloucester, represented 'the only harbour in which we can hope to give effectual protection' to the navy, though both settlements were low-lying and building defences would be a difficult job.

Clinton had another wild card to contend with. The French admiral, the Comte de Grasse, had twenty-six ships in the Caribbean, and it was known that he would use some of them to support another French fleet under the Comte de Barras that was already off Rhode Island. But how many ships would he send and where would he strike? If it were not for the French, the rebellion would have petered out by now. Rebel troops had mutinied at the beginning of 1781, and in April Washington wrote: 'We are at the end of our tether.' When the Comte de Rochambeau arrived with 4,000 French soldiers to support their flagging efforts, he was not impressed with his American allies, muttering 'do not count on these people'. The two generals disagreed on where they should attack. Washington favoured New York, but Rochambeau argued for Virginia, and the argument was effectively settled when news came in August that de Grasse was heading to

Virginia with ships and men, but would stay only until October. As the month wore on, more and more British spies were warning Clinton that Washington's true design was to attack Cornwallis, and on 25 August, de Barras and his squadron left Rhode Island. Four days later, the British fleet off Boston commanded by Rear Admiral Thomas Graves sailed for Virginia to join more ships being brought by Sir Samuel Hood from the Caribbean. There seemed no reason for alarm. As de Grasse would surely have to leave some ships in the West Indies, the French would still be outnumbered. Two days after Graves's departure, a lieutenant on the British frigate *Charon*, part of a small naval force off Yorktown, sighted a French fleet dominated by de Grasse's 104-gun flagship, the *Ville de Paris*. By that night three French ships were anchored at the entrance to the York River effectively blockading Cornwallis's forces. Cornwallis, meanwhile, was anxious about the rate of progress of the fortifications, complaining that his men were being slowed down by 'this warm season'. A week earlier he had warned Clinton that it would take at least six weeks to put Yorktown and Gloucester 'into a tolerable state of defence'.

Two days after the arrival of the French fleet, Cornwallis reported that the enemy were landing troops to try to prevent any breakout to North Carolina. Clinton believed that Cornwallis could have escaped at this stage, marching out '5,500 as good troops as any in the world'. Cornwallis's view, though, was that it was too early for desperate measures. He had provisions, and the Royal Navy was on the way, so he dug in. On 5 September, Graves's fleet encountered the enemy off the Virginia coast. They fought for an hour and a half, but it was the British who found themselves outnumbered, and withdrew with three ships badly damaged and two more leaking dangerously. Graves was inclined to return to New York, but the French had suffered too, and Hood urged that the fleet should stay in order to 'succour' Cornwallis. Then for eight days, to the second-in-command's growing anger, they did nothing except drift off Chesapeake Bay. Sometimes they could see the French. Sometimes they could not. Graves was not the most enterprising of admirals, and when he sent a message to Hood asking what he suggested, Hood replied that he 'would like to send an opinion but he really knows not what to say in the truly lamentable state we have brought ourselves'. Meanwhile, Graves sent a message to Clinton telling him the situation was 'ticklish'. The enemy had 'so great a naval force ... that they are absolute masters'. Then he sailed north. At the same time, 2,500 men from Washington's army, along with Rochambeau's 4,000, were heading in the opposite direction to join the attack on Cornwallis. French money had been dispensed to overcome the normal reluctance of American soldiers to travel too far from their homes.

In New York, Clinton was wondering how he could best help Cornwallis, when an armed galley dispatched by the beleaguered general arrived on 16 September, having cleverly given the French fleet the slip. It carried a message saying that he was 'working very hard' on his fortifications and that he had six weeks' provisions. Three days later, Graves's fleet limped into port for repairs. There were some who advocated immediate action, such as the governor of New York, General James Robertson, who argued that 'America is at stake', but Clinton wanted to wait until the new admiral, Robert Digby, arrived from England with three more ships. The 23 September brought two letters from Cornwallis. The first was calm: the general did not propose anything so 'desperate' as a breakout since Digby was 'hourly expected'. The second was alarmed, and alarming: Cornwallis had discovered that his route to the sea was barred by a fleet of thirty-six French ships! De Grasse must have brought every ship he had from the West Indies and now he had linked up with de Barras. 'If you cannot relieve me very soon' warned the general, 'you must be prepared to hear the worst.'

The next day, Clinton told Graves that Cornwallis needed 'the most speedy assistance' and outlined his plan. The fleet would carry 5,000 men under Clinton's own command, and, using the strong tide, they would blast their way through the French fleet anchored at the entrance to Chesapeake Bay, then form a defensive ring in front of Cornwallis's positions, allowing the troops to land at Yorktown or Gloucester. That night, Clinton wrote to Cornwallis: 'there is every reason to hope that we shall start from hence the 5th October.' Every day, the dockyard worked on Graves's ships from dawn until ten at night, but it began to look more and more as though the fleet would not be ready to leave on the appointed day. Clinton started floating other ideas – how about striking by land at Philadelphia, to force Washington to divert troops from Yorktown? The scheme was rejected, and instead on 30 September the commander sent Cornwallis a new message saying they would not be able to start until 12 October 'if the winds permit and no unforeseen accident happens. This, however, is subject to disappointment.' However, he would stick with his plan 'even to the middle of November' if Cornwallis thought he could hold out. If not, 'I will immediately make an attempt on Philadelphia by land.' Clinton noted privately: 'I see this in so serious a light that I dare not look at it.'

Before Cornwallis arrived, Yorktown had been a small tobacco port of about seventy houses. Two creeks gave it some protection, but the British had to build most of their defences. They created redoubts, stockades, and parapets from earth and felled trees, and sank ships to make a barrier in the channel that separated the town from Gloucester, but more and more enemy troops kept arriving, and on 28 September the Yorktown garrison saw 16,000 moving into position to surround the town. Captain Samuel Graham of the 76th Regiment of Foot said they 'came on in the most cautious and regular order', but that the garrison had only one wish: 'that they would advance'. British gunners opened up, but inflicted few casualties. The defenders faced many problems. Two deserters told Washington's forces the following day that Cornwallis's troops were 'very sickly to the amount of 2,000 in the hospital ... and their cavalry was very scarce of forage'. The same day, Cornwallis's artfully dodging galley got back through the French fleet again with Clinton's message that Graves would sail on 5 October. Cornwallis immediately pulled back troops from most of his outer defences, which the enemy began to take over and use for their own batteries. The British had held on to just three redoubts. On 30 September the French tried to take one of them, but were driven back.

Believing cavalry would be of little use at Yorktown, Cornwallis had sent his dragoons with their dashing and ruthless commander, Banastre Tarleton, across the water to Gloucester. The British command thought the enemy were unaware of this, and so on 3 October, they attempted to set up a trap for the Duc de Lauzun and his French cavalry. While a big British foraging party set out, Tarleton and his dragoons hid in a wood. As expected, Lauzun and his cavalry charged at the foragers. Immediately, the dragoons broke their cover and rushed the enemy. Tarleton himself headed straight for Lauzun, pistol drawn, but before he could shoot, one of the French cavalry plunged a lance into the mount of another dragoon, which fell, knocking over the British commander and pinning him beneath his horse. Tarleton's men fought off an attempt to take him prisoner, and he got up and tried a second attack, but it was beaten back by disciplined supporting infantry.

Now the noose tightened. The night of 6 October was very dark, with low clouds hiding the moon. The British guns kept firing whenever officers thought they detected enemy movement, and one of the remaining redoubts had to fight off another attack, but daylight revealed that the enemy had made very good progress on digging a trench 600 yards from them. In spite of British fire, they kept working all through the next day.

Cornwallis now sent a message to Clinton saying that he did not think an attack on Philadelphia would be of any use. Two days later, the enemy guns were in position. First the 12 pounders opened up, and then it was the turn of the heavier 18 and 24 pounders, with Washington himself firing the first shot. It hit a house where British officers were having dinner, killing one of them. According to James Thacher, a surgeon with the rebel army, the bombardment was 'tremendous and incessant'. About 3,600 shots were fired on the first day. The British tried to retaliate, but 'with little effect'. The second day saw forty cannons and sixteen mortars pounding their positions 'without intermission'. Cornwallis now had only about 3,250 men fit for duty against the 16,000 besieging him. At midday on 11 October, he wrote to Clinton that he had lost seventy of his troops, and had his defences 'considerably damaged'. He warned that he could not 'hope to make a very long resistance'. By 5.30pm he had lost another thirty men, and by midnight, he reported that the enemy had started work on a new trench just 300 yards from the town. One of their guns set fire to the frigate *Charon* and a couple of boats.

On 14 October, Rear Admiral Graves finally announced that his ships were ready, but Clinton now began to agonise over whether it was too late to do anything. One of his subordinates grumbled: 'Our generals and admirals don't seem to be in earnest about this business.' That night, the rebels stormed two of the remaining Yorktown redoubts and incorporated them in their new trench. Inside the town, things were going from bad to worse. Food was running short, horses had to be killed, mutilated bodies lay unburied, and more men were falling sick. One British soldier wrote: 'We could find no refuge in or out of the town.' Local people 'fled to the waterside and hid in hastily contrived shelters on the banks, but many of them were killed by bursting bombs'. Cornwallis wrote to Clinton that the situation was now 'very critical'. He was expecting the enemy to have their new batteries in operation by the following morning, and he knew that his earthworks would not be able to withstand 'their powerful artillery, so that we shall soon be exposed to an assault in ruined works, in a bad position, and with weakened numbers'. Indeed, the general concluded, their situation was 'so precarious that I cannot recommend that the fleet and army should run great risk in endeavouring to save us'.

The next day in desperation, Cornwallis sent 350 of his best troops on a sortie to put the enemy's guns out of action. Just before dawn, they attacked silently with fixed bayonets, literally catching the enemy napping, killing and wounding 100 French soldiers and spiking eleven guns, but it seems they had been issued with the wrong sort of spikes, because as the general ruefully noted, the artillery was 'soon rendered fit for service again', and by nightfall the new batteries were almost complete. The next day, they began firing. Now there was only one thing for it: he had to get as many men as he could across to Gloucester, where the enemy had far fewer numbers and a breakout might be feasible. One group made it across safely, but then a storm blew up, the boats were scattered and the enterprise had to be abandoned. By 17 October, the British had almost run out of ammunition, and after a few hours of further bombardment 'the walls were in many places assailable'. If the firing went on much longer, they would be impossible to defend, so Cornwallis decided it would be 'wanton and inhuman … to sacrifice the lives of this small body of gallant soldiers'. He sent out a drummer boy followed by an officer waving a white handkerchief to arrange terms for surrender. In reply, Washington said he had 'an ardent desire to spare the further effusion of blood'.

The capitulation was signed on 19 October. Cornwallis did not attend the ceremony, pleading illness, and sent Brigadier-General Charles O'Hara to represent him. One American officer said his British counterparts 'behaved like boys who had been whipped at school: Some bit their lips, some pouted, some cried.' Captain Graham agreed that many of the British wept from 'mortification and unfeigned sorrow', but he also paid tribute to the 'great delicacy and forbearance' of the Americans, while he said the French were 'profuse in their protestations of sympathy'. More than 7,000 soldiers and sailors surrendered. That same day, Clinton's rescue fleet of thirty-six ships finally set off carrying 7,000 men. Five days later they were off Chesapeake Bay when three men in a boat told them Yorktown had fallen. The fleet promptly sailed back to New York. It took five weeks for the tidings to reach England, and when the prime minister, Lord North, was told, witnesses said he looked as though he had been shot. Then he paced up and down the room, shouting: 'Oh God! It is all over!' King George III tried at first to maintain that Yorktown was just a setback, but the clamour for peace grew louder and louder, and in February 1782, the House of Commons voted to abandon the war. Lord North resigned the following month, and the king went so far as to draft a letter of abdication. In September 1783, the treaty of Paris brought an end to the war, and gave independence to the United States of America.

For a battle with such momentous consequences, casualties at Yorktown were fairly light. The British lost around 150 killed and 300 wounded.

The French had sixty killed and nearly 200 wounded while American casualties were twenty-eight killed and about 100 wounded. Sir Henry Clinton was recalled in February 1782, and never again commanded an army in the field. He spent the last thirteen years of his life trying to defend his conduct of the war, engaging in long pamphlet battles with a number of critics, including Cornwallis, who escaped blame for the disaster, and went on to become governor-general of India and lord-lieutenant of Ireland (see chapter ten). George Washington was elected first president of the United States. When he received news of Yorktown, King Louis XVI of France ordered the people of Paris to 'illuminate' their houses to celebrate the overthrow of the British crown in America. Eight years later, he would himself be overthrown and then executed in the French Revolution.

10

The 'Castlebar Races', 1798

When British soldiers encountered a French force sent to support Irish rebels at Castlebar in 1798, they ran from the field at such speed that the event earned the nickname 'the Castlebar Races'. It was one of the smallest encounters in this book, involving perhaps only 3,500 men, but it was one of the most ignominious in the history of Britain's army.

Having helped the American rebels against the British in the 1780s, in the 1790s the French were considering assisting Irish rebels, though the small matter of the French Revolution had occurred in the meantime. Wolfe Tone's United Irishmen wanted to free the country from British rule, but they knew they would need outside help. In 1796, they persuaded the current French regime, the Directory, who were already at war with Britain, to mount a raid, but it failed when a storm scattered the fleet. In 1798, tension mounted again, and a rising broke out in parts of Ulster and Wexford, so who should Prime Minister William Pitt send for to be the new Lord Lieutenant but our old friend, Lord Cornwallis? None of the mud from Britain's loss of the American colonies (see chapter nine) seemed to stick to him, and in 1786, he had been appointed governor-general of India. By the time he arrived in Ireland on 20 June, the trouble appeared to be all over and the next day Lieutenant-General Gerard Lake routed the rebels at Vinegar Hill. There followed some pretty brutal repression, with one gaoler inventing a gallows that could hang thirty people at a time. Cornwallis was soon horrified at what he regarded as the bloodthirsty sectarianism of the Protestant loyalists, complaining that 'murder appears to be their favourite pastime' and came to the conclusion that the Lord Lieutenant's job was 'perfect misery'.

Across the Channel, the Directory had been humming and hawing about how much help it should give the rebels, and its doubts were aggravated by the way Irish exiles in Paris kept bad-mouthing each other. Still, as the rebellion waxed and waned, it allowed preparations for an invasion to keep meandering on. Finally it came up with a plan for three separate expeditions to land at three different places. The overall command of this 'Army of Ireland' was given to a French general named Hardy, while in charge of the force that was going to sail from La Rochelle was General Joseph Humbert, who had been a dealer in animal skins before the Revolution broke out. Then he had joined the army and been elected an officer by his fellow soldiers. He soon won a reputation for bravery, and made rapid progress through the ranks. Humbert, who was said to have 'the eye of a cat preparing to spring on its prey', had taken part in the abortive expedition of 1796, when the warship on which he was sailing, *Les Droits de l'Homme*, was intercepted by the Royal Navy on her way back to France. During a 15-hour battle in a fierce gale, she was wrecked on a sandbank with the loss of nearly 1,000 men.

Now even though the Directory had supposedly made up its mind what to do, all three expeditions were held up in port because it would not release the money they needed. Humbert got tired of languishing in the pending tray, and borrowed from private lenders. On 6 August, he set sail with three frigates and just over 1,000 men, as well as ammunition and arms for the Irish rebels he had been told would be itching to join them. Just off the French coast, he brilliantly evaded a British patrol, and on 22 August, flying a British flag, the expedition landed near Killala, a small town in County Mayo. A British officer rowed out to offer them some fish, and was promptly taken prisoner. When the French appeared in the town, the local force of yeomanry made a half-hearted attempt to repel them, and Humbert quickly took the town. He issued a proclamation, headed 'Liberty, Equality, Fraternity, Union!' Declaring that the French had 'great affections' for the Irish and that they were finally here 'after several unsuccessful attempts', it assured local people that the expedition had come 'to share your dangers ... to mix their blood with yours in the sacred cause of liberty'. What was more they were just 'the forerunners of other Frenchmen whom you shall soon infold in your arms' – another 30,000 would be following soon. Could there be any Irishman 'base enough' not to join them? If so, let him be chased from the country and have his property confiscated. The rationale of coming to this part of Ireland was that British troops were thin on the ground there. The reason for that, though, was that it was an area where there had been little disaffection. Still the Directory believed that an insurrection would 'certainly break out on the first favourable opportunity' and one of Humbert's Irish officers, Wolfe Tone's younger brother Matthew, told a friend: 'The People will join us in myriads.'

Certainly, wherever Humbert's soldiers went, the local peasantry turned out to cheer, and a handout of weapons and uniforms attracted thousands. The French rather turned up their noses at the quality of the Irish who joined them, and complained about their laziness and their pilfering, moaning that most could not even load a cartridge and that those who could shoot wasted their powder aiming at birds. The more politically conscious invaders were horrified to be welcomed as crusaders taking up arms for 'the Blessed Virgin' after the battles they had fought with the Roman Catholic Church back at home. Of the 5,000 men the French issued with arms, they found only about 500 who they considered fit to be formed into regular companies to fight alongside them, and even those, thought Humbert, might run at the first sound of cannon. The general's instructions were to act with 'the greatest caution' until he had linked up with Hardy, or had attracted enough local men to his colours 'for important operations'. He had a bit of wriggle-room, though, because he had also been told to do everything he could to boost Irish morale and stoke up hatred of Britain, so, leaving behind 200 of his men at Killala, ostensibly to protect local Protestants, but in fact to secure a line of retreat in case he needed it, Humbert advanced inland, brushing aside some feeble attempts to check him. Of the 'numerous and well-disciplined army, headed by the gentry and chief landowners' that, according to an Irish newspaper, he had been told would join him, though, there remained no sign.

As he approached Ballina, 10 miles to the south, Humbert dispatched 250 men to reconnoitre. The town was garrisoned by local yeomanry, who sent out a squad to attack the enemy, and had a few men killed. This seemed to unnerve the whole force, which abandoned Ballina to the invaders without firing another shot. By now Humbert had heard that a force of 3,500 British regular soldiers was closing in on him. Boldness seemed the best policy. He would strike at Castlebar, the county town of Mayo, and catch the enemy by surprise. What Humbert did not know was that back in France, Hardy was still stuck in port, delayed by lack of money, adverse winds, and a British blockade, and that on 26 August, the Directory had decided for the moment to give up any idea of sending any more men to Ireland. That very day, the general set out from Ballina with 700 infantry and cavalry and about the same number of Irish volunteers. The road to Castlebar went via Foxford, where an enemy force barred his way, but Humbert had been told, perhaps by the local priest, of a rough track climbing over a ridge that his column should just about be able to negotiate, and which was completely undefended. The general put out the word that he was taking the road via Foxford, advanced that way for a few miles, and then dodged off onto the mountain track. The way was certainly rough, and the soldiers had to march all night, until at 6am, they saw the town walls of Castlebar ahead of them, but they also saw that the British were entrenched outside, and had brought up artillery. A French officer remarked that it would be 'a tough nut to crack for a little army like ours'.

In charge of Castlebar's defence when Humbert had left Ballina was Major-General John Hely-Hutchinson. Cornwallis regarded him as 'a sensible man, but no general'. Hely-Hutchinson had about 1,700 men at his disposal. A few were regular soldiers, but most were Irish militia and yeomanry, along with some Scottish Fencibles: volunteers raised to defend the British Isles against invasion, who were commanded by regular army officers, and intended to be used for garrison and patrol duties. Hely-Hutchinson had sent an officer under a flag of truce to Killala, supposedly to inquire after a wounded officer, but in fact to check out the strength of the enemy's forces. What he learned had given him enough confidence to move forward to confront the foe, but just as he was putting his plan into operation, an express messenger had appeared from Cornwallis warning him not on any account to advance with such a small force as his, so Hely-Hutchinson had to change tack and start preparing a defensive position instead. Then at 11pm on the night of 26 August, while the enemy were still toiling along the mountain track, General Lake, the victor of Vinegar Hill, arrived with orders from Cornwallis to take over command. Lake had become well known for the harshness with which he had put down the rebellion, at one point ordering his soldiers to take no prisoners.

Just four hours later, at about 3am on 27 August, a member of the yeomanry who had been to check on his farm, returned with a story of a large body of men in uniform marching along a wild, rocky track, but no one much believed him, and it was another two hours before an officer was sent out to investigate. Humbert's advance guard shot at him, and the officer did not loiter, but raced back to Castlebar with the news. The garrison had to scurry into position. On Sion Hill just outside the town, Lake stationed several hundred musketeers, mainly from the Kilkenny militia under the command of Lord Ormonde. They also had four mobile guns, two of them manned by experienced artillerymen from the Royal Irish Artillery. Behind were a second line of musketeers – Fraser Fencibles from the highlands of Scotland – with two more guns and a corps of Galway yeomen. Then four companies of the Longford militia under their landlord, Lord Granard, formed a third line. The cavalry and other troops were held in reserve, while another mobile gun was kept in the market place to reassure local people.

Humbert must have realised that this did indeed represent a 'tough nut'. Lake's artillery had a range of around 1,000 yards, while the French muskets would be no use until they had closed to within about 100 yards of the enemy. By that point, they could expect to have been cut to ribbons by grape and canister shot, and then the cavalry could be unleashed on them. Besides, by now they had lost the advantage of surprise. Most regular generals would have called the whole thing off, but Humbert was not a regular general, he was a son of the Revolution, so he ordered the attack. As one of his captains shouted that there was 'no alternative to victory but death', Humbert's second-in-command, Colonel Sarrazin, led a charge along the line of a ditch with undergrowth deep enough to give them a modicum of shelter from the artillery fire that was now 'falling everywhere like hail'.

Most of the local recruits, what Humbert called his 'Irish Legion', did indeed flee at the first cannon shot, but then there was an astonishing development. Was it the changes of plan, the arrival of a new commander, the haste with which men had had to take up their positions, or secret sympathy for the rebel cause? Whatever the reason, Lake's Irish militia suddenly threw down their muskets and packs, turned and ran for it. While the artillery and the Fencibles looked on aghast, French grenadiers were suddenly upon them with fixed bayonets in a charge of such ferocity and determination that they captured the guns. A few of the British rearguard fought valiantly, and a solitary Fraser was said to have shot down attacker after attacker until he was finally hurled to the ground and had his brains knocked out. Lord Granard found himself fighting alone, while Ormonde tried to rally his men. First he 'begged and beseeched' them, then he 'upbraided and swore' at them, and finally he burst into tears, but all to no avail. The French had still not fired a shot, and now Lake's force were falling over each other in a desperate race to get away. Leaving behind guns, flags and munitions, they poured through the narrow streets of Castlebar, and out into the country beyond. The French, exhausted by their long night march, soon gave up the chase, but many of their enemy kept running until they reached Tuam, 30 miles away, and some even covered a further 30 miles to Athlone. In fact, they fled with such speed and enthusiasm that wags were soon dubbing the engagement 'the Castlebar Races'.

The Times produced a fairly muted account of the *débâcle* for home consumption. The assault had come before Lake's forces were ready, so although they 'sustained the attack of the French with great gallantry' the Fencibles had 'given way'. The enemy had captured half a dozen guns, and the general had 'found it necessary to retreat with some loss'. The messenger who galloped into Cornwallis's camp at Athlone gave a rather less bowdlerised account of events. Lake had found it 'impossible to manage the militia'; their panic had been 'beyond description'. Hely-Hutchinson said all the troops had failed in their duty apart from the artillery and some of the Fencibles. British losses amounted to nine guns, fifty-three killed and thirty-six wounded. French casualties had been somewhat higher: up to 200.

Humbert took possession of Castlebar, holding a victory ball and appointing a young Roman Catholic lawyer 'President of the Provisional Government of Connaught'. 'In the name of the Irish Republic' he ordered all men between the ages of sixteen and forty to rally to his camp. He also sent for the 200 men he had left at Killala to come and join him. Cornwallis remained calm. In spite of the disaster at Castlebar, he knew the odds were stacked strongly in his favour, and even many of Humbert's men believed the best the future could offer them was surrender. Wolfe Tone had insisted that the militia would desert to the French in droves, but even after the Castlebar Races, only about 100 men of the Longford and Kilkenny levies came over. As Humbert marched north, still hoping to rendezvous with other French forces, Lake followed, harassing him from a respectful distance.

Then the French general got word of an uprising in County Leitrim and met a rebel chief, who was decked out, according to a French officer, like a medieval knight errant. The chief asked them to hang on for twenty-four hours while he mustered 10,000 men, but the next day, he sent word that he considered them too small a force to take on the British and that he would not be joining them after all. On 8 September Cornwallis cornered Humbert's little army at Ballinamuck. After a short, token fight, they surrendered. The French prisoners were treated with great respect, and taken to Dublin, where a banquet was given in their honour, then they were put on a ship for home. For the Irish who had supported them, things were less pleasant. Many had been cut down as they had tried to flee. As for those who were captured, Cornwallis tried to spare the rank and file, but of the ones who had served in positions of authority, ninety were executed, including Wolfe Tone's brother, Matthew.

Ironically, twelve days after Humbert's surrender, another French force finally did land at Rutland Island off Donegal. When they arrived, some local peasants told them that County Mayo was in open insurrection against the British, but the postmaster, who was rather better informed, said this was all nonsense, and that Humbert had thrown in the towel. The French promptly sailed away again. The same month, Wolfe Tone himself was captured. He later slit his throat with a penknife the day he was due to be hanged for treason. In 1800, the Irish Parliament voted itself out of existence, and an Act of Union bound Ireland more closely to Britain. Hely-Hutchinson got his revenge against the French in Egypt, where he fought and defeated them. Lake went on to serve with some distinction in India, and was made a viscount in 1807. Cornwallis, disgusted at the British government's refusal to end discrimination against Irish Catholics, retired from public life in 1801, but was prevailed upon to return, first to help in the struggle against France and then to do another stint as governor-general of India. As for Humbert, he would play his part in another British military disaster. After becoming disillusioned with Napoleon's dictatorship, he fled to the United States, and fought for them as a volunteer private at the Battle of New Orleans (see chapter eleven).

11

The Battle of New Orleans, 1815

The year of Waterloo began with a stunning defeat for the British Army, as the redcoats were routed by untrained American frontiersmen outside New Orleans, with the British barely able to inflict a casualty on the foe. The battle need never have been fought. Unbeknown to the contending forces, Britain and America had already made peace.

Britain's attitude after its defeat in the American War of Independence (see chapter nine) was similar to that of the football manager whose team have gone down in a match that featured a couple of dubious refereeing decisions: 'We was robbed!' Indeed, the idea took hold that as British forces had *surrendered* rather than being beaten on the battlefield, then they had never really lost at all, so some people were not too concerned when the year of 1812 brought a rematch. Antagonism had grown between the New World and the Old during the titanic struggle of the Napoleonic Wars, as both Britain and France tried to stop America trading with their enemy. Indeed, at one point it looked as though the United States might find itself at war with its erstwhile liberators, until Britain found other ways to upset the Americans, like press-ganging its sailors into the Royal Navy. When hostilities began, the American government was in a confident mood, with Thomas Jefferson looking forward to the 'final expulsion of England from the American continent'. In fact, when an American army invaded Canada, it was driven back tail between legs, and the pursuing British captured Detroit. In August 1814, they took Washington, put President Madison to flight, and set the Capitol and the White House alight. The same month, peace talks began in Ghent, but by now it was the British who had grandiose ambitions, as a fleet of more than fifty ships sailed into the Gulf of Mexico, planning to attack New Orleans. The idea was for British soldiers to take the city then head up the Mississippi valley to join troops coming down from Canada, reducing Americans to, in the words of Foreign Secretary Lord Castlereagh: 'little better than prisoners in their own country'. Vice-Admiral Sir Alexander Cochrane had thought this could be achieved with as few as 3,000 regular troops, as Indians, black slaves and the Spaniards (who ruled Florida) would join them, while most American people would rejoice at being 'liberated'. London approved the plan, but just to be sure, they decided to commit more men than Cochrane suggested.

Standing in Britain's way at New Orleans was 47-year-old General Andrew Jackson. Jackson hated the British. As a thirteen-year-old, he ran messages for the American rebels, and the redcoats had caught him. When he was ordered to clean a soldier's boots, the young Jackson refused, so the soldier slashed at him with a sabre, scarring him for life. The whole of his family died in the war, and Jackson later told his wife: 'I owe to Britain a debt of retaliatory vengeance.' When peace was made, he studied law, and became a senator and judge. He first won military fame for his brutal suppression of the Creek Indians in 1813. 'We shot them like dogs' said the legendary frontiersman, Davy Crockett, who fought with him. Then in August 1814, 'Old Hickory', as Jackson became known because of his toughness, was put in command of US troops in Tennessee, Louisiana, and Mississippi. Early in December, the British fleet reached Cat Island on the edge of Lake Borgne, about 70 miles from New Orleans, and on 14 December, they defeated a force of American gunboats. When Jackson heard the news, he was alarmed and sent a dispatch to General John Coffee at Baton Rouge telling him to get his soldiers to New Orleans 'by forced marches', while he ordered General William Carroll at Natchez 'to proceed night and day' with his 1,400 men. Old Hickory then warned the people of New Orleans that if the British attacked, their liberties, their property and 'the chastity of [their] wives and daughters' would be in danger, reminding them of gruesome stories of rape and pillage by the British when they had taken Hampton, Virginia, the previous year. He trusted all good citizens would all be at their posts with their guns, and in case there were not enough good men, criminals were released from prison provided they promised to enlist. The city was placed under martial law, with no one allowed to leave without written permission.

The British had planned to attack New Orleans quickly 'before any effectual preparation could be made for its defence'. The most promising invasion route would involve sailing into Lake Pontchartain, then landing at Bayou St John, immediately north of the city. For this, Cochrane needed shallow-draft boats, but they had not arrived, so instead the troops would have to be rowed to Pea Island at the northern end of Lake Borgne, then to Bayou Bienvenu at its extreme western edge – a total journey of 60 miles. It took five days to move the British forces to Bayou Bienvenu, and conditions were dreadful. Pea Island was just a bare, damp sandbank, and the soldiers had no tents or shelter. The rain drenched them by day, then the frost froze them by night, and some began to sicken and die. At the mouth of Bayou Bienvenu was a fishing village, where the locals gave conflicting stories of the size of Jackson's army. Some said he had just a few thousand men; others said 20,000. The British commander, Lieutenant-General Sir Edward Pakenham, had been delayed by adverse winds, so in charge for the moment was Major-General John Keane, who had served with Wellington in the Peninsular War. As his men drew closer to New Orleans, they started to encounter American deserters who excited them with stories of the city's wealth, while telling them that its people hated Jackson because of his 'tyranny and violence', and were ready to rise up against him. According to a nineteen-year-old British lieutenant, George Gleig: 'from the general down to the youngest drummer-boy, a confident anticipation of success seemed to pervade all ranks'.

By 23 December, Keane had about 1,800 men ashore at Bayou Bienvenu, just 10 miles from the city, without Jackson knowing. That morning they entered a plantation on the east bank of the Mississippi and captured the owner's son, Major Gabriel Villeré, but he knocked down the soldiers holding him, leapt out of a window, and ran to a fence, dodging bullets as he went, then hurdled it before finally making his escape through a cypress forest. Colonel William Thornton urged Keane to march on New Orleans immediately, but Keane was worried about those reports of Jackson having 20,000 men, and about his long supply lines, so he decided to wait for the rest of his forces to join them. By 1.30pm the British presence was a secret no longer. Major Villeré had managed to reach Jackson and tell him the news. Old Hickory decided that he must confront the British immediately. Their army was considered to be as professional and disciplined as any in Europe, and they had beaten Napoleon (they would have to beat him all over again after he escaped from Elba in a couple of months' time), but

Jackson knew his ranks held many crack shots, with long rifles that were much more effective than anything the enemy had, and they had learned military discipline fighting the Indians. Anyway, there was no choice. He could not allow the British to advance on the city, which had no real defences. The general gathered together around 2,000 men, and by that evening they had reached the Laronde plantation just north of the Villeré estate where Keane was waiting for his reinforcements. They formed up so quietly that British pickets 500 yards away had no idea they were there. At the same time, the warship USS *Carolina* anchored in the Mississippi close to the enemy. The British were so confident that their presence was still undetected that some waved to the vessel believing it was a merchant ship.

At 7.30pm, as the British were cooking dinner, the *Carolina* opened up on them. The Americans then fell on Keane's men with their toma-hawks and hunting knives and a fierce hand-to-hand fight went on for two hours, before Jackson withdrew to his original position. The British had lost forty-six killed and 167 wounded, while twenty-four Americans had been killed and 115 wounded. Neither side could claim victory, but Jackson's men had acquitted themselves well, and the skirmish had a very important consequence. It strengthened Keane's determination not to march on New Orleans without reinforcements. Jackson now pulled back 2 miles to the Plains of Chalmette to make his main defensive line at the dried-up Rodriguez Canal, just 8 miles south of the city, with two further lines behind it. On Christmas Eve, a peace treaty was signed in Ghent, but nobody in New Orleans knew it, and the Americans, and their slaves, dug all day, making the old canal wider and deeper and erecting a rampart of earth along its northern rim, where artillery pieces were placed at regular intervals. The barrier stretched about three quarters of a mile from the Mississippi to a cypress swamp. By the end of the day, all Keane's troops had arrived, but the hardships of Pea Island had taken their toll, with 200 men lost to death or sickness, and on Christmas Day, Lieutenant-General Pakenham finally arrived. Pakenham, aged thirty-seven, had won a reputa-tion for being brave, if impetuous, in the Peninsular War, and Wellington said that though he might 'not be the brightest genius', he was 'one of the best we have' while Lieutenant Gleig described him as 'admired and beloved by both officers and men'. Pakenham brought with him as second-in-command another admired Peninsular veteran, Major-General Samuel Gibbs. The new commander was not impressed with what had gone before. He told his staff that the men available on 23 December should have been plenty to take New Orleans and that they ought to have advanced on the city immediately. He also thought their present position between a swamp and a river was very ill-chosen, and considered withdrawing to another point and starting all over again, until Admiral Cochrane piped up that far too much respect was being accorded to the Americans, and that if the army 'shrinks from attack' his sailors and marines would do the job.

On Boxing Day, Pakenham went out to have a look at the Americans, but he could see nothing that looked like an army: just a collection of horsemen galloping around in an apparently disorganised fashion, taking the odd pot-shot at British sentries. So no cause for alarm there, but Pakenham decided he had to do something to stop the fire that was coming from the *Carolina*, and another warship that had now joined it, the *Louisiana*. This meant haul-ing a battery of guns 60 miles from the ships in the Bayou, and, in the view of some of the British force, wasting precious time when they could have been marching on New Orleans. Still, on 27 December, the British gun-ners blew the *Carolina* to bits. They also hit the *Louisiana*, but her crew leapt into rowing boats, and pulling like fury, towed her to a position out of range of the British guns, but from which hers could still be deadly. While all this was going on, Jackson's force had been steadily growing as more 'dirty shirts' (as the British called them) kept arriving. The following day, Pakenham ordered a general advance. The British came forward in smart, professional order. Then, when they were 600 yards away, Jackson's batter-ies opened up from in front, while the *Louisiana* bombarded their flank. The British artillery maintained a steady fire, and also deployed their secret weapon, a new rocket, which caused some consternation at first, but turned out not to be very accurate. The American guns, on the other hand, were devastating. Lieutenant Gleig said the 'dirty shirts' were 'excellent marksmen, as well with artillery as with rifles.... Scarce a ball passed over, or fell short of its mark, but all striking full into the midst of our ranks, occasioned terrible havoc.' Soon the redcoats were leaping into ditches in a desperate search for cover, and a number of British guns were destroyed or captured. Pakenham called off the attack, but many of his men had to wait until nightfall before they could creep back to their lines. The Americans had lost just seven killed and ten wounded, while British losses were more than 150. The mood in the camp, wrote Gleig, was one of 'shame and indignation'. They had retreated in the face of an enemy for whom they felt 'the most sovereign contempt'.

Pakenham decided he needed heavier guns, so over the next three nights, sailors hauled ten 18 pounders and four 24 pounders from the fleet.

Jackson also brought in more guns, some of which he put on the far, west bank of the river. Although he had more men now, many of them did not have weapons. Still, he made sure the enemy got no rest. The British were horrified that American sharpshooters kept picking them off throughout the night, and Gleig decided they were ignorant of 'chivalric notions'. During the night of New Year's Eve, the British crept forward to build gun emplacements just 600 yards from the American lines, as Pakenham's artillery officers, confident after their successes against Napoleon, assured him they could silence the American guns within three hours. New Year's Day 1815 began with thick fog, and visibility down to 20 yards. Deciding there would be no action, Jackson ordered a review of his entire army on the open ground between his lines, but at 10am the fog began to clear, and thirty British guns opened up. The Americans were running hither and thither, and British cannon balls demolished Jackson's headquarters, though he and his staff escaped. 'Oh that we had charged at that instant!' lamented Gleig later. Even if the artillery had simply switched to anti-personnel ammunition it might have had a decisive effect. Instead they stuck to cannonballs, most of which buried themselves in the thick earthen walls the Americans had put up and did little damage. Gradually, Jackson's men recovered their composure, and for two hours, the gunners blasted away at each other, while Old Hickory rode up and down the line, dodging rockets and encouraging his soldiers. By the end, the British had undeniably come off worse. More of their guns were damaged or destroyed, and they had lost forty-four killed and fifty-five wounded, against American casualties of thirty-four killed and wounded. 'We were completely foiled' admitted Gleig, while another British officer gloomily noted: 'Our intention in the morning was to attack but now it was entirely dropped.'

It had got pretty miserable in the British camp. Food was scarce, there were no tents to protect the men against the continuing foul weather, and the Americans kept up a constant bombardment. At this point, said Gleig, 'something like murmuring began to be heard'. These men considered themselves elite troops, and look what had happened to them: they had been dragged through a wilderness to mount an invasion from a position that looked completely hopeless, and now they were trapped. Pakenham, though, had a plan. He decided he needed to begin his offensive on the far side of the Mississippi, seize the American guns there, and turn them on the enemy on the eastern side before the main British attack came in. It would mean transporting Colonel Thornton and 1,400 men with a few artillery pieces across the river. Cochrane decided the best method was to dig a 2-mile canal from the British camp to get the barges they needed to the river. This was a very tall order for men already exhausted, and some asked why they could not drag the craft on rollers just as they had done with much heavier cannon over a much longer distance, but Cochrane would not be budged. So spadework it was, and just when they finished late on 6 January, there was some encouragement, as Major-General John Lambert arrived with another 1,700 men – all veterans of campaigns in Spain and France – which meant that, including sailors and marines, Pakenham now had more than 8,000 troops. He divided his main force into three, with Gibbs on the right commanding 2,200 men to attack the part of Jackson's line commanded by General Carroll, and considered the most vulnerable. Keane would be on the river side with about 1,200 troops, with Lambert holding his force in reserve about a mile to the rear. To confront them, Jackson had just over 4,000 men. Looking out from a vantage point at the top of a plantation house, he could watch the enemy preparing scaling ladders and building batteries.

Thornton's force was meant to cross the Mississippi just after dark on 7 January, but rain had softened the ground, and the banks of the newly dug canal kept caving in, so the barges still had to be dragged the last 200 yards overland, and eight hours after the scheduled departure time, the colonel's men were still waiting by the crossing point. At 3am he decided he could not hang on any longer, but there were only enough boats to take 440 soldiers over, and when the craft were launched, they were swept down-stream by the current, ending up 1½ miles south of where they should have been, and 4½ miles from the American lines. This would greatly delay Thornton's offensive and could be a major blow to Pakenham's plan. The Americans on the west bank were alarmed, though. They had heard the boats being launched, and did not believe they were strong enough to with-stand a British assault, so they sent a messenger across to Jackson to ask for reinforcements. He replied that he could not spare a single man. Pakenham had probably hoped to launch his main attack while it was still dark, but now the sun was rising, though it was misty, and there was no sign of action on the west bank. It is not clear how much the commander knew about Thornton's problems, but perhaps he calculated that delaying any longer might damage the morale and performance of his troops, or maybe he just felt sure that his veterans could see off these American amateurs. Not that everything was going to plan on the eastern side. Gibbs was furious because the 44th Irish Regiment, commanded by Lieutenant-Colonel Thomas Mullens, had failed to appear with the scaling ladders.

A rocket soared into the air to signal the attack, though unfortunately no one had told Keane about this arrangement, and he and his men hesitated until the British artillery began the 'most vehement' fire, while the Americans replied with 'murderous' muskets, grape, canister and round-shot. The British made a promising start as Colonel Robert Rennie's men on the left drove the Americans along the river from their outposts, and forced them to flee back to their lines. Rennie and two other officers gallantly climbed the main American rampart, and the colonel even shouted: 'The day is ours!' before they were all shot. The rest of the column turned and ran, pursued by deadly American fire, and scores of dead and wounded were left along the riverbank. Rennie's attack, though, was only meant to be a diversion to help Gibbs's main thrust. As the rocket soared into the air, his redcoats had moved forward, attired in splendid uniforms, with drums beating, bugles sounding and flags flying, though there was still no sign of the 44th or the ladders. Many a foe might have been overawed, but not this one. The American artillery punched great holes in their lines. They crammed a 32 pounder with musket balls right to the muzzle, and that single blast caused 200 casualties. The British kept their discipline, filled the gaps, and kept coming on. Carroll made his men hold their fire until the enemy were within 200 yards, then rifles opened up along the whole parapet. The frontiersmen operated in well-organised rotating lines to keep up a relentless and highly accurate fire, while the British could not even see their tormentors. One of Pakenham's aides said he had never witnessed anything more destructive, and Gleig saw his comrades 'mowed down by the hundreds'. Even those few redcoats who got as far as the ditch had no means of crossing it or of scaling the rampart.

With Mullens still AWOL (he would later be court-martialled), Pakenham came across the 44th and their ladders, and led them to the fray himself. He was wounded and then his horse was shot, so he leapt on a pony. By now, many officers in Gibbs's column had been killed or wounded, and his men started to break. The major-general tried to rally them, but to no avail. Keane had held back the crack highlanders of the 93rd Regiment until he could see where they were most needed. Now he threw them in to support Gibbs's failing attack. Their appearance brought a brief rally, but once again the Americans waited for the right moment, then cut them down with shot of every description. When 600 had been felled, Gibbs's column turned for the last time and fled in disorder.

Pakenham now ordered up Lambert's reserve, but almost immediately, the commander was hit several times by grapeshot, and mortally wounded. Gibbs had managed to get within 20 yards of the rampart when he met the same fate, while Keane too was badly wounded, and had to be carried from the field. Virtually the entire British leadership had been eliminated and Lambert now had to use his reserves to cover the retreat of what was left of the other two brigades. A few redcoats had reached the rampart, but most had no ladders, and just slid down in the mud when they tried to climb it. Gleig managed to get to the top, and was about to spring in among the enemy when a bullet struck him in the head and he was carried to safety by his men. The Americans were astonished at the courage of Major Wilkinson, Lieutenant Lavack and twenty of their men, who climbed on each others' shoulders to surmount the obstacle. Wilkinson died, riddled with bullets, while Lavack leapt in among the enemy and demanded the surrender of the first two American officers he saw, but they laughed, told him he was alone, and took him prisoner.

The action had lasted just twenty-five minutes, and as the smoke and mist began to clear, it was plain that for 200 yards in front of Carroll's position the field was literally covered with dead and dying. Jackson went around his army, congratulating them on their efforts, but just as he was nearing the end of his progress, the sound of guns rose from the other bank of the Mississippi. Thornton's men, supported by three gunboats, soon overwhelmed the Americans, who were poorly armed and had only rudimentary earthwork defences, though British sailors, attacking on the right, suffered heavy casualties from their artillery. The 'dirty shirts' had the presence of mind to spike their guns so that those the British took could not be turned on Jackson. Lambert, who had taken overall command, sent over his artillery chief to examine the situation, and ordered Thornton to come back across the river after he had destroyed what American weapons and stores he could. That, effectively, was the end of the Battle of New Orleans. For all the bravery shown by the British, it had been an unmitigated disaster. Their casualties were at least 291 killed, more than 1,200 wounded, and nearly 500 taken prisoner, while the Americans had suffered only fifty-five killed, 185 wounded, with ninety-three missing. Fortunately for the redcoats, Gleig was wrong about the Americans lacking chivalry, and a British officer said the wounded were 'treated with the greatest humanity'.

The British had not completely given up on New Orleans though, and on 9 January a naval force sailed up the Mississippi. Barring the way was Fort St Philip. For nine days they bombarded it, but they could not take it. In retaliation, Jackson unleashed his guns on the remnants of the British Army still on the Plains of Chalmette, and on 18 January, Lambert began to pull them out – an action he completed with such skill that he was knighted. As they were leaving, they met another 1,000 infantry arriving from England. Cochrane then persuaded Lambert they should attack Mobile to open the way for another assault on New Orleans, and they were well on the way to taking the town when on 11 February news finally reached America of the peace agreed at Ghent. The treaty gave no significant gain to either side, but New Orleans remained a stunning victory for the United States: its first significant military success, and one that would launch it on the path to becoming the most powerful nation in the world. It turned Jackson into a national hero. The secretary of war, James Monroe, told him: 'History records no example of so glorious a victory obtained with so little bloodshed on the part of the victorious.' Jackson put it more simply: 'I have beaten this boasted army of Lord Wellington.' He would go on to be elected the seventh president of the United States in 1828. Keane recovered from his wounds and would serve in India and Afghanistan (see chapter twelve), while the pain of Britain's defeat was alleviated just six months later by the triumph of Waterloo, where Lambert commanded a brigade of infantry in Wellington's army. But the stain was never washed out, and nearly a century and a half after the event, the skiffle star Lonnie Donegan, would have a top ten hit with a song about the battle which contained many hurtful lines on the British Army's performance, including:

We fired our guns and the British kept a-coming,
But there wasn't as many as there was a while ago.
Fired once more and they began a-running
On down the Mississippi to the Gulf of Mexico.

12

The First Afghan War, 1842

We have been reminded in recent years that Afghanistan is a difficult place to subdue. The British first learned that lesson the hard way in 1842. Alarmed by signs that Russia was trying to get a foothold, Britain mounted an expedition to install a puppet king. Early victories were followed by the most disastrous retreat in the history of the British Army.

The 'Great Game' was a description coined in the first half of the nineteenth century for the struggle between the British and Russian empires for domination of Central Asia. Russian expansion threatened India, the jewel in Britain's imperial crown, but Afghanistan seemed like a formidable buffer: a desolate, mountainous land of warlike, independent tribesmen who fought each other with a ferocity exceeded only by the fury with which they would turn on any interloper. The country was largely unmapped, and Europeans knew little about it, though they were aware that its highlands were pierced by deep, narrow ravines, and that its roads were seldom more than rough tracks. Its people regarded trade of any description as rather 'infra dig', and made their living through farming, plundering or both. The atmosphere of intrigue was heightened by the fact that its women were concealed from head to foot in burqas, while its men wore shirts with great wide sleeves that were very convenient for concealing weapons. The Afghans were split into competing tribes, which were in turn split into rival clans, and there had been eight changes of royal dynasty in the past half century.

Afghanistan, in short, sounded like a good place to leave very well alone. Unfortunately, in 1837, as Queen Victoria came to the throne, it seemed the Russians might be taking a different view. Indeed, there were rumours that an agent of the Czar was active in Kabul, and that the Russians were supporting a Persian siege of Herat. Alexander Burnes, a celebrated and daring explorer, but also a political official in British India, was dispatched by the governor-general, Lord Auckland, on what was ostensibly a commercial errand, but which provided an opportunity to check out the stories. Burnes tracked down the Russian agent, Captain Ivan Viktorovich Vitkevich, without any trouble, and even invited him to Christmas dinner. He reported back that Vitkevich had been sent to offer Russian help to the Afghans against one of Britain's allies, the Sikh king Ranjit Singh. The 'Great Game' had kicked off!

The current king of Afghanistan was Dost Mohammad Khan, who had emerged from the long power struggle that followed the removal of the ineffectual Amir Shah Shuja-ul-Mulk by rebellious chiefs in 1809. Shuja had been fortunate to escape being blinded, a fate that befell another Afghan king who failed to come up to scratch, and he was now living in India on a comfortable British pension with his dozens of wives and concubines, though he had lost his prized Kohinoor diamond to Ranjit Singh. Burnes was impressed with Dost Mohammad. He seemed intelligent, competent, and well disposed to the British as long as he could get back Peshawar, once an Afghan city, but now ruled by the Sikhs. That gave Burnes a problem: his masters thought the Sikhs with their French-trained army were far more formidable than the divided, ragtag Afghans, and that it was more important to keep Ranjit onside than Dost Mohammad. All the same, Burnes recommended that Dost should be cultivated as a potential ally.

Auckland saw it differently, and, as it took three months for a question to wend its way to London and three more months for the answer to wend its way back, what he thought was what mattered. On 1 October 1838 along with Chief Secretary Sir William Macnaghten, an Ulsterman, he issued his Simla Declaration. Immediate action was needed to halt the foreign intrigue that was threatening India. Dost Mohammad and his supporters had shown themselves 'ill-fitted ... to be useful allies to the British government', so Britain would restore the rightful king – Shuja – who was 'popular throughout Afghanistan' and would enter the country 'surrounded by his own troops'. The only role for the British Army would be to assist him 'against foreign interference' and as soon as he was secure and the 'independence and integrity of Afghanistan established', the British would withdraw. It was pure spin. Shuja did not have any troops, and even if any Afghans remembered a king they had thrown out thirty years before, there was no evidence they wanted him back, and even less that they would welcome a British army.

Still, knowing on which side his bread was buttered, Burnes quickly fell into line with the new orthodoxy, and decided that it would be a good idea to get rid of Dost Mohammad after all. Back in London, directors of the East India Company, whose army was the real power in India, were horrified. Auckland's predecessor, Lord William Bentinck, considered the plan 'folly', while Britain's greatest living soldier, the duke of Wellington, could not understand why we would wish to occupy a land of 'rocks, sands, deserts, ice and snow'. The press attacked Auckland's declaration as dishonest, and Parliament demanded publication of all the relevant documents. The foreign secretary, Lord Palmerston, agreed, but carefully removed anything favourable Burnes had said about Dost Mohammad. Anyway, events were now moving to Auckland's timetable. Apart from the East India Company's own army, Ranjit Singh's was the biggest on the subcontinent, and the governor-general wanted to rope it into the invasion. So the British invited the Sikh king to a dazzling ceremony, at the end of which Ranjit wished them all the best in their enterprise, and took his own troops home.

As the British were about to march off into Afghanistan, news came through that the Persians had raised the siege of Herat, thanks partly to the efforts of Major Eldred Pottinger, an East India Company officer who had travelled there disguised as a horse dealer, and then helped to organise resistance. Not only that, the Czar had disowned Viktevich, who then killed himself. The only tangible effect of all this on Auckland was to make him cut back on the number of soldiers he would send. What was now known as the 'Army of the Indus' comprised Shuja's contingent of 6,000 hastily recruited mercenaries, along with 9,500 troops drawn from the British Army and the East India Company's force, which was mainly made up of sepoys recruited from all of India's wide assortment of races and religions. Its officers, though, were British – educated at the company's own military academy – and they did not buy their commissions like officers in the British Army, but were generally promoted according to merit. The number of fighting men might have been reduced, but the army that moved off on 10 December 1838 did not stint on the baggage train. One brigadier needed sixty camels for his provisions, while another couple were occupied just carrying cigars for the 16th Lancers. No wonder 30,000 of the beasts were needed, and in addition, a staggering 38,000 camp followers tagged along. Each officer was allowed at least ten domestic servants, then there were wives, children, aunts, uncles, saddlers, blacksmiths, water carriers, tailors, laundrymen, cooks, stable boys, herdsmen and butchers, not to mention fortune tellers and prostitutes. In spite of the presence of all those camels, the poor old infantryman carried his own musket and ammunition, plus clothes weighing another stone, over the tough terrain.

The army appeared to be in no hurry. Shuja made a detour to subdue a few unruly elements, and it was spring before the great crocodile crossed the Indus River and marched up the mountain valleys towards Kabul. At the passes, they were sometimes harassed by Afghan marksmen. Their long, old-fashioned matchlock jezail rifles might look rather quaint, but they were horribly accurate at anything up to 800 yards, as they picked off stragglers. Tribesmen also stole camels, while the Sikh grooms, hired to look after them, deserted. It took six days to clear the Bolan Pass, and the way was left strewn with dead camels and discarded baggage. Soon many camp followers were on half rations. The main military obstacle before Kabul was the formidable fortress of Ghazni, which the British took on 23 July 1839 for the loss of seventeen killed and 165 wounded. Afghan losses were estimated at 500. For them, this was a terrible shock. Ghazni was supposed to be impregnable. Dost Mohammad marched out of Kabul to confront the invader, but so many of his army deserted that he fled, and then fought a guerrilla war, before finally giving himself up, and being sent into exile in India.

The Army of the Indus entered Kabul on 6 August 1839 and re-installed Shah Shuja to his throne in its great citadel, the Bala Hissar. Local people received him in stony silence. The British commanding officer, General Sir John Keane, a veteran of the Battle of New Orleans (see chapter eleven), was seized by a sense of foreboding, writing to a friend: 'Mark my words, it will not be long before there is here some signal catastrophe' though he did not share these fears with Auckland. Any such catastrophe would not be Keane's problem. Officially, it was 'mission accomplished', and much of the army, including the general himself, was recalled to India. Shuja might enjoy the pomp, but the real rulers of Afghanistan were Macnaghten, who had never been to the country before but was now the Envoy and Minister at Shuja's court, and 34-year-old Alexander, now Sir Alexander, Burnes, who, as the British Resident, was effectively Macnaghten's number two. Kabul lay on a desolate gravel plain surrounded by mountains, but the occupiers turned it into something of a little Britain. They skated on frozen ponds, built a racetrack and played cricket, even initiating a few Kabulis into the mysteries of the game. There were amateur dramatics, concerts and gardens. Much admired sweet peas and cauliflowers were grown by Lady Florentia Sale, the wife of Brigadier Sir Robert 'Fighting Bob' Sale, who had played a courageous role in the taking of Ghazni. Food and drink were plentiful, and the officers entertained each other lavishly. Burnes gave weekly parties at his fine walled house in the city. One or two officers took Afghan wives, others brought their wives and children from India, including Macnaghten, whose spouse arrived with crystal chandeliers, choice wines and an army of servants. Sepoys' families also began to flood in. Some of the British were drawn to less innocent pleasures, though. Sir John Kaye, a contemporary historian and civil servant, who had access to secret reports, diaries and cor-respondence, later wrote that it became an 'open, undisguised, notorious' scandal that British officers made free with local, often married, women. This proved a highly effective way of making enemies of Afghan men. Shuja, meanwhile, surrounded himself with decaying and petulant advisers, and made no serious attempt to win the hearts and minds of his new sub-jects, dismissing them as 'dogs'.

Macnaghten and Burnes, at least outwardly, were the soul of confidence. The resident remarked that he led 'a very pleasant life', while Macnaghten's wife felt 'the perfect tranquillity of the country' was 'miraculous'. The army, though, was not in Kabul. They could have gone into the Bala Hissar, but Shuja was not keen. He needed the space for his well-populated harem, so the soldiers were accommodated in a camp on the open plain 1½ miles from the city, surrounded by dilapidated forts. It had walls, but they were 'beyond measure contemptible', according to Kaye, and the army's food, powder and ammunition were kept in two of the forts outside the camp. One young artilleryman considered the arrangement 'a disgrace to our military skill and judgment'. There were also garrisons at Kandahar, Ghazni and Jalalabad, while, to maintain the veneer of 'miraculous tranquillity', Macnaghten's political officers were always buzzing about dispensing bribes or uttering threats to keep the Afghans in line.

As time went on, the danger signs grew. In the south of the country, the half-naked corpse of a political officer was found chained to a camel pan-nier. Soldiers began to be insulted and harassed in the streets. Macnaghten still maintained that everything was 'quiet', but fewer now believed him. Major-General William Nott said: 'Unless several regiments be quickly sent, not a man will be left to note the fall of his comrades.' Major Colin

Mackenzie also believed the expedition was skating on very thin ice: 'Our gallant fellows in Afghanistan must be reinforced' he said, 'or they will all perish' while at Jalalabad, Colonel William Dennie expressed a similar fear: 'you will see: not a soul will reach here from Kabul except one man, who will come to tell us the rest are destroyed'. Lady Sale, who knew how busy 'Fighting Bob' had been battling with rebellious tribesmen outside the capital, considered the envoy was 'trying to deceive himself into an assurance that the country is in a quiescent state' while, even in faraway London, Wellington believed the Army of the Indus was now in a 'precarious and dangerous position'. Macnaghten though was not interested in bad news. He was due to return to India to become governor of Bombay, and did not want anything to rock the boat. On 15 September 1841, he declared: 'Our prospects in this country are brightening in every direction.'

By then, the army had a new commander – Major-General William Elphinstone – who had served with distinction in Wellington's army at Waterloo. Indeed, he had not seen action since then, and now he was so crippled by gout and a variety of other infirmities, that he could hardly walk. He made no secret of the fact that he did not think he was up to the job, being 'done up in body and mind' but Auckland had sent him off anyway, telling him that Afghanistan's mountains would be much better for his health than the hot plains of India. Elphinstone was generally regarded as a delightful, kind, courteous man, but he was also, according to Nott, 'the most incompetent soldier that was to be found among officers of the requisite rank'. Even Elphinstone, though, could see how dangerously located the camp was, and how precarious were the lines of communication through narrow passes to India, but the outgoing commander told him: 'you will have nothing to do here, all is peace'.

Back in the summer, under pressure from Auckland, who would soon be returning to England, Macnaghten agreed to a major budget cut, halving the handouts he was making to the Afghan chiefs. According to an old saying, you can rent an Afghan, but you cannot buy him, and the Ghilzai, who controlled the passes that were Kabul's lifeline, were furious. They plundered a valuable caravan, and blocked some crucial routes. Macnaghten said that they were just 'kicking up a row', and that although they had 'completely succeeded in cutting off our communications for the time being', they would be 'well trounced'. However, when a force of sepoys were dispatched to administer the 'trouncing' on 9 October, the Ghilzai fell on them, inflicting twenty-four casualties. 'Fighting Bob' then went and cleared the passes, but lost 100 men killed and wounded, and Macnaghten also had to hand over a substantial payment.

Burnes could call on a useful network of informers, headed up by his Kashmiri secretary, Mohan Lal. Now they were telling him that Dost Mohammad's ablest son, Akhbar Khan, a handsome, impulsive and charismatic figure who had been in exile, was back in Kabul, and that a group of Afghan chiefs were hatching a plot to expel the British. One of their number was determined to kill the resident, who had allegedly seduced his mistress, and this act might provide the signal for a general rising. Burnes was advised to move into the army's camp, but he stayed put. On the night of 2 November, with Macnaghten already packing to leave, a mob besieged Burnes's house. He ordered his sepoy guards not to shoot, and then, accompanied by his brother and his assistant, William Broadfoot, he went out onto the balcony to appeal for order, but the crowd were having none of it. Shooting began. Broadfoot picked off half a dozen rioters in the garden below, but then he was shot dead, through the heart. As the mob set fire to the stables, a stranger appeared and told the Burnes brothers to follow him. They wrapped themselves in Afghan robes and went with him, but as soon as they were in the garden, the stranger told the crowd who they were, and they were cut to pieces. Then all the sepoy guards and their wives and children were murdered. The paymaster, Captain Johnson, who lived next door, escaped only because he was spending the night in camp, but the mob killed everyone in his household, and took all the money they could find. The much-maligned Shuja ordered one of his regiments out of his palace to put down the rebellion. They lost 200 dead and wounded, and had to beat a hasty retreat, but at least it was more impressive than Elphinstone's response to the murder of the British resident and his assistant. The commander wrote to Macnaghten that he was 'considering what can be done'. He had come to the conclusion that 'our dilemma is a difficult one'. If the army marched into town, they would 'only have to come back again … we must see what the morning brings'. Some senior British officers had treated Elphinstone with contempt from the first moment he arrived, but this they could scarcely believe. Macnaghten, meanwhile, moved into the camp.

Even the bravest Afghan insurgent must have been waiting with some apprehension for the inevitable British response. When none came, riot turned into revolt. Elphinstone, now even more ill and virtually bedridden, sent Lady Sale's son-in-law, Lieutenant John Sturt, to the Bala Hissar to try to agree a co-ordinated response with Shuja, but as he went inside, he was stabbed, and had to be brought back by an armed escort. Meanwhile, more and more Afghans began to assemble around the camp, and blocked the road that connected it with the food, medicine and ammunition stores. Lady Sale expressed alarm that inside the camp, they had only a few days' provisions. The next day, Ensign Warren, who was defending the stores with eighty sepoys, said that without reinforcements he could not hold out. Three times, Elphinstone sent out detachments to try to punch their way through, but each one was too small to succeed. After this, the commander seemed ready to give up the stores, but Macnaghten and others protested. At 9pm that night, Elphinstone held a council of war, and, after a lot of talking, finally agreed to prepare to make a sortie at 4am the next morning, but just as they were getting ready to move out, Warren and the surviving defenders appeared to say they had been forced out. The Afghans promptly plundered, then burned the stores. Not only did this deprive the army of supplies, and cut them off from Kabul, but according to Lieutenant Vincent Eyre, it also seemed to reveal such defeatism that it encouraged those chiefs who had so far remained neutral to 'join in the general combination to drive us from the country'.

There followed long frustrating days of endless discussion about what the army should do. Elphinstone prevaricated, wondered, kept changing his mind, and often launched into lengthy reminiscences about the Peninsular War. Macnaghten favoured getting the entire garrison and camp followers to make a night march to Bala Hissar, but Elphinstone's number two, Brigadier John Shelton, who had lost an arm in the Peninsular War, opposed it. Shelton was a difficult man: bad tempered – perhaps because the amputation of his arm had left him in constant pain – and deeply unpopular with his soldiers. Lady Sale wrote in her diary: 'General Elphinstone vacillates on every point.' She thought it was 'a very strange circumstance that troops were not immediately sent into the city to quell the affair in the commencement, but we seem to sit quietly with our hands folded, and look on'. Shelton took to bringing a bedroll to Elphinstone's meetings and curling up on the floor, pretending to be asleep. The commander complained bitterly about the attitude of his deputy. He also noticed that the soldiers were becoming openly contemptuous of him. When he ordered: 'eyes right', they would all look the other way. On 23 November, Shelton led the garrison's most ambitious sortie, to try to maintain communications with a village from which they had been buying grain. The British Army still used the Brown Bess musket, the weapon of Waterloo, which was effective to a range of only about 150 yards, while the

Afghans' jezails could kill at over five times that distance. The brigadier drew the men up in squares, making them a perfect target for the Afghan marksmen: a tactic Lieutenant Eyre thought little short of suicidal. Watching from a rooftop, dodging bullets behind the chimney stack, Lady Sale saw that 'the fire of the enemy told considerably more than ours'. In fact, repeated British volleys seemed to have no effect. After about three hours of fighting: 'our whole force, both horse and foot, were driven down the hill, and our gun captured – a regular case of *sauve qui peut*'.

It was the last throw of the dice. Food was running out, snow was falling, animals were eating the bark from the trees. Elphinstone went to meet Akhbar with an offer. The British, he said, were in Afghanistan only for the welfare and happiness of the Afghan people, and since their presence had grown displeasing, they would go immediately. Their protégé, Shuja, could do as he pleased. Dost Mohammad would be allowed to return as soon as they had safely left the country. In return, the Afghans would send provisions to their camp, and guarantee them safe conduct. Akhbar was probably astonished to receive such an abject submission, and accepted at once. The garrison were to leave in three days. Unfortunately, Macnaghten believed he was cleverer than the Afghans, and did not want his mission to end in failure, so he started trying to play one chief off against another, promising money he did not have. Then an Anglo-Indian cavalry officer, Captain 'Gentleman Jim' Skinner, who had been trapped in Kabul when the rioting began, appeared in the camp, saying Akhbar had befriended him and offered a secret deal. Shuja could remain king, while Akhbar would be his vizier, and would pick up a handsome fee and then a pension for life from the British. Elphinstone's army would be allowed to stay for another eight months, and then leave apparently of its own free will. The envoy, seeing a way of avoiding a fiasco that might severely blight his prospects, snatched the messenger's hand off, and signed a statement saying he accepted the terms. A number of people warned Macnaghten that it might be a trap, but he simply replied, 'trust me' while he confided to his assistant, George Lawrence, that he had felt so humiliated by the events of the last few weeks, that 'rather than be disgraced', he 'would risk 100 deaths'. Two days before Christmas, Macnaghten rode out to meet Akhbar with three officers, a small detachment of cavalry and a fine Arab mare as a present. The prince was with a group of chiefs and a crowd of warriors. A carpet was laid on the snow and Macnaghten and Akhbar sat down. The prince asked whether the envoy was prepared to implement their agreement. When the Ulsterman said: 'Why not?' Akhbar shouted: 'seize them', and the Afghans fell on Macnaghten and his comrades. Their escort fled and one of the officers was killed. Macnagten appears to have been shot and wounded in the struggle by a pistol he had once presented to Akhbar. The other two officers saw the envoy being dragged off head first, before they were imprisoned in a nearby fort. Later that day his head was paraded through Kabul's streets, while his corpse was hung from a meat hook in the great bazaar.

The Afghans braced themselves again. This time there surely must be a British reprisal! Instead, Elphinstone meekly reopened negotiations as though nothing had happened. Now Akhbar dictated the terms: the British would leave at once, handing over all of their treasure and most of their guns, plus hostages, to ensure that Dost Mohammad was safely returned. For their part, the Afghans would provide 'an escort of trustworthy persons' to see their unwanted guests to the Indian frontier. There were plenty in Elphinstone's camp who did not believe Akhbar. Major Pottinger, the saviour of Herat, had been seriously wounded while serving as a political officer to the north of Kabul and had still not recovered when he was handed the poisoned chalice of Macnaghten's old job. He complained: 'I was hauled out of my sick room, and obligated to negotiate for the safety of a parcel of fools who were doing all they could to assure their destruction.' Lady Sale wrote that the chiefs' real plan was to capture all the women, and kill all the men except one, but it was bitterly cold, and food was running out. A day's ration for a soldier now might be a little flour with some melted ghee. Pottinger advised against accepting the terms, and urged trying to move to Shuja's citadel to wait for a relief force, while Burnes's old secretary, Mohan Lal, warned Elphinstone not to trust the Afghan prince, but when the general put the plans to a council, they were accepted, and a total of 130 hostages were handed over. Lady Sale summed up her fears: 'We are to depart without a guard, without money, without provisions.'

The promised Afghan escort did not arrive, but on the morning of 6 January 1842, 700 European soldiers, 3,800 Indian sepoys, including most of Shuja's remaining troops, and 12,000 camp followers, as well as bullocks pulling carts, camels, mules and ponies, began the retreat from Kabul, with the snow thick on the ground. They had about eight guns. To reach the safety of Jalalabad, where 'Fighting Bob' was still holding on with a British garrison, they would have to travel 90 miles. The thirty or so European women and children on the march were in camel panniers, while the camp followers would have to struggle along on foot carrying babies, bundles, baskets, cooking pots and all manner of things. About 100 Afghans gathered around the gate to watch them go. No attempt was made to harass the party until the rearguard, under Shelton's command, had exited the camp. Then the mob rushed in to plunder or destroy anything left behind, while snipers began firing at the retreating British from the ramparts. Fifty were killed or wounded, and they had to leave two guns behind. The column's progress was painful, with the camp followers slowing everything down, and spreading confusion as they broke up the soldiers' formations with their milling around, jostling and trying to push to the front. The first mile took two and a half hours, and by the end of it, some people were already frostbitten. Eyre wrote: 'the very air we breathed froze in its passage out of the mouth and nostrils' while icicles formed on moustaches and beards. Already baggage was being abandoned, and many Indian bearers simply fled into the wilderness. Parties of Afghans, some on horseback, began shadowing the column. At first, it was assumed they were the escort. Then they launched an attack on the rearguard who beat them off, but the marauders just turned their attention to the virtually defenceless centre, cutting down unarmed men and women with their swords, grabbing as much plunder as they could, and then riding off unopposed. On the first day, the fugitives managed to travel just 5 miles, and scores of exhausted sepoys and camp followers, said Eyre, 'sat down in despair to perish in the snow' while the rearguard arrived hours after everyone else, having spent the whole day fighting running battles. By the next morning, most of Shuja's troops had deserted, some to join the Afghans, while hundreds of sepoys abandoned their regiments and their weapons to walk with their families.

The next morning the column was a good deal smaller, but the advance guard had to fight its way through the camp followers who had set off before they should. Lady Sale noted: 'Discipline was clearly at an end' and when a group of tribesmen swooped on the column to steal two guns, the regular British troops guarding them 'made themselves scarce', though another group of regulars put an Afghan band to flight with a bayonet charge. Elphinstone sent Captain Skinner to complain to Akhbar about the attacks, but the prince said they were happening because the army had moved off before its escort could be organised, even though it had started at the agreed time. Friendly Afghans had warned the British that they must cover at least 15 miles on the first day and get through the first pass, the Khoord-Kabul. Instead they halted early on the second day, with just 10 miles covered, and more and more armed Afghans closing in on them. Shelton was beside himself with fury. Then, wrote Eyre: 'Night again closed over us, with its attendant train of horrors – starvation, cold, exhaustion, death.'

On 8 January it was hard even to get up with, in the words of Lady Sale: 'nearly every man paralysed with cold, so as to be scarcely able to hold his musket or move'. At last they reached the long Khoord-Kabul pass, said to be so narrow and enclosed that the sun 'rarely penetrates its gloomy recesses'. Up above, thousands of Ghilzai were waiting for them. Akhbar seemed to motion them away, but they just waited until the whole column was in the gorge, and then opened fire. 'Bullets kept whizzing by us', wrote Lady Sale. Many fell, never to rise again. She was wounded in the wrist, while another three bullets passed through her coat without harming her. Her son-in-law, Lieutenant Sturt, was seriously wounded in his abdomen, and died the following day. By the time they got to the end of the pass, 2,500 civilians and 500 soldiers lay dead or dying. From now on, there seemed to be horsemen at every gulley and deadly marksmen on every ridge. One lieutenant, who had been speared in the back, tried to crawl after the column on his hands and knees. Akhbar offered to convince the Ghilzai to stop firing if he was given more hostages. He particularly wanted Shelton, but the brigadier flatly refused, so instead he was given Pottinger, George Lawrence and Major Mackenzie, whose native troops had all been killed or had fled.

The next day, the column moved off at first light without waiting for Elphinstone's order. After they had gone a mile he called them back, though many of the camp followers ignored him. Once again, Shelton was livid. Another day's march would have got them below the snow line. The reason for the recall was an offer from Akhbar. He would take all the women under his protection. Eleven, including Lady Sale and Lady Macnaghten were handed over, plus a few husbands, such as Lieutenant Eyre, who had been wounded, and about twenty children. They were taken to an old fort and given some mutton bones and greasy rice to eat. The rest of the column spent the whole day in camp. By now its fighting strength was down to fewer than 1,000, and there were still 70 miles to go. The sepoys could no longer hold their guns, and, wrote Kaye, the Afghans came among them with long knives, and 'slaughtered them like sheep'. On the fifth day of the march, 10 January, the column had to enter the Tunghee Tareekee gorge. It was quite short, but only 4 yards wide. The Ghilzais resumed their slaughter and soon the path was strewn with dead bodies that the living had to clamber over. The rearguard faced repeated waves of attack. Shelton's shortcomings were many, but he was a brave man, and he and his troops steadfastly resisted. Akhbar watched from a nearby peak, and if anyone tried to remonstrate with him, he just said that he could not restrain the tribesmen. The next gorge they found strewn with the bodies of camp followers who had run on ahead of the column, while the Ghilzai stood around admiring their handiwork. Once again the soldiers had to battle their way through, and once again Shelton was praised for his 'persevering energy and unflinching fortitude'. By the end of the day, there were only about 450 soldiers left. All the sepoys were missing, though some were with the camp followers – now down to perhaps 4,000 in number, and they were still 50 miles from Jalalabad. Akhbar made a new offer: all the Europeans should lay down their arms and enter his custody, but he could do nothing for the Indian civilians. Elphinstone rejected it.

Instead, that night, amid growing desperation, the remaining officers decided that to try to outwit the Afghans, what was left of the column should make a surprise night march on to Jagdalak, just over 20 miles away. Having spiked their last gun, they set off at about 7pm and, for a long time, they encountered no resistance. Then at Seh-Saba, shots were fired at the rear of the column. As was their wont, the camp followers surged to the front. Then when shots were fired there, they rushed to the back again, maddened with fear. This human tsunami effect overwhelmed the handful of soldiers, and the Afghan marksmen took a terrible toll even in the dark. The column was still 10 miles from Jagdalak when dawn broke on 11 January, and Shelton fought off attacks all day until they finally reached the village in the late afternoon. Then they halted for a day while Skinner went to negotiate with Akhbar. He came back with the news that the prince wished to hold a conference with Elphinstone, Shelton and Captain Johnson. They were received politely with food and tea, and then Akhbar told them they were now his hostages. Elphinstone demanded to be allowed to return to his men, but Akhbar refused, and then a tribesman shot and killed Skinner. Perhaps he knew too many secrets about the prince's machinations.

It left the remains of the column under the command of Brigadier Thomas Anquetil and facing the worst obstacle of all, the Jagdalak Pass, a gloomy, winding, gorge between immense crags. As they struggled warily through it, the survivors found themselves confronted by a 6-feet high barricade made from thorny holly oak. While the soldiers desperately tried to pull it apart with their bare hands, the Ghilzai unleashed furious fire on them from the ridges above, and horsemen galloped in among them, mercilessly hacking down anyone they could catch. Anquetil was one of the first to die, and eleven other officers were killed with him, among the hundreds who perished at the barrier, so that only about fifty troops managed to reach Gandamak village at daybreak on 13 January. At first the local people seemed friendly, but a fight began when they started trying to grab the soldiers' weapons. As the troops ran out of ammunition, they were slaughtered, apart from about half a dozen who were taken prisoner. That left just a dozen horsemen who had managed to gallop clear from the slaughter at the Jagdalak Pass, bypassed Gandamak, and now found themselves apparently in the clear. They were the only survivors still at large from the 16,000 or more who had started out from Kabul a week before. At the village of Futtehabad, about 16 miles from Jalalabad, one of them, Captain Bellew, stopped to ask for food. A villager raised a red flag, and soon Afghan horsemen were descending on them from all sides. Bellew was killed instantly, and only five of the group got away.

Three of them raced off to an unknown fate, leaving behind just Lieutenant Steer, who was wounded, as was his horse, and an army surgeon, Dr William Brydon, who had been given a pony by a wounded Indian soldier. After a time, Steer could go no further, and, in spite of Brydon's pleas, insisted on being left behind. As the surgeon got closer to Jalalabad, a group of tribesmen circled around him, throwing stones and swinging their swords. He defended himself as best he could until all he had left was the hilt of his broken sword, which he threw in the face of one of his assailants. Exhausted, he dropped down onto his pony's neck, and then suddenly found himself alone. Had the tribesmen thought he was reaching for a pistol, and fled? Anyway, frostbitten and wounded in four places, Brydon finally spotted the Union Jack flying above Jalalabad. He took off his forage cap, and feebly waved it. The gates of the fortress opened, and a group of officers ran out to meet him, while Colonel Dennie reminded his comrades of his extraordinary prescience: 'Did I not say so? Here comes the messenger.' The garrison lit beacons and sounded bugles every half hour to guide home any other survivors, but no one came.

So ended the first of Queen Victoria's colonial wars. It had been a disaster for the British, but an even bigger one for the Indians who accompanied them. Most of the 16,000 native servants, sepoys, and their families perished. A few children were kidnapped by Afghan tribesmen, and some camp followers and Indian soldiers turned up in Kabul as beggars. These were the invisible victims. Lady Sale had forty servants, but none were ever mentioned by name in her diary. Lieutenant Eyre's son was saved by an Afghan woman servant who galloped through an ambush with the boy strapped to her back, but her name is also unknown. Elphinstone died in April, still in Akhbar's custody. The prince had his body respectfully wrapped in aromatic blankets and sent to Jalalabad, attended by the general's valet. Poor Shuja had had most of his soldiers taken away by the retreating British, and did not long survive their departure. At first he stayed holed up in his citadel, but in April he emerged to inspect his remaining troops and was promptly shot dead by his godson. In September, a British 'Army of Retribution' led by Major-General George Pollock appeared in Kabul, having defeated Akhbar's forces twice. He had dealt with the problem of negotiating the treacherous passes by the tactic of 'crowning the heights' which involved sending out flanking units to secure the high ground above to protect the troops below from snipers. In the capital, Pollock executed men he took to be 'rebels' and blew up the grand bazaar where Macnaghten's body had been hung. Brydon recovered from his ordeal, though his pony did not. Fifteen years later, he was again seriously wounded in the Indian Mutiny, but survived to die in his bed in 1873. In captivity, Lady Sale had to endure a number of forced marches, and earned the nickname the 'Petticoat Grenadier'. She was liberated by her beloved husband, 'Fighting Bob', who would die in battle against the Sikhs in 1845. Lady Sale passed away in South Africa eight years later. The inscription on her grave reads: 'Underneath this stone reposes all that could die of Lady Sale.' Shelton was liberated by the British Army in September, and faced a court-martial for his disrespectful attitude to Elphinstone, for acting without authority, and for allowing himself to be captured. He was exonerated, and the court praised his 'personal gallantry'. In 1845, while he was serving in Dublin, his horse threw him and, after three days of agony, he died. It is said that his regiment gave three cheers when they heard the news. Akhbar died suddenly in 1847 at the age of twenty-nine. Some believe he was poisoned.

Auckland, who had set the whole disaster in motion, was anxious to 'move on', as they say nowadays. He blamed everyone else, and anyway dismissed the loss of a whole army as a 'partial reverse'. It worked. He got himself appointed First Lord of the Admiralty. Others though, were determined that the catastrophe should not be so easily forgotten. Sir John Kaye, who published his *History of the War in Afghanistan* in 1851, described it as a 'totally overwhelming' failure. He proved that, to justify the war, the government had issued a dodgy dossier, and revealed how all the good things Burnes had to say about Dost Mohammad had mysteriously disappeared from the dispatches that were published. Sir John Cam Hobhouse, president of the India Board of Control, replied that making these comments public 'would have answered no good purpose'. But the scandal did not die so easily, and in 1861 the radical MP, John Bright, called for an inquiry into who was responsible for doctoring Burnes's missives. Palmerston, by now prime minister, said the resident had severely misjudged the situation and that there was no point in publishing papers that had not influenced government decisions. Bright exploded. If Burnes's views were of no importance, why had they been falsified? The war had cost more than 15,000 lives, he fumed, but still the prime minister showed the British people 'documents which are not true – which slander our public servants, and which slander them most basely when they are dead and are not here to answer'. The MP failed to get his inquiry, and Palmerston complained that it was 'really too bad to put us on our defence about a transaction which happened upwards of 20 years ago'. All those lives had been lost in the name of getting rid of Dost Mohammad, and yet after Shuja's murder, the British helped him regain his throne; for his part, he would show himself a true friend of the British Empire until his death in 1863. He always remained baffled by the invasion of his country, though, once remarking to a British visitor: 'I cannot understand why the rulers of so great an empire should have gone across the Indus to deprive me of my poor and barren country.'

13

The Charge of the Light Brigade, 1854

Half a league, half a league,
Half a league onward,
All in the valley of Death
Rode the six hundred.

It was perhaps the best, certainly the most memorable, work ever produced by a poet laureate in the line of duty, and Alfred, Lord Tennyson explains the reason for the destruction of the Light Brigade very succinctly. 'Some one' — the poem does not say who — 'had blunder'd'.

The Crimean War arose from a demand by the Czar to have the right to protect the Christian subjects of the Ottoman (Turkish) Empire. Suspicious of his motives, the Christian British and French promptly took the side of the Muslim Turks against the Christian Russians, and sent their forces to the Crimea to fight on the Ottoman side in September 1854. One of the allies' first acts was to lay siege to the Russian fortress city of Sevastopol. By mid October the Czar was demanding that his generals took action to relieve it, and they decided to strike at the British Army's lifeline — its supply route — that ran about 15 miles from the port of Balaclava. Every item of food, ammunition and equipment had to come this way, and it was poorly defended because the invader's forces had been severely depleted by sickness. Just over a mile out of the port, the only road from Balaclava to Sevastopol – the Voronzov Road – ran along the top of a ridge known as the Causeway Heights which divided the plains of Balaclava into two valleys, the North and the South. To try to keep control of the road, the allies had built a chain of six redoubts along the heights, housing British naval guns manned by Turkish soldiers. The plains themselves were a natural amphitheatre, about 3 miles long and 2 miles wide, surrounded by hills. By 24 October, the Russians had gathered a formidable force there – 25,000 men and thirty-eight guns.

The British commander was Lord Raglan, who had served with some distinction in the Peninsular War, and had lost an arm fighting at Wellington's side at Waterloo. By then he had married the duke's niece and become his military secretary. For the next forty years, Raglan was an army administrator. Then at the age of sixty-five, although he had never commanded an army in the field, he was chosen to lead the expeditionary force in the Crimea. On 24 October, a Turkish spy warned him that the Russians would attack in force on the plains the next day. His lordship replied: 'Very well'. Unfortunately, three days before, a similar warning had been delivered, the cavalry had stood by in bitter cold for fourteen hours, a major had died of exposure, and there had been no assault. On this occasion, history would not repeat itself. Before dawn on 25 October, the Russians moved their guns onto the undefended Fedyukhin Hills commanding the northern side of the North Valley. Then they attacked and captured four of the redoubts on the Causeway Heights, all before Lord Raglan put in an appearance at 8am. The British cavalry commander, Lord Lucan, tried to disrupt the Russians by ordering the Heavy Brigade and the Horse Artillery to advance a little and fire a few rounds, but he knew it could only be a bluff because his orders were to hold these forces back for the defence of Balaclava itself, and the manoeuvre failed to halt the enemy. Ironically, the only real experience Lucan had had of war was with the Russian Army when he served on its staff during a campaign against the Turks in the late 1820s. A reputation for being over-cautious had seen the troops dub him 'Lord Look-on'. His brother-in-law, Lord Cardigan, commanded the light cavalry, the Light Brigade. The pair detested each other, and were barely on speaking terms, while most of their soldiers seemed to hate them both. One commented: 'two such fools could hardly be picked out of the British Army. And they take command. But they are Earls!' Another remarked: 'We call Lucan the cautious ass and Cardigan the dangerous ass.' Cardigan was supposed to be junior to Lucan, but he kept trying to establish the Light Brigade as an independent fiefdom, something that Raglan, by accident or design, seemed to encourage. Vain, and a notorious womaniser with a foul temper, Cardigan once had an officer arrested for drinking porter at a mess dinner, while earlier in the campaign he had made his exhausted men keep moving their tents around until he was satisfied that they were arranged in a sufficiently symmetrical manner. He had no experience of combat either, and if Raglan was late to the fray, he was even later. While Lucan shared the lice, the mud, the scant food and the icy winds of the camp with his men, by special permission of Lord Raglan, Cardigan slept in Balaclava harbour on his yacht, drinking champagne and consuming dishes served up by his French cook. So it was not until 9am that the commander of the Light Brigade arrived on the scene.

Raglan watched the action from the hills above, giving him a grandstand view on a lovely, clear day. Seeing the British were hopelessly outnumbered, he sent orders for two infantry divisions to come from the siege of Sevastopol. Even if the order had been obeyed promptly, it would have taken a couple of hours for them to arrive, but it was not, because of more squabbling between the top brass. One of the infantry commanders, Sir George Cathcart, who had been secretly designated as Raglan's successor if he should die, felt that the commander-in-chief was freezing him out, and inundated him with constant complaints. It would be 10am before Sir George could be persuaded to start moving his men. In the meantime, the Heavy Brigade inflicted a stunning reverse on the Russian cavalry in the South Valley, even though they were heavily outnumbered. It was an act of sufficient valour to earn a poem of its own from Tennyson, 'The Charge of the Heavy Brigade at Balaclava'. While Lucan and the Heavy Brigade were giving the Russians a hard time, Cardigan's Light Brigade looked tamely on, even though Captain William Morris pleaded with Cardigan to let them pitch in and exploit the disorder in enemy ranks. As it was, the Russians were able to regroup, cross the Causeway Heights, and set up their guns at the end of the North Valley. At the end of the action, Lucan sent Cardigan an angry message demanding to know why he had not supported it.

Throughout the campaign, Raglan had been worried that he did not have enough cavalry, and was reluctant to commit what he had. At the Battle of the Alma, just two weeks before, for example, his horsemen had been, in the view of the great *Times* war correspondent, William Russell, 'improperly restrained from charging'. This had led to a feeling 'that our cavalry had not been properly handled since they arrived in the Crimea, and that they had lost golden opportunities from the indecision and excessive caution of their leaders.' Now as Raglan looked down on the valley below, he grew increasingly concerned about what was happening. The first problem was that the Russians might take command of the crucial Voronzov Road. The second was that his French allies, who were also watching, could mark this engagement down as a British defeat. Raglan's grandstand view had a number of drawbacks. It took half an hour before an order from him could reach the plain, and it gave him a very misleading impression. The valley floor was broken up not just by the Causeway Heights but by many mounds and hillocks, so there were lots of things that Raglan could see from up above that Lucan could not, and unfortunately the cavalry commander had done no reconnaissance to ascertain where exactly the Russian forces were. Lucan had obeyed his first order from Lord Raglan that morning with great reluctance because it left Sir Colin Campbell's Highland Brigade infantry in a very exposed position. They had then been attacked by a formidable force of Russian cavalry, and managed to fight them off only thanks to Campbell's resourcefulness and the courage of his men.

Now Raglan thought he spotted an opportunity. The Russians on the Causeway Heights seemed dangerously isolated, and he believed there was a chance to recapture the redoubts and naval guns they had taken and re-establish control of the Voronzov Road. He dispatched an order to Lucan: 'Cavalry to advance and take advantage of any opportunity to recover the Heights. They will be supported by infantry which have been ordered to advance on two fronts.' Lucan read this as meaning he should wait for the infantry before he advanced. After all, as Russell put it in *The Times*: 'It is a maxim of war that "cavalry never act without a support"'. Anyway, the order seemed to be a disaster in the making – requiring a charge uphill against Russian artillery and infantry. So for the moment all Lucan did was to order the Heavy Brigade forward into a position from which an attack would be possible. Watching up above, Raglan grew more and more impatient, not to say embarrassed, with all those French eyes on him, and his discomfiture got worse as it looked as though the Russians were going to start removing the captured guns from the redoubts.

Time for another order. As usual, the commander dictated it to his quartermaster-general, General Richard Airey, but this time, unusually, Airey specifically included Raglan's name: 'Lord Raglan wishes the cavalry to advance rapidly to the front, follow the enemy, and try to prevent the enemy carrying away the guns – Troop Horse Artillery may accompany – French cavalry is on your left. Immediate.' Had the quartermaster-general realised the dangerous implications of this instruction? It was in the hand of an aide-de-camp (ADC) who was about to set off with it, when up bounded one of his colleagues, Captain Lewis Nolan. A fast and daring rider, Nolan said he would carry the message. As he plunged onto the precipitous path to the valley at breakneck speed, Raglan called after him: 'Tell Lord Lucan the cavalry is to attack immediately.' Nolan was headstrong and brave. Indeed, according to Russell, 'a braver soldier than Captain Nolan the army did not possess'. He had written two books on cavalry warfare and believed that light cavalry could do almost anything: 'break squares, take batteries, ride over columns of infantry', as Russell put it. The captain was furious about the way the cavalry had been, in his view, misused; in fact, 'in some measure disgraced' so far in the Crimea, and he blamed it all on wretched leadership by Lucan, who he despised. The feeling was mutual. Nolan rode up to the cavalry commander sitting on his horse, and handed him the order. From his position, Lucan could not see a single Russian soldier or a single Russian gun. He read the order slowly and carefully, but did not understand it. Which guns did it refer to? Those on the Heights, mentioned in Raglan's earlier order but not referred to this one, or some others? When he sought clarification, Nolan brusquely replied that he must attack immediately. 'Attack, sir! Attack what? What guns, sir?' asked Lucan. Nolan then threw back his head, in, as the commander would put it later, 'a most disrespectful' manner, gestured theatrically towards the end of the North Valley, and replied: '*There*, my Lord, is your enemy; *there* are your guns.' The captain's manner was so insolent that some observers felt he should have been arrested on the spot. As for the content of the order, military orthodoxy was that, as Russell put it: 'infantry should be close at hand when cavalry carry guns, as the effect is only instantaneous'. Everyone knew that to send cavalry alone against artillery was likely to result in their annihilation. Lucan said later that he 'urged the uselessness of such an attack and the dangers attending it'. By now, Nolan was beside himself with impatience. He cut the commander short, saying again: 'Lord Raglan's orders are that the cavalry are to attack immediately.'

Lucan went to see Cardigan and ordered him to advance with the Light Brigade while he followed with the Heavy Brigade. The pair might loathe each other, but this fateful conversation was conducted with impeccable propriety. Cardigan said politely: 'Certainly, sir; but allow me to point out to you that the Russians have a battery in the valley on our front and batteries and riflemen to both sides.' Lucan shrugged his shoulders and replied: 'I know it, but Lord Raglan will have it. We have no choice but to obey.' Cardigan said nothing and saluted, while Lucan instructed him to 'advance very steadily and keep his men well in hand'. Seldom have upper lips been stiffer. While this was going on, Nolan had gone to see Captain Morris, who was a friend of his, and got permission to join in the charge. It was 11.10am. In the front rank, Cardigan put the 13th Light Dragoons and the 17th Lancers. His own regiment, the 11th Hussars, formed the second, while in the third were the 4th Light Dragoons and the 8th Hussars, accompanied by their mascot, Jimmy, the Irish terrier. Cardigan took up his position seven lengths in front of the first rank, with his staff just behind him. Quietly, he gave the order: 'Walk. March. Trot.'

> 'Forward the Light Brigade!'
> Was there a man dismay'd?
> Not tho' the soldier knew
> Some one had blunder'd:
> Their's not to make reply,
> Their's not to reason why,
> Their's but to do and die:
> Into the Valley of Death
> Rode the six hundred.

These men were probably the best light cavalry in Europe – the Russians feared them as 'those terrible horsemen'– though their mounts had been weakened by the long journey to the Crimea and by lack of food. Now was their chance to show the 'damned Heavies' what they could do. A mile and a half ahead of them at the end of the North Valley stood twelve Russian guns and the main body of enemy cavalry. On the Fedyukhin Hills to their left were fourteen guns as well as infantry and cavalry, while on the Causeway Heights to their right were thirty guns and eleven infantry battalions. Tennyson did not exaggerate. Truly they were riding 'into the jaws of death, into the mouth of Hell'.

As they moved forward, an eerie hush fell. Russell watched the Light Brigade go 'proudly past, glittering in the morning sun in all the pride and splendour of war. We could scarcely believe the evidence of our senses! Surely that handful of men are not going to charge an army in position? Alas, it was but too true.' Cardigan rode as stiff and upright as a ramrod, staring straight ahead. Raglan said he had 'the heart of a lion'. Another observer thought he looked 'the very incarnation of bravery'. The enemy themselves seemed to hesitate. They could not believe their eyes either. Then the first salvo rang out. At that moment, Nolan suddenly emerged from the ranks and dashed diagonally in front of Cardigan, turned, pointed with his sword, and shouted. No one could hear him above the guns. Was he trying to redirect the assault towards the Heights? Had he suddenly realised that this was not what Raglan wanted at all? Perhaps, but he had been talking to Captain Morris for quite a while before the advance, and had never said anything to disabuse his friend of the notion that they would be attacking the guns at the end of the valley. Anyway, we shall never know, because at that moment Nolan was struck by a shell fragment, and with a terrible scream, he died instantly, though Cardigan did not realise it. As far as he was concerned, he had just witnessed an act of appalling insubordination, a takeover bid for command of the brigade!

The earl had taken Lucan's instruction to heart, and as his men tried to speed up, he kept slowing them down. Indeed, in this, one of the most famous charges in history, no order to charge was ever given. Soon, though, the pressure from behind became intolerable. Captain White of the 17th Lancers said the men were simply 'anxious to get out of such a murderous fire and into the guns as being the lesser of two evils'. Russian round-shot and shells ripped gaping holes in their lines, the men closed up to fill them, then fresh gaping holes appeared. The troopers in the rear ranks found themselves riding over their dead and dying comrades and their horses. Sergeant Mitchell of the 13th Light Dragoons, on the right of the first line, said 'the number of men and horses falling increased every moment'. His horse was wounded and fell, trapping him beneath it. Then he heard the second line galloping up, and 'lay down expecting to be trampled' but somehow he escaped. One of Raglan's entourage began to weep. As the brigade broke into a gallop, troopers cheered and yelled. Riderless, often wounded, horses careered in and out of the ranks. The French *Chasseurs d'Afrique* mounted a brave attack on the Fedyukhin Hills and managed to disrupt the bombardment from there, but as the Light Brigade got within 80 yards of the guns, with Cardigan still 'steady as a church', a frontal salvo wiped them out by the dozen. Watching aghast from above, the French general, Pierre Bosquet, famously observed: '*C'est magnifique, mais ce n'est pas la guerre*' though the continuation of his remark: '*C'est de la folie*' – it is madness – is less often quoted.

As the Light Brigade sped up, the slower Heavy Brigade fell further behind. It too came under withering artillery fire. Lucan was wounded in the leg. His horse was hit in two places, and his ADC was killed, as were many other men. Watching the commander's steadiness under fire, one of those who most hated him had to admit through clenched teeth: 'damn him, he's brave'. Now, though, he ordered the halt to be sounded. 'They have sacrificed the Light Brigade' he said, 'they shall not the Heavy, if I can help it', and he pulled the soldiers out of range of the guns, deciding the only useful thing they could do was to 'protect the Light Cavalry against pursuit on their return'.

When Cardigan was just two or three lengths from the guns, he felt a torrent of flame rush down his right side, and believed for a moment he had lost a leg, but he had no time for any further thoughts as in an instant he found himself the first man into Russian artillery. However, he considered it was 'no part of a general's duty to fight the enemy among private soldiers' so he galloped on beyond the guns until, through the smoke, he caught sight of a mass of Russian cavalry. As luck would have it, one of its officers, Prince Radzivill, recognised Cardigan, who he had met in London at dinners and balls, and sent off a troop of Cossacks to take him alive. At the cost of a slight wound to his thigh, the earl evaded them. Having 'led the Brigade and launched them with due impetus' he decided his 'duty was done'. So, amid the continuing Russian fire, at a leisurely, dignified pace, he made his way back to the British lines, past the dead, dying and wounded.

For those of Cardigan's men who were still alive, things were rather more frenetic:

Flash'd all their sabres bare,
Flash'd as they turned in air
Sabring the gunners there

In smoke so thick that a trooper could not see his arm in front of him, they cut, hacked and thrust like madmen. 'Cossack and Russian reel'd from the sabre-stroke', but they too fought bravely, and the massive superiority of Russian cavalry numbers soon told. Captain Morris managed to kill a senior Russian officer, but was then left lying unconscious with his skull cut open in two places. The 4th Light Dragoons secured some enemy guns for a time, but were soon driven off. The surviving officers desperately searched for their commander, but in the end all they could do was gather together any soldiers they could find and retreat down the valley. The way back was, if anything, even worse than the advance. Horses were wounded and exhausted and so were the men, many now on foot: 'some running, some limping, some crawling'. No one knew who was alive and who was dead, no one gave orders, and all the time the guns kept firing while Russian lancers swooped down, cutting off stragglers and taking prisoners. The Heavy Brigade did what they could to help, and suffered heavier casualties than in their own charge a couple of hours earlier. Lord George Paget, leading the 4th Light Dragoons called it 'a scene of havoc ... strewn with the dead and dying, and all friends!' He had been astonished to see Cardigan 'riding composedly' back, and wrote an official complaint, saying the earl had abandoned the Light Brigade to its fate.

Cardigan, though, had other things on his mind. When he saw Brigadier-General the Hon. James Scarlett, commander of the Heavy Brigade, he launched into a tirade against Nolan, accusing him of insubordination and of 'screaming like a woman when he was hit!' 'Say no more, my lord,' Scarlett replied, 'You have just ridden over Captain Nolan's dead body.' With that matter off his chest, Cardigan went to see the survivors. Jimmy the terrier had escaped with just a small cut to his neck, but there were only 195 men mounted and fit for action: more than 300 were killed, wounded or captured, and 475 horses were dead or about to be shot. The whole affair had taken just twenty minutes. And for what? If it had not been for the carnage, it would have been like the Grand Old Duke of York. The Light Brigade's commanders had sent it charging up to the end of the valley, and charging – or, more truthfully, staggering – back again. Cardigan said: 'Men, it is a mad-brained trick, but it is no fault of mine' and a voice answered: 'Never mind, my lord, we are ready to go again.'

Not everyone was so easily satisfied, though. One British lieutenant described it as 'a most dreadful disaster.... We all pray that whoever is to blame for this may be made to answer for it.' Another officer declared it 'the most useless and shocking sacrifice of the lives of hundreds of brave men that was ever witnessed' while a French colonel said the Light Brigade 'might as well have been ordered to charge the walls of Sevastopol'. When Raglan saw Cardigan, he began shaking with rage: 'What did you mean, Sir' he demanded, 'by attacking a battery in front, contrary to all the usages of war and the customs of service?' Cardigan replied: 'My lord, I hope you will not blame me, for I received the order from my superior in front of the troops.' Then he rode serenely off to his waiting yacht. So if the blame could not be put on Cardigan, how about Lucan? 'You have lost the Light Brigade' thundered Raglan. Lucan waved Raglan's own order in front of him. The commander-in-chief then made the rather surprising suggestion that Lucan should have disobeyed it. He ought to have 'exercised discretion', and if he disapproved of the charge, he 'should not have caused it to be made'. Lucan was incensed; his own regiment, the 17th Lancers, had just come close to being wiped out. He pointed out that under Queen's Regulations 'all orders sent by aides-de-camp … are to be obeyed with the same readiness, as if delivered personally by the general officers to whom such aides are attached.' Rather than disobey such an order, he would 'blow his brains out' and he warned Raglan that he would not 'bear one particle of the blame'. While the top brass wrangled, the poor, bloody cavalry, most of whom had had nothing to eat since the day before, had to wait without food for another six hours before they were stood down. After the charge, the Battle of Balaclava rather fizzled out, but it did have one important strategic consequence. The British lost control of the Voronzov Road, so that from then on supplies could only be carried from Balaclava on steep, treacherous paths, condemning men and horses to a winter of shortage, suffering and death.

One way to defuse a disaster like this was the creation of a myth, and it began with William Russell's report in *The Times*. He had witnessed 'the exhibition of the most brilliant valour, of the excess of courage, and of a daring which would have reflected lustre on the best days of chivalry… Don Quixote in his tilt against the windmill was not near so rash and reckless as the gallant fellows who prepared without a thought to rush on almost certain death.' The correspondent gave the myth a villain. Not Raglan, or Lucan, or Cardigan, but the dastardly Russians – 'a savage and barbarian enemy' who committed 'an atrocity without parallel in the modern warfare of civilised nations'. As the Light Brigade retreated 'to the eternal disgrace of the Russian name, the miscreants poured a murderous volley of grape and canister' on them, and also hit some of their own men. It was stirring stuff, though as the Light Brigade had not surrendered and were still an enemy in the field, it was not altogether clear that any other army would have acted much differently, and the myth proved insufficiently powerful to still the awkward questions.

As commanding officer, Lord Raglan held the commanding heights in the impending PR war, and he quickly got *The Times* to print a dispatch that blamed the charge on 'some misconception of the instruction to advance'.

For some unaccountable reason, Lucan had thought it meant 'he was bound to attack at all hazards'. Raglan also praised Cardigan for 'the most spirited and gallant manner' in which he had obeyed the order. Lucan did not find out what his commander had written until the end of November when copies of *The Times* reached the Crimea. He demanded to see Raglan. His request was refused. So he wrote him a letter, explaining that he had queried the order with Nolan, but that Nolan had insisted that Raglan's instruction was that they should attack and that he had had no alternative but to obey – anything else would have amounted to 'direct disobedience of orders'. Raglan tried to get Lucan to withdraw his letter, but the cavalry commander insisted on sending it to the secretary for war in London, the duke of Newcastle. Raglan then reiterated his own case to Newcastle – that Lucan had misunderstood the order, that there was nothing telling him to attack 'at all hazards' and so on.

Whatever the rights and wrongs of it all, the government decided they could not have two senior commanders on such bad terms, and recalled Lucan. Many in the army considered he had been unfairly treated, but few were sorry to see him go. 'He was a horrible old fellow' said one young officer. Lucan arrived back on 1 March 1855 to find Cardigan, who had already got himself home on the grounds of ill health, being fêted everywhere as the hero of Balaclava. The queen invited him to Windsor, he was showered with honours and appointed inspector-general of cavalry. He also kept telling everyone that the charge of the Light Brigade was all Lucan's fault. Lucan tried everything to clear his name: he requested a court-martial and attempted to start a debate in the House of Lords no fewer than four times. That summer, Lord Raglan died of fever, a few days after an allied assault on Sevastopol failed. Perhaps it was a blessing. After seeing his army starve during the winter, he had said: 'I could never return to England now. They would stone me to death.'

The Crimean War ended in 1856, with the Russians agreeing not to interfere in Turkey's internal affairs, and promising not to establish any military bases on the Black Sea, but as the veterans started returning home, Cardigan's reputation began to receive more and more dents. 'Who was the first man out of action after the charge?' asked some, while others circulated stories that he had sat out the whole thing on his yacht. When Raglan's nephew and ADC, Colonel the Hon. Somerset Calthorpe, wrote a book that criticised his conduct, Cardigan took him to court. Bad move. This second battle of Balaclava would shred his reputation almost as comprehensively as the first battle had shredded the Light Brigade. The proceedings exposed what seemed to most people to be an extraordinarily callous lack of concern for the brave men who served under him. A hero no longer, he died after falling from his horse in 1868. Lucan also brought, and lost, a libel action against the *Daily News*, but then he had never been a hero. He survived Cardigan by twenty years, and was promoted to field marshal just before his death.

There may be some debate about the exact portions of blame due to Raglan, Lucan and Cardigan, but it is clear that none of them emerge with much credit from the story. Unlike the Light Brigade itself, whose bravery inspired a great poet to write the words that would immortalise them:

> When can their glory fade?
> O the wild charge they made!
> All the world wonder'd.
> Honour the charge they made!
> Honour the Light Brigade,
> Noble six hundred!

14

The Battle of Isandlwana, 1879

It would be no contest, surely. Well-trained imperial troops with artillery against savages armed mainly with spears. That, at least, was the view in British military circles when they mounted an invasion of Zululand, but at the Battle of Isandlwana, the Zulus out-thought and out-fought the redcoats, and brought about perhaps the greatest military humiliation in British colonial history.

King Cetshwayo of the Zulus was a confirmed Anglophile. In 1875, he told a missionary: 'I love the English' adding, by way of proof, that he considered himself more the son of Queen Victoria than of his own father, but he also said: 'I am a king in my own country and must be treated as such.... I shall not hear dictation... I shall perish first.' When the British annexed the Boer republic of the Transvaal two years later, he welcomed it. The Boers were always trying to steal bits of his land.

The British prime minister, Benjamin Disraeli, was just as keen on maintaining good relations between Britain and Zululand. In 1878, he had scored a major diplomatic triumph at the Congress of Berlin, halting Russian expansionism without a shot being fired. The last thing he needed now was a war in Africa that might stir up the animosity of other European powers, as well as costing a lot of money. Indeed, his cabinet declared a Zulu war would be a 'serious evil'. Others in London, however, were committed to expanding British rule in South Africa, like the then colonial secretary, Lord Carnarvon, who believed the annexation of Zululand was simply a matter of time. Such views were also common in South Africa itself, among men such as Sir Bartle Frere, high commissioner of native affairs, who saw himself becoming governor-general of a mighty new South African confederation, and with the fastest message from London taking more than two weeks to arrive, they had lots of room for manoeuvre. Many others were simply afraid of the formidable Zulu military machine, which could put 30,000 warriors in the field, and in January 1878, Sir Theophilus Shepstone, secretary for native affairs in Natal, had proclaimed: 'no permanent peace can be hoped for until Zulu power has been broken up'.

Shepstone had once been a champion of Cetshwayo, and had attended his coronation, but now he was the administrator of the newly annexed Transvaal, and he needed to pacify its people, who were deeply unenthusiastic about British rule. An opportunity soon arose. For years, the Boers had been laying claim to a piece of territory on the north-western border of Zululand. Shepstone had always rejected their demands, and Cetshwayo's father had even offered to hand over the land in question to the British. In October 1877, Shepstone did a u-turn, telling the Zulus they must give the disputed land to the Boers. Cetshwayo was furious. His messengers did not mince their king's words, telling Shepstone he was a cheat and a fraud.

Sir Theophilus told London that Cetshwayo must go, or he would become a role model for every African chief who felt like defying the British. Then he launched a smear campaign against the Zulu king in the press, drawing on the testimony of whisky and gun runners, and disgruntled missionaries who had been signally unsuccessful at converting the Zulus. People were warned about the 'black shadow' lurking across the border. The governor of Natal, Sir Henry Bulwer, was appalled by this sabre rattling, and announced a commission of inquiry into the ownership of the disputed territory. Even though Sir Theophilus's brother, John, was one of the committee, in July 1878 it found in favour of the Zulus. It could hardly do otherwise. The Boers had produced not a shred of credible evidence in support of their claim.

Frere reacted by trying to impose a news blackout while he endeavoured to get the result changed. When this failed, he presented Cetshwayo with an ultimatum on 11 December. Like so many ultimatums, it was designed not to ensure that the recipient complied, but that they would find it impossible to comply. The king had thirty days to disband his army and accept a virtual British protectorate, or his country would be invaded. When the ultimatum expired, a British force of 7,000 crossed the Buffalo River into Zululand on 12 January 1879. They established a depot at Rorke's Drift, then advanced carefully eastwards, slowed down by the muddy ground.

An engraving by Andrew Birrell based on the depiction by the Gothic painter, Henry Fuseli, of the ancient Briton Caratacus successfully pleading for his life before the Emperor Claudius in Rome, following the conquest of Britain. (*US Library of Congress*)

The famous statue of Queen Boudicca on the Thames Embankment close to the Houses of Parliament. (*Paul Baillie-Lane*)

A nineteenth-century view of the speech that the historian Tacitus put into the mouth of the Caledonian leader Calgacus before his troops did battle with the Romans at Mons Graupius. (*The Pictorial History of Scotland*, London, 1859)

A seventeenth-century view of the arrival in England of the brothers Hengest and Horsa in AD 449; by tradition, the start of the Anglo-Saxon conquest. (*A Restitution of Decayed Intelligence*, 1605)

The Battle of Hastings was a close-run thing, but in the end, the Norman cavalry were able to cut down the English fighting on foot. This is how an eighteenth-century artist, Philip James de Loutherbourg, saw it. (*Hume's History of England*, 1804, courtesy of *LIFE Photo Archive*)

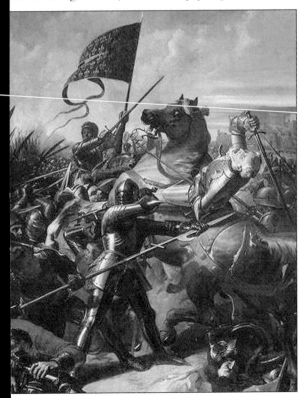

The death of Talbot, the 'English Achilles', at the Battle of Castillon which virtually ended the Hundred Years' War. In reality, Talbot was not wearing armour, having previously sworn never again to put it on against the French. (From a painting by Charles-Philippe Lariviére, 1798–1876)

One of Britain's greatest naval disasters, and one of the Netherlands' greatest triumphs – the burning of the English fleet in the Medway. This is a Dutch view. (A painting by Jan van Leyden

'The defeat of the British Armada.' In 1741, a huge force of ships and men was sent against Spain's South American Empire, but, amid bitter inter-service rivalry, it suffered a humiliating defeat at the fortress of Cartagena de Indias in modern-day Colombia.

Forty years after Cartagena, the surrender of Lord Cornwallis's army at Yorktown effectively sealed Britain's defeat in the American War of Independence. (*US Library of Congress*)

When British soldiers encountered a French force sent to support Irish rebels at Castlebar in 1798, they ran from the field at such speed that wags dubbed the event 'the Castlebar Races'.

At the Battle of New Orleans in 1812, General Andrew Jackson's motley band of frontiersman routed a professional British army that considered itself the best in Europe. (*US Library of Congress*)

Did I not say so? Here comes the messenger.' A prescient colonel had said that only one man would be left alive at the end of the retreat from Kabul in 1842, and that he would recount the story of the disaster. Dr William Brydon was the man. (A painting by Elizabeth Butler)

Perhaps the most famous military mistake in British history. The Light Brigade is sent to its destruction in a head-on charge against Russian artillery. (courtesy of James Bancroft, *Echelon*)

George W. Joy's famous painting of Gordon's Last Stand. There are a number of different accounts of how the general met his death, but all agree that Khartoum fell after a siege lasting ten months.

In the foreground of this picture, the British seem to be doing rather well against their Zulu enemies. In fact, the Battle of Isandlwana was a comprehensive defeat. (*Illustrated London News*)

Most people in Britain expected the Boer War to be a walkover, but the Boers proved tough and resourceful enemies, inflicting three humiliating reverses on the British in just six days of 'Black Week' in 1899.

British artillery in action during the Gallipoli campaign. Designed to sidestep the murderous stalemate of the Western Front, the offensive was soon bogged down in bloody deadlock.(*The War Illustrated*)

Men from the 11th Battalion, the Cheshire Regiment manning a British trench near the Albert–Bapaume road at Ovillers–La–Boisselle, during the Battle of the Somme. Nearly 100,000 British and British Empire soldiers would be killed. (*Crown Copyright*)

Captured British and French troops at Veules-les-Roses in 1940. Dunkirk was a masterpiece of escape, with 300,000 allied troops snatched from under the noses of the Germans, but Britain still lost 66,000 killed, wounded or captured. (*Picture Post*, 1940)

The surrender of General Percival at Singapore, described by Churchill as 'the worst disaster and largest capitulation in British history'. The fall of the supposedly impregnable fortress island left 85,000 prisoners in Japanese hands. (*Cody Images*)

The commander was Lord Chelmsford, a brave and conscientious, but not noticeably talented, soldier. He divided his army into three separate columns and eight days later, the 4,000 under his direct command pitched camp on a hillside beneath a strange-looking rock the Zulus called Isandlwana. Their tents spread over half a mile. A Boer veteran warned Chelmsford that he was facing a dangerous enemy, and advised him to set his wagons in a laager, and indeed the general's own field regulations said camps should be entrenched and laagered, but he made no attempt to erect defences, complaining: 'It would take a week.'

King Cetshwayo was still hoping for peace, and, even when the British began burning Zulu villages and stealing cattle, at first he ordered his troops to fight only in self-defence, but as the scale of the invasion became clear, he decided it would have to be confronted, and on 17 January he dispatched his army of about 24,000. He knew Britain's enormous resources meant that in any long war, it was bound to emerge victorious, but he believed that if he could gain a quick victory over the invasion force, and threaten Natal, then just maybe he could make a peace that would save his country before the enemy could send reinforcements. His plan was to throw his best warriors against the main column, and defeat it in a pitched battle.

Chelmsford, on the other hand, was worried the Zulus might try to avoid fighting. Shortly after midnight on 22 January, he learned that while out reconnoitring, Major John Dartnell had spotted some of the enemy, and had requested two troops of soldiers so he could attack them. Chelmsford decided to go one better – or worse. He would split his army yet again, and would personally take most of the forces at Isandlwana, including four of the six guns and all the mounted infantry, to join Dartnell. Left in command at the camp was Lieutenant-Colonel Henry Pulleine. For most of his career, Pulleine had been a desk soldier, and had only seen action for the first time during the last couple of years. Now he was ordered to act 'strictly on the defensive'. Chelmsford also instructed Lieutenant-Colonel Anthony Durnford to bring up his contingent of 300 mounted native troops plus a rocket battery from Rorke's Drift, 12 miles away, though it was not made clear whether they were to reinforce Isandlwana or support Chelmsford's advance. Durnford was an interesting character. He carried his left arm in a sling after an assegai wound received fighting the Hlubi tribe in Natal, and was a great admirer of the valour of African warriors. A champion of native rights, he had served on the commission of inquiry that awarded the disputed territory to the Zulus. Now, as a soldier, he said he could not deny his excitement about the invasion, but 'as a man' he condemned it. He was officially senior to Pulleine, but unfortunately Chelmsford's orders did not make clear who was to be in command at Isandlwana.

Meanwhile, the commander of the Zulu Army, Chief Ntshingwayo, was keeping his main force hidden about 6 miles from Pulleine, lighting fake camp fires and sending out soldiers in other places to mislead the enemy. It was twenty years since the Zulus had fought a war, and none of his army had ever been in a battle against the white man. When he saw Chelmsford's column leave at dawn, he knew he had been presented with an unrepeatable opportunity to strike a blow that might be decisive enough to induce the British to make peace. To defend his camp, Pulleine had about 1,250 soldiers, including nearly 900 Europeans, along with about 350 wagon drivers and other camp followers, and the two remaining guns. He had a core of battle-hardened men, experienced in colonial war, but many of his other 'soldiers' were not really frontline troops, but clerks, cooks or bandsmen. Ntshingwayo's scouts reported that they 'were scattered about on the hills around the camp like a lot of goats out grazing'. It looked as though the spirits of the Zulu nation had put the British into their hands to be killed.

By the time Durnford reached Isandlwana at about 10am, there had been reports of Zulus in the vicinity of the camp, sometimes of very large numbers, and just after 8am, Pulleine had sent a message to Chelmsford saying the enemy were 'advancing in force'. Even now he made no attempt to put his wagons into a circle, causing some of his men to wonder whether he was trying to invite a Zulu assault. A trooper claimed later that from a lookout point, he had seen a force of between 25,000 and 30,000 Zulus. He had reported this to an officer, but 'no heed' was taken. He and his comrades then decided they would make themselves scarce if the enemy did attack. The overall picture was still confused. A lieutenant accompanying Durnford reported seeing Zulus apparently running away. Perhaps this was all part of the deception plan and the British were meant to think that the enemy were heading off in pursuit of Chelmsford's column. Anyway, Durnford was convinced that if there was any danger, it was to Chelmsford, and following a brief conversation with Pulleine, he set off after the commander to intercept any of the enemy who might be thinking of attacking his force.

As Durnford's men advanced, small groups of the enemy kept retreating before them, drawing them on. He detached some horse soldiers to deal with a group of Zulus and as they chased them over a ridge, they were the first to encounter the main enemy force. Durnford's commissariat officer,

James Hamer, reckoned there were at least 12,000 'in perfect order, quiet as mice'. Faced with this army, Captain George Shepstone, Sir Theophilus's son, ordered a fighting retreat, though some native troops just fled back to the camp. Meanwhile, Durnford was in the valley pursuing groups of Zulus that he feared were on their way to assault Chelmsford's column. Hearing the sound of gunfire, he set off towards it, and suddenly, he too came on the enemy host about 800 yards away. When they saw him, they opened fire. Fortunately for him, most of the Zulus' guns were out-dated muzzle-loading muskets and rifles – no match for the Martini-Henry weapons carried by the British, and anyway, firearms were not key to Zulu tactics. Normally, they would just fire a ragged volley from a distance, then try to close in with their assegai, but the realisation quickly dawned on Durnford that the British had been outwitted and outmanoeuvred. There was no option but to turn back.

He tried to conduct an orderly withdrawal, but the Zulus were on them too quickly. His rocket battery managed to get just one poorly aimed shot off before it was overwhelmed and its escort of African troops fled. He and his men reached a dried-out watercourse about half a mile from the camp where he decided to make a stand. At Isandlwana, however, all was calm. Some men were even having their dinner. An artillery officer said later that no one dreamt there was 'the least danger, and all we hoped for was that the fight might come off before the general had returned'.

Chelmsford had received Pulleine's message about Zulus 'advancing in force' at about 9.30am. When asked what should be done, he replied: 'nothing'. Still, he ordered Commandant Browne to take one battalion of Natal native troops back to the camp, and sent two officers up a hill to look at Isandlwana through their telescopes, but they reported nothing unusual. By now the general was getting frustrated at the difficulty of coming to grips with the Zulus and was resigned to having to get his men to bivouac out on the plain that night, so he dispatched Captain Alan Gardner to ask Pulleine to send out tents for them, and to carry an order to entrench the camp. Gardner galloped into Isandlwana at about the same time that Shepstone arrived with his disturbing news about the huge Zulu Army. Pulleine seemed perplexed, but Gardner told him that when Chelmsford had given the order to entrench the camp, he had not known about the large force of Zulus who were about to attack. So the lieutenant-colonel decided not to obey it, but he did split his already diminished force, sending two companies to help Durnford while detaching a force of mounted men to an advanced position a quarter of a mile in front of the camp. Gardner sent a message to Chelmsford saying that there was heavy fighting but that there were reports that the Zulus were 'falling back'.

A Zulu army is supposed to attack like a charging buffalo, with the centre held back, and the horns stretched forward to encircle the enemy. For a time, the shells from the two British field guns, placed about 1,000 yards to the left of the camp, seemed to be holding the centre, while the left horn was finding it hard to advance in the face of withering fire from Durnford's reinforced group in the watercourse. One of his native soldiers said later that the lieutenant-colonel rode up and down on his charger, encouraging them: 'he was very calm and cheerful'. They held back the Zulus for a long time, but finally when they were nearly out of cartridges, and in danger of being outflanked, they had to retreat back to the camp. After about half an hour British soldiers all over the field were running short of ammunition, and many were a long way from fresh supplies, but even now, some must have thought the day would still be theirs. Many were veterans of wars with Africans, and believed case shot from artillery and concentrated rifle volleys would never fail to break up an attack. On the other hand, according to testimony after the battle from a trooper who survived, there seemed by this time to be 'a great deal of confusion, no kind of formation being made for the defence of the camp'. It was even difficult to get ammunition boxes open, because there were not enough screwdrivers.

In the face of everything the British could throw at them, these Africans kept coming – perhaps 20,000 of them. Belatedly, Pulleine ordered everyone to withdraw to the camp, but his soldiers were outpaced by the more lightly clad Zulus and: 'In a very short time' said the trooper, Isandlwana 'was invaded by vast numbers'. They shrieked their war cries, fired their muskets, stabbed with their assegais, and most of the native infantry on the British side broke and fled. The artillery had switched to case shot for only a couple of rounds when they received the order to retire, but by the time they got back to the camp, the Zulus were already in control.

A few miles away, the four guns that Chelmsford had taken with him had fallen behind the rest of his force. At about 1pm, the artillery commander, Lieutenant-Colonel Arthur Harness, was astonished to hear the sound of field guns coming from the camp. He grew even more alarmed when a galloper drew up with a message from Commandant Browne, saying: 'For God's sake, come back. The camp is surrounded.' Harness immediately started heading back with his guns, but he was spotted by Chelmsford's senior ADC, and told to pay no attention to Browne's hysterical message. In fact, just after noon, two terrified Zulu prisoners had said that a great army of about 20,000 was expected to arrive that day, but Chelmsford still seems to have thought that a camp with 1,000 rifles and two field guns could look after itself – a belief that may have been confirmed when at about 2pm, he got that report from Gardner about the Zulus 'falling back'.

At Isandlwana, though, it was turning into a rout, and such a rapid one that few British soldiers were able to fix their bayonets before the enemy were upon them. An interpreter named James Brickhill said he saw men running in all directions with no sign of an officer. James Hamer later described a scene of complete chaos: 'oxen yoked to wagons, mules, sheep, horses and men … all wildly trying to escape.' He also saw Durnford gallantly making a stand with about seventy men to cover the retreat of those now trying to escape to Rorke's Drift. After the battle, a Zulu warrior would speak of a one-armed soldier who killed many with his revolver. The lieutenant-colonel and his men held on until they had run out of ammunition, then fought with knives before they were finally overcome. Later Durnford's watch would be found, stopped at 3.40pm.

George Shepstone's body would be recovered from a clump of about thirty corpses. Like Durnford, he had let his horse go, spurning the chance to escape. A Zulu eyewitness said he had fought 'very bravely' trying to hold back the right horn of the attack, but he was finally killed while he was reloading. Captain Reginald Younghusband was also praised by his foes. His company had retreated in good order and made a last stand beneath the rock of Isandlwana. They kept shooting until they ran out of ammunition, then attempted a suicidal charge down the hill. Sixty-eight bodies were found here. There were other stories of small groups fighting back to back until their ammunition ran out. The last British soldier to fall was said to have taken cover in a cave and shot every Zulu who came near until a volley finally silenced him. It is not known how Pulleine met his end; he was last seen by Gardner close to his tent and some said he was on his way to write a final note to Chelmsford.

The bravery of those who tried to buy time for others to escape was to little avail. The main track out of the camp was soon blocked by panic-stricken men, many of them wounded. According to a Zulu warrior, one group of sixty, who had been surrounded, pleaded for mercy, only to receive the reply: 'How can we give you mercy when you have come to us to take away our country?' One man who did get away was Lieutenant Horace Smith-Dorrien, who just a few hours before – though now it must have seemed like a lifetime – had delivered Chelmsford's message to Durnford to come to Isandlwana. He told how, when the Zulus entered the camp, he and some others had made for the place where their ranks seemed thinnest to try and burst through. They went 'pell-mell over ground covered with huge boulders and rocks' until they reached a deep gulley. 'How the horses got over I have no idea' said Smith-Dorrien, but they ran into more Zulus there whom they had to 'go bang through'. Many of the men with him were killed there. The lieutenant said he had many 'marvellous escapes', firing away with his revolver while he galloped along. The pursuing Zulus 'were going as fast as the horses' and killing fugitives all the way.

At last, he came to a 'kind of precipice' leading down to the Buffalo River, which was now in flood and 80 yards wide. He led his horse down, but just as he jumped back on it, it was hit by an assegai. Now Smith-Dorrien found himself surrounded by Zulus who were finishing off the wounded, so he ran off on foot, and leapt into the 'roaring torrent'. As he was swept along he managed to grab the tail of a loose horse and get safely to the bank. Even then the Zulus kept firing, killing men fleeing close by him. His boots were full of water, and the enemy chased him for another 3 miles, but he evaded them and staggered on until he reached Natal. He had been very lucky. Only fifty-five Europeans, including just five officers, one of whom was Captain Gardner, and 350 African auxiliaries had survived.

By 3pm, Chelmsford realised that the main Zulu force had escaped him, and began to lead his column back towards Isandlwana. On the way, he met Rupert Lonsdale, commandant of one of the native battalions, who told an extraordinary story. He had become separated from his soldiers while they were chasing Zulus, and in the mid afternoon he had gone back to the camp to try to organise rations for his men, who had had hardly anything to eat for thirty-six hours. As he approached, a sentry shot at him. The camp was full of redcoats, but a closer look revealed that they had black faces. There was not a white man to be seen, and the Zulus were looting the place. More shots rang out, but he managed to gallop away. Many officers refused to believe his story, but Chelmsford did. He got his men together, and told them that the Zulus had taken their camp, and that they must take it back 'at any cost' and then cut their way to Rorke's Drift. The soldiers answered with a cheer. As Isandlwana came into distant view, they saw masses of Zulus retiring with oxen and wagons. It was pitch black by the time they finally got there, but they could see campfires, and wagons drawn up to block their approach. They shelled the wagons, and then advanced, only to find the camp deserted. The enemy had evaded them once again. Over Rorke's Drift, though, there was an ominous glow in the sky.

The next morning, before it was light, Chelmsford ordered his men to retreat to the depot there. They had not even had time to bury the dead, though the general may also have wanted to spare them the sight that greeted a news reporter – their comrades lying dead, stripped and often mutilated with a ritual slash across the abdomen. The Zulus had captured more than 1,000 rifles and a lot of ammunition and supplies, along with the oxen and wagons. Zulu losses were estimated at about 1,000 killed, while a similar number are thought to have died from their wounds in the months that followed. When Chelmsford reached Rorke's Drift, the mission station was still burning, but the garrison of just 120 had held out against up to 4,000 Zulus, killing about 500 of them. In other words, they had been more heavily outnumbered than the men at Isandlwana. Rorke's Drift had demonstrated the value of defences, even when rapidly improvised. A wall built of biscuit tins had helped the garrison to survive. According to one of his staff, Chelmsford was 'awfully cut up' about the disaster at Isandlwana, and they were afraid he might have a breakdown. He raced off to the Natal capital, Pietermaritzburg, while all over the province, people built laagers and braced themselves for a Zulu invasion. Cetshwayo, however, had ordered his men not to cross the frontier.

It was not until 12 February that first reports reached London: more than 1,000 men massacred by some African rabble, and Chelmsford scurrying back into Natal with his tail between his legs! It must be a hoax, was the first reaction of the new colonial secretary, Sir Michael Hicks Beach. As it became clear that the unthinkable had actually happened – an incredible defeat for British arms at the hands of a supposedly primitive foe, Disraeli was dumbfounded. This might bring his government down. He had to admit to Parliament that it had been 'a terrible military disaster'.

But Chelmsford quickly got down to work at Pietermaritzburg – rewriting history and salvaging his career. He dispatched a long letter to Colonel the Hon. Frederick Stanley, Secretary of State for War, putting the blame for the disaster squarely on Durnford. An excellent choice – being dead, he was in no position to argue. If only the lieutenant-colonel had not left the camp with his force, but had 'taken up a defensive position' and made a rapid entrenchment, Chelmsford was 'absolutely confident' that the Zulus could have been held at bay. He also convened a 'court of inquiry', though it is not clear what entitled it to the term 'inquiry'. It heard from just eight witnesses, none of whom were cross-examined, and was told, falsely, that Durnford had been ordered to take command at Isandlwana. At the conclusion of its brief proceedings, the court, 'very properly' in Chelmsford's view, expressed no opinion on what had gone wrong. The 'inquiry' may have expressed no view, but Colonel William Bellairs, Chelmsford's deputy adjutant-general, did, and once again it was the ghost of poor Durnford that was cast as the villain. If he had not 'interfered' with Pulleine's defence of the camp: 'it cannot be doubted that a different result would have been obtained'.

Chelmsford plainly understood an important rule of propaganda – that a lie can be halfway around the world before the truth has got its boots on – but right from the start there were people in London who did not buy his account. An Intelligence Department memorandum noted that he did 'not seem to have fortified the camp at Isandlwana'. He had allowed himself to be decoyed away by the Zulus. When he left, he had not kept up proper communications. How could an army of thousands of Zulus have been concealed so close to the camp? Why did his scouts not discover them? The British people were furious at the humiliation, with the *Illustrated London News* demanding that the Zulus must be 'defeated; their tyrant deposed', and then put under British rule. Disraeli also faced calls for Chelmsford's head, but he did not accede to them. Instead, to bring the Zulus to heel, the general was sent everything he asked for – cavalry, artillery, stores – and more. He had requested three battalions of infantry: he got five. As the months wore on, though, Chelmsford made further dubious military judgments, and in June, a rising army star, Major-General Sir Garnet Wolseley, said to be Gilbert and Sullivan's 'very model of a modern Major-General', was sent in over his head as the new commander of all forces in Southern Africa. As Cetshwayo had foreseen, once the British really turned their minds to the war, there could only be one winner, and on 4 July 1879, Chelmsford scored a decisive victory over the Zulus at Ulundi. Five days later, he resigned. He was received coolly in England, though Queen Victoria was still a fan, and heaped on him whatever honours she could, such as the position of Gold Stick at court.

Disraeli had been urged to take action against Sir Bartle Frere, and in this case he responded rather more quickly. The high commissioner of native affairs was censured, and then effectively demoted. The Conservative leader still lost the general election of 1880 heavily, though economic troubles were probably a more significant factor than Isandlwana. But what of Cetshwayo, the man who looked up to Queen Victoria like a mother? He was captured in August 1879 and sent into exile, while Wolseley broke Zululand up into little principalities under many separate chiefs. As the country was riven by a civil war between Cetshwayo's supporters and those of the puppet rulers appointed by the British, he was brought back in 1883, but was unable to establish peace, and he handed himself over to the British once again. Within a few months he was dead – officially from a heart attack, though his followers claimed he had been poisoned. Ntshingwayo, the general who had masterminded the Zulus' great victory, also perished in the Zulu civil war.

15

Khartoum, 1885

Prime Minister W.E. Gladstone was desperate to avoid getting entangled in the Sudan, but he allowed himself to be manoeuvred into dispatching a renegade soldier with a famously dismissive attitude towards official orders to the country. General Gordon ignored instructions to evacuate exposed garrisons, and instead made a last stand at Khartoum and turned himself into a British imperial martyr.

General Charles George Gordon was one of the loosest cannons ever to infiltrate the upper echelons of the British Army. Before he had reached his mid twenties, he had distinguished himself by his enterprise and reckless bravery during the Crimean War, and had been awarded the *Légion d'Honneur* by Britain's French allies. In the 1860s, he went to China to fight in the Second Opium War, and personally directed the burning down of the emperor's summer palace. Then, when rebels began threatening Shanghai, foreign merchants in the city raised a force of Chinese and put him in charge. Although heavily outnumbered, Gordon completely outmanoeuvred the enemy and won an impressive victory. These successes made him rather disrespectful towards his superiors. Returning to England as 'Chinese' Gordon, he commanded the Royal Engineers at Gravesend, but became better known for running clubs for street urchins, and tending the sick in the workhouse hospital. The dying would often send for him rather than a doctor. During a mild bout of smallpox, he had found God, and become a devout, though mystical and unorthodox, Christian. He once told a friend he had just walked arm-in-arm with the

Almighty along the street, and he took to posting religious tracts on trees or throwing them through train windows. Gordon believed the earth was enclosed in a golden globe with God's throne directly above, and that the Garden of Eden was on the seabed near the Seychelles. Unmarried and a chain smoker, he stood only 5 feet 5 inches tall, and had a sweet smile and piercing blue eyes.

In Gordon's time, Egypt was officially part of the Turkish Ottoman Empire, but in practice, the Khedive, who ruled as the Sultan's viceroy, was virtually independent. Khedive Isma'il Pasha often employed Europeans in important positions, and he recruited Gordon to be governor-general of the Sudan, a troublesome 1 million square miles of desert that had been a dependency of Egypt for half a century but which seemed to be in a constant state of turmoil. After insisting that the salary he had been offered should be reduced by four-fifths, Gordon took the job and launched into hyperactivity: mapping the Upper Nile, establishing a line of stations that extended as far as Uganda, crushing rebellions and suppressing the slave trade in the south of the country. He also abolished torture in the prisons and public floggings. In Darfur, the slavers rose in revolt, so Gordon rode into their camp in full dress uniform with just an interpreter and a small escort. He was so persuasive that some of the rebels joined him, while others gave up, and the revolt petered out. Eventually, though, the governor-general grew tired and frustrated and returned to England in 1880.

He then served in a variety of posts and places including Mauritius, where he scandalised Europeans by sitting at the back of the church with the natives. His behaviour became, if anything, even more mercurial. Once he travelled all the way to India to be private secretary to the new viceroy, then resigned after just a few days. The diplomat Sir Thomas Wade confided to the Foreign Office: 'His nerve is perfectly unshaken, but his judgment is no longer in balance, and … his very devoutness is dangerous' while an official in the Chinese service, Sir Robert Hart, put it more bluntly: 'Much as I like and respect him, I must say he is "*not all there*".' By 1883, Gordon was at a loose end, and agreed to go and take charge of the Congo Free State for King Leopold of the Belgians. This might have proved a highly challenging appointment for the pious Gordon as the Free State regime became one of the most spectacularly brutal in history, wiping out perhaps half the native population, up to 15 million people, over the next two and a half decades. But just as he was about to take up the job, on 18 January 1884, he received a telegram inviting him to the War Office to attend a meeting with the

British government. Gordon, now aged fifty, was about to become the most famous man in the world.

Two years after he had left the Sudan, the British had been alarmed by a revolt in Egypt on a 'foreigners out' ticket. Egypt was seen as the key to India, the jewel in the imperial crown, especially after Disraeli bought shares in the Suez Canal. General Sir Garnet Wolseley was dispatched to sort out the problem. He defeated the rebels at Tel-el-Kebir and occupied Cairo in short order, describing the operation as 'the tidiest war in British history'. Britain kept assuring the rest of the world that it had no designs on Egypt, so the Khedive stayed Khedive and the Turkish Sultan remained head of state, though now the most powerful men in the land were British 'advisers'. But what about the Sudan? Was it included in this British sphere of influence? Lots of Egyptians, and many more Britons, had little interest in it, but imperial expansionists argued that unless Britain controlled this inhospitable territory, Suez would never be safe, and slavery would never be ended, while some anti-imperialists argued that we should be trying to help establish a genuinely independent Sudan. As the debate continued, another religious mystic became prominent there, but this one was a Muslim – Muhammad Ahmad ibn as-Sayyid 'Abd Allah, who in 1881 proclaimed himself the Mahdi – the 'Expected One', a new prophet divinely appointed to purify Islam and the governments that defiled it. He declared a holy war, and in the summer of 1883, an Egyptian army of 10,000 men led by a British mercenary, Colonel William Hicks, set out to put him in his place. Sometimes described as the worst professional army in history, some of its members were kept in chains to stop them deserting. Fifty thousand of the Mahdi's supporters fell on them in the desert near El Obeid, and virtually wiped them out. Just a few hundred Egyptian soldiers escaped, while Hicks and the other British officers were never seen again. Now the Mahdi controlled much of the Sudan, meaning the remaining Egyptian garrisons there were extremely vulnerable.

So it was that the government of William Ewart Gladstone sent for Gordon to extricate the Egyptians and their families. The general was what Sir Humphrey Appleby in *Yes, Minister* might have called a courageous choice. Gladstone, never keen to throw the nation's money around, was anxious to avoid any entanglement in the Sudan, but there were plenty of other voices, including many in the press, demanding that Hicks must be avenged, and that it was cowardly and a betrayal of British missionaries to hand over the country to slavers and Muslim fanatics. Gordon's views were at least partially known already. He had given an interview to the *Pall Mall Gazette* newspaper in which he said that, as governor-general, he had brought honesty, loyalty and a real sense of community to the Sudan, that the Mahdist revolt had happened because he had left, and that evacuation was impossible: 'You must either surrender absolutely to the Mahdi or defend Khartoum [the Sudan's capital] at all hazards.'

When Gordon arrived at the War Office, there was no Gladstone. The 74-year-old prime minister was ill. Those present included the war minister, Lord Hartington, rather more hawkish than Gladstone; the foreign secretary, Lord Granville and Sir Garnet Wolseley, now adjutant-general at the War Office, who Hartington greatly admired and consulted constantly. Wolseley had a hidden agenda. He had grown up in poverty after his father, a major, died when he was only seven. Clever and ambitious, when he joined the army, he decided the only way to get on was to put himself in harm's way whenever possible. He was seriously wounded in Burma before he was twenty, and in the Crimean War he lost an eye, was promoted to captain and met Gordon. Wolseley reached the rank of general well ahead of most of his contemporaries. Queen Victoria considered him an opinionated egotist, but the press dubbed him 'our only general'. He despised Gladstone, and thought him negligent of Britain's honour – he was said to have trained his dog to bark at the sound of the prime minister's name – and he considered the Liberal leader's wish to abandon the Sudan 'the worst of ignorant, cowardly folly'. Wolseley's ideology dovetailed nicely with the requirements of his career. The army was dominated by two rival factions: the 'Wolseley Gang' and the 'Roberts Ring' centred around Major-General Sir Fred Roberts. To show who was top dog, Wolseley felt he needed a big success, and he knew that if a British army were sent to the Sudan, he would be the man to lead it because of his experience in the Ashanti and Zulu wars (see chapter fourteen). His admiration of Gordon, though, was genuine. He described him as 'infinitely superior to every man in our Cabinet'. For his part, Gordon prayed for Wolseley every night.

The meeting ended with an agreement that Gordon should go to the Sudan to 'report on the military situation' and consider the best way of evacuating the Egyptian garrisons. Gladstone approved the arrangement by telegraph. Mission creep began almost at once, as Gordon dashed off a memo to Granville suggesting the Khedive should make him governor-general of the Sudan for the 'time needed to accomplish the evacuation'. Granville approved the request and relayed it to Britain's top man in Cairo, the consul-general Sir Evelyn Baring. That same night, Gordon set off on the first leg of his journey. Wolseley carried his kit bag to Charing Cross station, while Granville bought his ticket, and as Gordon had no money, the adjutant-general handed him the contents of his wallet plus his watch and chain. Only Baring objected to the appointment, saying that no one who knew Gordon would suppose 'for one moment that he would confine himself to mere reporting' adding that 'a man who habitually consults the Prophet Isaiah' could not be counted on to obey any lesser mortal. Wolseley had come to the same conclusion; sure that Gordon would obey what he saw as the dictates of his conscience rather than any orders he might be given. Before long, the general would be cut off in the Sudan, and there would be a popular clamour for a relief force to be sent to rescue him. Gordon, for his part, appears to have told Wolseley that once he got to the Sudan, he would decide on the best course of action.

The general had been reassuring everyone that the danger from the Mahdi was exaggerated, but Colonel John Stewart, the only British officer who was to accompany him, confided to a friend that it would be 'a very dangerous mission', a sentiment the queen herself echoed. By the time Gordon reached Cairo, the job had changed again. It was no longer to report, but to organise the withdrawal of the Egyptian garrisons 'with full powers civil and military'. His meeting with the new Khedive, Tewfik, must have been a bit tense to start with, as Gordon had to apologise for describing him as 'a little snake' in his *Pall Mall Gazette* interview, but soon the two of them were getting on like a house on fire, and the new governor-general emerged with yet another task: establishing some kind of government in Khartoum. Then an episode occurred which illustrates what a nightmare Gordon must have been to deal with. One of his sworn enemies from his previous stint in the Sudan was a former slave trader, Zubeir Pasha. The general had been partly responsible for having his son executed, and on his way to Egypt, he had cabled ahead asking Baring to send Zubeir into exile. Sir Evelyn refused, and in Cairo the two old adversaries happened to run into one other. Afterwards, Gordon told the consul-general that he had experienced a 'mystic feeling' and now realised that Zubeir was the only person who could set the Sudan to rights, and that he must take him to Khartoum. When the news reached the Anti-Slavery Society, they went ballistic, and the British government declared that under no circumstances should this 'ruffian' be involved with the mission. It was all very typical Gordon. The South African high commissioner, Sir Hercules Robinson, said he had never come across anyone 'so undecided in word or so decided in action: that he would telegraph one thing in the morning, another thing in the evening, and a third thing the next day.' Nor would Gordon have disagreed. He said: 'talk of two natures in one! I have 100, and none think alike and all want to rule.'

As he set off for Khartoum, Gordon cabled the garrison: 'Stand fast. I am coming, you are men, not women.' It did not sound like the language of evacuation. The general did not take a lot of luggage, but he did pack his full dress uniform. When asked why, he replied: 'when the British Army arrives in Khartoum to relieve me, I wish to receive it properly dressed'. As Gordon and Stewart crossed the Nubian desert on camels, they were warmly received at the village of Abu Hamed, with women ululating, young men asking for jobs and tribesmen kissing their hands. Encouraged, Gordon wrote to Baring that he had not 'the slightest anxiety about the Sudan'. Everything would be settled within six months. Gordon now wrote to the Mahdi, appointing him 'Sultan of Kordofan' – a region representing about one-seventh of the country, declaring that he had brought no soldiers with him, and that there was no need for war between them. He asked the Mahdi to free his Egyptian prisoners, and to allow a telegraph line he had cut to be repaired. The general's next stop was Berber, where he told the provincial governor and the local headmen that he was in the Sudan to evacuate the garrisons. It proved a major error. Rumours had been circulating that the Sudan was going to be abandoned, but few believed them. Now here it was from the horse's mouth. Any tribes who had been thinking of declaring their loyalty to the government in Egypt were now being driven into the arms of the enemy. Gordon's revelations had severely damaged his best chance of getting the soldiers out safely – doing it before the Mahdi realised how weak he was.

Khartoum stood on the Blue Nile, at its junction with the White Nile, and its shabby buildings extended perhaps a mile inland. About 34,000 people lived there, including 8,000 soldiers. Gordon and Stewart arrived on 18 February. They were mobbed by more than 1,000 people, including women carrying sick children, who hoped Gordon would cure them with a touch – a power the Mahdi was also supposed to wield. The general said how glad he was to see them, and how sorry to find that since he was last there four years before, the Sudan had become 'miserable'. He asked for their help: 'to put it right. I have come here alone without troops, and we must ask Allah to look after the Sudan if no one else can'. Gordon moved into the governor-general's palace on the Blue Nile, a dingy two-storey building, and had the old tax records and instruments of torture publicly burned. Soon there was a carnival atmosphere; the souk was festooned with bunting and coloured lamps, while Gordon was addressed as the 'Saviour' or the 'Father of the Country'. In addition to Stewart, Gordon was also accompanied by a young *Times* correspondent, Frank Power. He thought the reception the general received was 'wonderful', considering him 'the greatest and best man of this century' though he was also gentle and humble. One of the many, and often contradictory, ideas that had now moved into Gordon's head was that to keep Egypt safe, 'the Mahdi must be smashed up'. He said that at present the Expected One was unpopular and 'comparatively easy' to destroy, but that if the opportunity was not taken now, it would become much more difficult. Whatever he may have told the provincial governor, Gordon now wrote to Baring saying that if the garrisons were withdrawn, the country would collapse into anarchy. The government should immediately appoint as his successor Zubeir Pasha, who was the only man capable of holding the Sudan together. Meanwhile, he began to apply his skills as a military engineer to Khartoum's defences, first strengthening the ramparts so that the town could not be taken by a sudden assault, then building new fortifications outside Khartoum and garrisoning the fort at Omdurman across the river. An inspection of food stocks revealed that there should be enough to feed the garrison for six months. Khartoum's most reliable link with the outside world was a little flotilla of ten paddle steamers similar to those that carried day-trippers on the Thames. Gordon had them armour-plated.

The general had no illusions about what a loose cannon he was, confiding to his diary: 'I own to having been very insubordinate to Her Majesty's Government and its officers, but it is my nature and I cannot help it.... I know if *I* was chief I would never employ *myself* for I am incorrigible.' However, if Gordon had tried to carry out his instructions, the task would have been formidable. Turco-Egyptian troops and officials, and their wives and families numbered about 6,000, but if Gordon added in any other civilians who wanted to go, that might take the number up to 20,000. The first leg of the journey would entail going up to Abu Hamed by steamer. With the ten steamers and the boats that could be towed behind each one, it would require twelve journeys, and with each round trip taking fifteen days, that would mean six months to get everyone out. The Mahdi, meanwhile, laughed when he received Gordon's offer of the Sultanate of Kordofan. He already had that, and more! He was delighted to discover that Gordon had brought no troops with him. On 22 February, a traveller warned the general that it was only a matter of time before the Mahdi attacked. The same day, Gordon got a message from Granville saying there could be no successor to him as governor-general. Without Zubeir, Gordon now believed there could be no evacuation. He begged Baring to dispatch a small force to the Sudanese border, or to send a British officer to Dongola, in the north of the Sudan, to pretend to look for quarters for British soldiers in the hope of convincing the Mahdi that a large force was on its way. Baring was now coming to the conclusion that Gordon was 'half-cracked'.

Inside Khartoum, the Mahdi's agents were busy, and Gordon's popularity soon started to wane. He had to pull back some of the troops he had posted to Omdurman, but he began telling people that a British force was on the way. The general admired the Sudanese as staunch and stalwart, including those who supported the Mahdi, but he did not think much of the garrison now under his command: 2,000 or so Arab tribesmen were a 'dreadful lot', while he felt his 1,900 bashi-bazouks (Turkish irregulars), and 1,400 Egyptians were not much better. At the beginning of March, he sent Stewart and Power, now created British consul, on a six-day scouting mission. They reported that even in normally placid villages, the locals hurled abuse at them, and that at least 20 miles of the country to the south was controlled by the Mahdi's supporters. On 12 March, 4,000 Mahdists attacked Halfaya, 9 miles to the north, and cut the telegraph line to Cairo. From then on, messages would have to be carried through hostile territory by native runners. Six days later, the enemy laid siege to Khartoum. One by one, the other Egyptian garrisons in the Sudan began to surrender. A force of Egyptians led by a disgraced British officer, Colonel Valentine Baker, was sent out to relieve one of them, but was heavily defeated with the loss of about 2,300 officers and men. Believing that the crucial Red Sea base of Suakin was under threat, London dispatched three battalions of British soldiers under Lieutenant-General Sir Gerald Graham, who defeated the Sudanese in two battles, but only after the tribesmen had broken a British square, inspiring Kipling to praise them in verse, in the assumed voice of a British soldier:

So 'ere's *to* you, Fuzzy-Wuzzy, at your 'ome in the Soudan,
You're a pore benighted 'eathen, but a first-class fightin' man

Graham suggested sending a 'flying column' to Berber, 150 miles north of Khartoum, but Cairo forbade it as too dangerous. Apart from a small garrison dispatched to Suakin, the whole force was withdrawn.

Now Gordon got an offer from the Mahdi. If he surrendered immediately he and his supporters would be saved. Otherwise, they would die. The general's only response was to evacuate about 400 ailing members of the garrison. When London asked why he did nothing more, he replied: 'because Arabs have shut us up and will not let us out'. Some of the rebels advanced to positions opposite Khartoum, set up camp, and started taking potshots at the governor's palace. Gordon sat in his usual place by a window and ignored them, but with the enemy now entrenched at Halfaya, any of his vessels trying to head north up the Nile might face hostile fire, while more and more tribes were deserting to the Mahdi. Evacuation looked a dead duck, but Gordon understood the importance of public relations, and made sure he was constantly seen around the city, seeming the very soul of confidence. He printed his own currency, personally signing the most valuable notes, and continued to tell everyone a British relief mission was on the way. In fact, in London, Gordon's rescue had not got beyond the stage of debate, though there was now plenty of that. Queen Victoria wrote to Hartington: 'Gordon is in danger. You are bound to try and save him.' Granville replied that it would be 'unjustifiable' to send a force to Khartoum, but now even Baring was pleading the general's cause: having sent Gordon to Khartoum in the first place 'it is our bounden duty, both as a matter of humanity and policy, not to abandon him'. Wolseley was even more forthright: it would be 'an indelible disgrace if we allow the most generous, patriotic, and gallant of our public servants to die of want or fall into the hands of a cruel enemy'. With the public sector dragging its feet, private enterprise, in the person of Baroness Burdett-Coutts, started trying to raise the money for an expeditionary force. Gladstone was furious. Gordon was 'turning upside down and inside out every idea and intention with which he had left England, and for which he had obtained our approval'. The Sudanese people were simply 'struggling to be free', and we should not be making war on them. Gordon was already a great national hero, however, and the prime minister was censured in Parliament and hissed at in the street. There were mass demonstrations, and people stuck white feathers on cards calling them 'Gladstone primroses'. Then, on 31 July Hartington threatened to resign. His departure might bring down the government, so Gladstone agreed to mount a rescue, though he fretted that it was likely to mean 1p on income tax. The prince of Wales volunteered to join the expedition, but the queen forbade it. As Wolseley had foreseen, he was chosen to lead the enterprise, and on 9 September he arrived in Cairo.

By then Gordon was increasingly isolated, with few messages able to pass between him and the outside world. His forces managed to sortie out of the city and inflict a few defeats on the Mahdi's men, but on 4 September, his best commander, along with about 1,000 troops, were lured into a wood and destroyed. So on the very day that Wolseley arrived in Cairo, Gordon sent Stewart and Power off on the steamer *Abbas* to tell the outside world about his plight. The colonel tried to persuade Gordon to go with them, but he refused, saying he intended to die in Khartoum. For reasons that are not clear, Gordon gave them his cipher key, so that from now on he would no longer be able to read any encrypted messages that did reach him. The *Abbas* slipped safely past Halfaya in the dark, and steamed along quite happily for nine days, until she was holed on a rock. When her passengers had to come ashore to repair her, supporters of the Mahdi set upon them and killed Stewart, Power and most of the small force who were with them.

Wolseley, meanwhile, had to decide how his force was going to make the hazardous journey to Khartoum. He put together the British Army's first ever Camel Corps – more than 1,000 soldiers drawn from a number of top regiments – and also decided to enlist boatmen who had helped him get up the Red River in Canada to take his troops along the Nile in 800 small wooden vessels. The force would travel as one as far as Korti. Then part of it would form a desert column that would take a shortcut across the wilderness on camels to re-join the river at Metemma, where Gordon's steamers could meet it and carry a small advance force the last 75 miles up to Khartoum. The river column, meanwhile, would stay in its boats, knocking out Mahdi strongholds at Abu Hamed and Berber, and then re-join the main desert column for the final assault. It all meant more delays: delays while the boatmen arrived, delays because there was not enough coal for the steamers detailed to tow the boats to the first cataracts, and delays when the Nile proved more treacherous than expected and the boats kept getting damaged on rocks. Wolseley did not reach Korti until 16 December, and many of his craft were still well behind. En route he had received a message from Gordon begging for just a handful of troops in red jackets to make an appearance in Khartoum and convince the inhabitants that the British really were on their way.

When he arrived in the Sudanese capital, Gordon had said it was 'as safe as Kensington Park', and he did his best to maintain the illusion even now, especially when he heard rumours of Wolseley's expedition. Around the streets, his assurance never wavered. He told one merchant: 'When God was portioning out fear to all the people in the world, at last it came to my turn, and there was no fear left to give me; go, tell all the people in Khartoum that Gordon fears nothing.' There were musters, band concerts, hopeful proclamations, even fake messages from the relieving army. He put labourers to work building moorings for the boats that would bring their rescuers, he sent intermediaries to rent and furnish houses for their officers. He put up barbed-wire entanglements, planted mines made from old tins filled with dynamite, got the arsenal to produce thousands of rounds of ammunition, put up dummy wooden soldiers on the banks of the river, and built a new steamer, but even Gordon could not prevent the food running out. The few horses and donkeys left were butchered, then it was the turn of the dogs, cats and rats. Corpses began to litter the streets, while desperately weak soldiers tried to stand at their posts. Every day, Gordon peered through the telescope on the palace roof for some glimpse of the British, but in the end he told the civilians they could leave. They could even join the Mahdi if they wished. Perhaps as many as 15,000 accepted the offer. Knowing that any message he sent to Wolseley might be intercepted, he dispatched a series of upbeat missives.

By now, Gordon's ordeal was the biggest story in the world. Would the relieving force reach him in time, or would he die at his post? He was no longer just a British hero, he was an international celebrity, appealing for help to the Pope and to the millionaires of America. The general enjoyed war, but recognised that its victims were often the defenceless – women, children, the old – and that for them it simply meant 'murder, pillage and cruelty'. He gained exhilaration from fighting against impossible odds, but there is a question mark over how much he wanted to be rescued. Gordon had written to his sister that: 'Earth's joys grow very dim, its glories have faded' while he had confided to Sir Hercules Robinson that if Christianity did not forbid it, he would have killed himself long before, because 'his life was a burden and a weariness to him'.

A messenger carrying one of Gordon's misleading missives managed to evade the Mahdi's sentries and reached Wolseley on 30 December. The first word from Khartoum for six weeks was dated 14 December and written on a piece of paper the size of a postage stamp. It read: 'Khartoum all right', but the messenger said Gordon had asked him to deliver another message verbally: that the city was surrounded and to please come quickly. Wolseley had wanted to go and relieve Gordon himself, but Hartington said no, so the job was entrusted to Brigadier Sir Herbert Stewart. That day, Stewart led the Camel Corps out across the desert. Progress proved much slower than expected. Some of the men had never ridden camels before, and were surprised at how uncooperative they were – it was the devil's own job to get them to trot, and they were always liable to turn their heads and nip their riders' calves. As for their supposed qualities of endurance, they appeared to get sore backs in no time, though some of that may have been down to the inability of the British to load them correctly. Or had canny Arab traders sold them inferior beasts? Whatever the reason, they began to die by the dozen, their bodies strewn across the desert. In fact, the 19th Hussars' tough little Egyptian ponies seemed to do much better.

Stewart had no idea how much opposition he would face on the way to Metemma, but the Mahdi had heard about the relief column back in October, and had had plenty of time to get prepared. He knew the British would be desperately short of water, and that they would have to come to the wells at Abu Klea, so he sent 10,000 tribesmen there to wait for them. On the morning of 16 January, Stewart's men believed they were within reach of their precious water when a party of hussars who had been scouting ahead reported that they had encountered an enemy force numbering several thousand, and had narrowly escaped with their lives. In fact, there were up to 14,000 Mahdists, and they outnumbered the British by perhaps six to one. The brigadier ordered the men to prepare for battle, but at 3pm, his number two, Colonel Frederick Burnaby, suggested that as there were only three hours of daylight left, they should wait until the next day. Stewart's force built improvised defences from boxes, trunks, sacks and barbed wire, then tried to rest, but for much of the night, the enemy kept creeping up and sniping at them. The next morning, the fire got heavier, but Stewart could see that the enemy was not going to attack. They had water. The British did not. So the brigadier formed his men into a square, with three guns and a machine-gun embedded among them and began to advance slowly on what seemed the main enemy position, occasionally halting to return fire. When they were about 200 yards away, a much bigger enemy force leapt from a ravine in which they had been hiding 'in the most perfect order' and charged at them in three arrowhead phalanxes, armed with spears, swords and hatchets. The British poured volley after volley into them, but they just kept coming, even when their dead had formed a wall of corpses.

As Lord Charles Beresford trundled out his favourite weapon, the machine-gun, a gap formed in the square. At first, he and his team were knocking down the enemy 'like ninepins', but then the gun jammed, and the Mahdist cavalry were among the troops 'with a roar like the roar of the sea'. Lieutenant-Colonel Charles Wilson saw 'a fine old sheikh on horseback [who] never swerved to the left or the right, and never ceased chanting his prayers until he had planted his banner in our square'. He was shot by a British corporal, but Stewart's men were having a terrible time. Many had their rifles give up on them and were forced to grab weapons from fallen comrades, while bayonets bent because they had been made from inferior steel. After a furious fight, British firepower finally told, and the enemy retired. As they pulled back, the square broke out into loud cheers. By then, Burnaby was dead, along with eight other officers and sixty-five men, with a similar number wounded. About 1,100 of the Mahdi's force had been killed. This action too generated a famous poem – Sir Henry Newbolt's *Vitaï Lampada* – 'There's a breathless hush in the Close tonight.' It tells how:

> The sand of the Desert is sodden red –
> Red with the wreck of a square that broke;
> The Gatling's jammed and the Colonel's dead,
> And the regiment's blind with dust and smoke.

Until:

> ...the voice of a schoolboy rallies the ranks:
> 'Play up! play up! and play the game!'

The Colonel was Burnaby, but the machine-gun was actually a Gardner and not a Gatling. Still, that night Stewart's men would have water and their first decent meal in days, but it was another 26 miles to Metemma and 100 to Khartoum, and the British soldier had learned something about the enemy. One private described them as 'the bravest of the brave. They did not know the meaning of fear.'

After burying its dead, the expedition set off for Metemma at about 4.30pm the following afternoon. No bugles were to be sounded, and orders were to be given only in a whisper. Progress was very slow even before they reached the thick forests of thorny acacia a native guide had warned them about. Although the men were close to exhaustion, Stewart decided they must press on to get within sight of Metemma by morning. A couple of hours after dark, the path got more difficult, and camels started to stumble. Big gaps appeared in the column, and when they reached the acacia forest, the confusion grew even worse as men got lost and camels had the loads torn off their backs. By 8am the next morning, they were through the forest, but still 4 miles from the Nile. Stewart ordered the soldiers to build a small stockade of stones and thorn bushes as scouts told him that thousands of the enemy were streaming out of Metemma. He believed that the Mahdists had had the stuffing knocked out of them by their defeat at Abu Klea, and he planned to fight them after breakfast. Just as the men settled down to eat, bullets started whizzing around them from snipers hidden in long grass. The fire got heavier as more and more arrived, but some British soldiers were so exhausted that they simply collapsed and were shot as they slept. Then, at about 8.30am, Stewart was mortally wounded. That left Lieutenant-Colonel Wilson in command, a man who had never before led an army in the field.

Wilson bided his time, hoping that the enemy would launch a charge, but at 3pm when they had shown no sign of it, he ordered about 900 men to form a square and advance. They moved, he said 'in a cool, collected way' even as casualties mounted, and then at last they saw the enemy collecting in force ahead of them. Count Albert Gleichen, a Grenadier Guards subaltern, said: 'Thank God! They're going to charge!' It was all over in five minutes, as British volleys felled the tribesmen in dozens. When about 300 lay dead, the Mahdists withdrew towards Metemma. Wilson's men headed to the Nile at a different point, and reached its precious waters before dark.

While the Desert Column had been trying to fight its way to Metemma, Omdurman had been besieged by the Mahdi's army, which seemed to grow bigger every day. By 13 January the garrison had run out of food and ammunition, and Gordon ordered them to surrender, allowing the Mahdi to move his guns closer to Khartoum. Eight days later and 75 miles to the north, one of the general's most trusted lieutenants, Sanjaq Mohammad Kashm al-Mus Bey, heard the artillery fire from Wilson's troops as they probed the formidable ancient fortress of Metemma searching for the best way to attack. Gordon had sent Al-Mus downriver with a small detachment to look for the relief force. The British shells were having little effect as most of them just sank into the soft walls of the fortifications, and Wilson's men had to pull back as the defenders poured rifle fire onto them from loopholes in the walls or shot heavy stones from their own guns. After an hour of fruitless bombardment, Wilson decided that trying to take Metemma would be too costly, and that instead he would establish a base at Gubba, also by the river, but a little closer to Khartoum.

Al-Mus brought another reassuring message from Gordon dated 29 December, saying that Khartoum could 'hold out for years' along with more disturbing news of the Mahdi's growing strength. He was also carrying Gordon's journal, and the last entry, for 14 December, said the town might fall within ten days, though in view of the message of 29 December, it presumably had not. It concluded: 'I have done my best for the honour of our country.' Wilson's force had already lost more than 300 killed and wounded, and the river column was not now expected to arrive until March. He decided, therefore, to ensure that, before he left for Khartoum, Gubba was properly fortified so that it could be a base from which a full assault could be launched once everyone had arrived, as well as a place to which Gordon could be brought if they could rescue him. Anyway, Al-Mus's steamers were so badly battered and holed that they desperately needed repairs. Taking all this into account, Wilson decided 'a delay of a couple of days wouldn't make much difference'. He made a quick reconnaissance trip upriver, and was fired on from both banks, then at 8am on the morning of 24 January he set out for Khartoum in two steamers with about twenty British regulars and 240 Sudanese troops, considered by Wilson to be 'absolutely without discipline'. The chances of getting there and back alive looked pretty slim. The lieutenant-colonel dismissed the boats as 'penny steamers' that 'a single well-directed shell would send to the bottom'. They were also short of fuel, and he would have to keep sending parties ashore to cut wood. He hoped that once the general spotted them approaching, perhaps 20 miles away, he would create some kind of diversion to help them. At this time of year, however, the level of the Nile began to fall sharply, exposing more rocks, and making the journey much more treacherous, so that even if the vessels got to Khartoum, they would never make it back, which would mean using some of Gordon's even smaller boats for the return journey.

Four days earlier in Khartoum, on 20 January, Gordon had heard the shrieks of women and the cries of children rising from the Mahdi's camp. He knew it must be something very serious, for the Expected One banned expressions of grief for those killed in battle, and one of his best spies, a girl, slipped across the river and came back with the news of the two defeats the Mahdi's forces had suffered. Gordon ensured the tidings spread quickly among the soldiers and civilians left in the city, but it cannot have cheered them much, with food now virtually exhausted. After the Mahdi took Omdurman, Khartoum had been under constant fire, but the general continued to sit at his usual window, with a light shining behind him. Gordon received and dismissed nine letters from the Mahdi urging him to give up, and offering him safe conduct to the British lines, but now the Expected One knew that Khartoum was starving, and he had also identified a weak point where the Nile had washed away some of the town's defences. Still he was reluctant to attack, remembering the heavy losses his troops had once suffered in an assault on a fortified Egyptian position, but he finally decided he must make his move before British reinforcements arrived.

On the night of Sunday 25 January, Gordon called a meeting of the committee that ran Khartoum. He did not attend himself, but sent word through his chief clerk that every male over the age of eight must be told to line up alongside the troops and man the defences. A merchant who called on him after the meeting noted that Gordon seemed more agitated than he had ever seen him before. 'I have nothing more to say' he declared. 'People will no longer believe me. I have told them over and over that help would be here, but it has never come, and now they must see I tell them lies.' Beside him were two full packets of cigarettes. 'Now leave me and let me smoke these' were his parting words. Gordon's ADC, Orfali, woke him at 3am the next morning to say that the Mahdi's men were attacking. Then there were reports that the assault had been broken off, but soon after, Gordon heard shooting, and his orderlies came running in to say that thousands of enemy troops were flooding into Khartoum. The tribesmen had come on so silently that many of the troops manning the ramparts did not hear a sound until the enemy had passed through the gaps in their ranks and were inside the city. Some of the defenders put up fierce resistance, firing until their rifles 'were too hot to hold', but others were too weak to fight. Gordon's commander-in-chief, Faraj Pasha, rode around on his horse, encouraging the men until he realised the game was up. Then he ordered them to stop firing and surrender. After about an hour, resistance had collapsed, and before dawn the Mahdists had reached the palace. Their leader wanted Gordon alive, but a lot of the Expected One's followers wanted him dead. At first they were reluctant to enter his headquarters, having heard, correctly, that he had put two huge mines in the basement, and was prepared to blow himself up rather than surrender.

It is not certain what happened next. George William Joy's famous painting 'General Gordon's Last Stand' depicts one version: the general standing in his uniform at the top of a flight of stairs, his sword sheathed, a revolver in his hand pointing down at the floor, as he silently defies the savage, spear-wielding enemy soldiers beneath. Other accounts have him fighting desperately from room to room with his last comrades, selling their lives as dearly as they could, accounting for dozens of the Mahdi's men. Yet another closes with Gordon making his last stand in the street. They all end with the general dead, and having his head cut off and sent to the Mahdi. The mines went undetonated, and now Gordon was on his way to 'the glorious gate of eternity, of glory and joy unmixed with a taint of sorrow'. Khartoum had fallen 342 days after he arrived. While the manner of his end might be unknown, what happened to those remaining in the town is not. For six hours, the conquering tribesmen looted, raped and killed. Thousands of men, women and children perished before the Mahdi called a halt.

Two days later, on what would have been Gordon's fifty-second birthday, Wilson's force was on the final leg of the perilous journey to Khartoum, blazing away at the enemy on both banks with every gun they had, as bullets constantly spattered against the sides of their boats. Around noon, they finally caught sight of the governor's palace, but there was no sign of the Egyptian flag that Gordon always flew. As they got closer, they saw hundreds of tribesmen gathered by the river under the Mahdi's banners, and they were hit with more deadly fire. It was plain that Khartoum had fallen and Wilson 'at once gave the order to turn and run full speed down the river'. They had an even more difficult journey back. As had been feared, both steamers were wrecked on rocks, and the commander had to get his men to improvise defences on an island and fight off determined attacks by the Mahdi's followers, but even though some of his Sudanese troops deserted to the enemy, he managed to hold out until another steamer picked them up and carried them back to Gubba on 4 February. At first light the following morning, he set out with an escort from the Camel Corps to deliver the bad news to Wolseley. When the story reached the outside world, black-draped portraits of Gordon went up in windows not just in Britain, but also in France, Germany and the United States. The poet laureate, Alfred, Lord Tennyson, commemorated this general turned Christian martyr declaring: 'The earth has never borne a nobler man.' Queen Victoria, who considered Gordon 'dear, heroic, noble', fired off angry letters to her ministers, and Gladstone was no longer 'GOM'

– 'Grand Old Man', but 'MOG' – 'Murderer of Gordon'. He narrowly survived a censure motion on 27 February, but then, with his party torn apart by dissension, he resigned as prime minister in June. This was far from being the end of Gladstone, though, and he went on to form two more governments.

Just five months after his capture of Khartoum, the Mahdi died at the age of forty-one, perhaps of typhus. Wolseley blamed Wilson for the abortive attempt to rescue Gordon, saying he had 'proved a great failure as a soldier', though many others, including Wolseley himself, had been responsible for much longer delays in getting to Khartoum than any Wilson caused, and the lieutenant-colonel had his defenders, including Hartington. Anyway, even if he had arrived a few days earlier, it is not clear what his little force could have achieved against the Mahdi's hordes, which by then numbered perhaps 100,000. After returning to England, Wilson was knighted, while thirteen years after Gordon's death, a British-Egyptian army under Major General Sir Horatio, later Lord, Kitchener inflicted a crushing defeat on the Mahdist forces at Omdurman, and Britain effectively took over the Sudan.

16

'Black Week': the Boer War, 1899

'When sorrows come', lamented Hamlet, 'they come not single spies, but in battalions'. A lot of people in Britain must have felt that way during the last days of the nineteenth century. The Boer War, like the Zulu War before it, was supposed to be a walkover, but the enemy grabbed the initiative right from the start, and over the course of six days inflicted three humiliating defeats in what came to be known as 'Black Week'.

The British authorities may have been prepared to start a war with the Zulus to ingratiate themselves with their new subjects in the Transvaal (see chapter thirteen), but the province did not remain part of the empire on which the sun never sets for long – just four years in fact, before it seized back its independence in 1881. Not that that put an end to friction between Britain and the Transvaal. If anything, things got worse. First, the discovery of gold in the republic in 1886 upped the stakes, particularly when Witwatersrand turned into the biggest gold mining complex in the world, and British miners began to flood into the republic. Then in 1895, an English adventurer named Leander Starr Jameson, the inspiration for Kipling's famous poem *If*, mounted an abortive raid designed to overthrow the Boer government. That led the Transvaal to arm itself and make a defensive alliance with its sister Boer republic, the Orange Free State. By 1899, foreigners in the Transvaal outnumbered Afrikaners by two to one, but the Boers refused to give them the vote, and in late September, British newspapers reported that 47,000 additional soldiers were being sent out to mount an invasion. The Boers were not going to sit back and wait to be attacked, though. The Transvaal and the Orange Free State both mobilised, and in early October they sent an ultimatum demanding that Britain withdraw all of her troops from the border areas, bring home the reinforcements they had already dispatched and promise not to send any more.

The ultimatum was greeted with euphoria in Whitehall and derision in Fleet Street. Who did these Boers think they were? For *The Times*, it was an 'infatuated step' by a 'petty republic', while when Colonial Secretary Joseph Chamberlain was woken up to be told the news, he joyfully exclaimed: 'They've done it!' He had been itching for a fight and wondering how to engineer it. Now the Boers themselves had provided the pretext.

So Britain dispatched its biggest overseas force since the Crimean War. Its leader would be Sir Redvers Buller, a tall, powerful man who had found fame while serving with Wolseley's Red River expedition in Canada in the 1870s, for, among other things, being able to carry a heavier barrel of pork on his back than anyone else. A fearless, tireless and outspoken member of the 'Wolseley Gang' (see chapter fifteen), Buller was a soldiers' soldier, who had been awarded the Victoria Cross for his bravery during the Zulu War. As for the monarch who introduced that decoration, Queen Victoria, she found him reserved, with 'rather a dry, gruff manner'. Now the general belief was that Buller's 'steamroller' would soon crush the Boers, and that it would be all over by Christmas. On paper, his force outnumbered the enemy two to one, and in addition to this, he also had 150 field guns. A noisy, enthusiastic crowd saw him off at Southampton on 14 October. Putting a brave face on things, he said he hoped he would not 'be away long', but privately Buller was deeply worried. Unlike the people expecting a walkover, he actually knew the Boers. He had fought alongside them against the Zulus, and learned how tough, resourceful and determined they were. The general had warned his political masters that the enemy might quickly conquer large swathes of British territory, and he was right. By the time their ultimatum had expired, the Boers had already assembled more than 20,000 men on the borders of Cape Colony and Natal, and by the time Buller reached South Africa, they had penetrated deep into both colonies, and laid siege to the strategic towns of Ladysmith, Kimberley and Mafeking.

The general had originally hoped to advance up the railway to Bloemfontein, the capital of the Orange Free State, and then onto Pretoria, capital of the Transvaal, but instead the first thing he had to do was to divide his army into three to try to stem the Boer advance and relieve the besieged towns. One of the three prongs of his trident was led by Lieutenant-General Sir William Gatacre, a short, lean, but brave man with a bristling moustache. A veteran of India and the Sudan, he had a reputation for driving his men hard, gaining him the nickname 'General Backacher'. Like Buller he was a recent arrival in South Africa, and on 9 December he set out to recapture the important railway junction of Stormberg, in the north of Cape Colony, with a force of about 1,800 infantry, plus 250 mounted infantry supported by artillery.

The idea was to march through the night and attack a hill that dominated the Boers' position at dawn on 10 December. Things had gone wrong right from the start. The soldiers had been left sitting in trains for hours under a hot sun while locomotives were found to take them to the start of their march, so they were dog tired even before they set off at 9.15pm that night. As they neared the enemy lines, they seem to have been at cross-purposes with their guides from the Cape police, and the exhausted soldiers were left completely lost, blundering about the veldt in the darkness looking for the Boer positions. At about 4am they at last came in sight of the crucial hill, and a small Boer force there opened fire. About half the infantry rushed forward to storm it, but it was ringed by a vertical rock face that was impossible to scale. Meanwhile, the British artillery opened up, shelling their own infantry. The other half of Gatacre's force now began to fall back in disorder, and the general ordered a retreat back to Molteno, which was where they had started. By this time however, Boer cavalry had suddenly appeared and launched an attack. The British mounted infantry did its best to cover the retreat, but two guns were lost. The engagement had only lasted about an hour and a half.

The Times' first account of the battle was reasonably reassuring: 'Owing to errors of the guides and other accidents' its correspondent recorded, 'the attack was delivered against the wrong part of the enemy's position, where the hill was quite impregnable. The troops were obliged to retire. They did so in admirable order.' Indeed, the withdrawal from the hill across a cornfield 'could not have been surpassed during peace manoeuvres'. Then, unfortunately, the paper noted, with the soldiers tired out after being under arms for sixteen hours and marching for seven more through the night, 'disorder ensued, augmented by constant shell fire from the heights'. In fact, when the men got back to Molteno, Gatacre realised that more than 600 had been left behind. Completely isolated, they had no alternative but to surrender, as did some of the stragglers from the retreat. Another sign of the lieutenant-general's confusion was the dispatch in which he gave his account of the battle, which placed the action 4 miles north of where it had actually taken place. When *The Times* received 'further accounts' of the battle, its doubts grew. It was 'clear that the British commander endeavoured to execute an operation which is always dangerous in circumstances that greatly enhanced the perils of the attempt'. Back at home, Field Marshal Lord Roberts, hub of the rivals of the 'Wolseley Gang', the 'Roberts Ring', was more blunt. He declared that Gatacre had shown 'a want of care, judgment, and even of ordinary military precautions', which should disqualify him from further involvement in serious fighting. The secretary of state for war, the Marquess of Lansdowne, sent a cable to Buller telling him to sack Gatacre, but Buller declined to comply.

Stormberg, though, was just the first instalment of bad news. A British force led by Lieutenant-General the third Baron Methuen was now making steady progress towards Kimberley. Methuen was an experienced, but perhaps more importantly, a well-connected officer, much favoured by the queen and the prince of Wales. Indeed, the South African High Commissioner, Sir Alfred Milner, had wanted him made commander-in-chief. He had successfully driven the Boers from their positions on three occasions during the previous three weeks, but he had never been able to drive home the advantage, and on one occasion he had been criticised for sustaining heavy losses.

His latest partial success had been at the Modder River on 28 November, when he was wounded in the thigh. Methuen would have liked to strike again before the Boers had time to regroup, but he was slowed down by his injury, and his men were exhausted and short of supplies. In the Boer command, meanwhile, the reverse set off a debate. The senior general, Piet Cronje, decided to withdraw 10 miles to a new defensive line, but General Koos De la Rey believed it would be better to retreat just 6 miles to Magersfontein. Over Cronje's head, he cabled Marthinus Steyn, president of the Orange Free State. Steyn in turn contacted Paul Kruger, president of the Transvaal, who suggested that his ally should go to the front himself, because this was 'the final moment of decision whether we are to defend the country'. Steyn went, carrying with him a stirring message for the troops from Kruger. The Free State president read it out aloud at each of the laagers he visited. It declared: 'even though we must lose almost half our men, we must still fight to the death, in the name of the Lord'. The following day, De la Rey's plan was adopted. Just as important as the Boer fighters were the hundreds of African labourers they had dragged off to do the donkey work in this white man's war. They were given the task of digging 12 miles of trenches at the foot of a line of kopjes (small hills). It took six days, and when the job was finished, the Boers concealed them with great skill. Methuen's scouts were hampered by the wire fences of farms and of the border between Cape Colony and the Orange Free State, and harassed by fire from the Boers' long-range Mauser rifles, and they never found them.

By 10 December the baron felt ready to take on the enemy. Like Gatacre, he decided on a night march followed by what he hoped would be a surprise attack. Unfortunately, because of the problems his scouts had encountered, he had only the haziest idea of the Boer defences. They appeared to be holding the line of kopjes and the key to the battle seemed to be the biggest of them: Magersfontein. The attack would be pressed by the Highland Brigade supported by five artillery batteries. Major-General Andrew Wauchope, a fearless soldier who had been wounded in the cause of his country many times, would lead it. Methuen later said that Wauchope appeared happy with his orders, though before setting off, he remarked to an officer commanding some of the reserves: 'Things don't always go as they are expected. You may not be in reserve for long.'

A drizzle had begun falling before the soldiers marched off at 3pm to bivouac for the night on the plain 3 miles from the enemy. Meanwhile, nearly thirty guns pounded the slopes where Methuen believed the Boers were dug in. After darkness fell, the drizzle turned into a downpour, but the troops were forbidden to light fires or even to smoke. Around midnight, they marched off again – this time to fight. In accordance with Methuen's orders, the 3,500 men were packed in a very tight formation. Progress was slowed by the rain and the thorny scrub, and they began to fall behind schedule. As it started to get light, the Highlanders found that they were still about 1,000 yards from the ridge. They did not know that the bulk of the enemy were not on the ridge, but in fact in the concealed trenches below. When the Scots were 400 yards away, a single shot went off from a kopje and then all hell was let loose. All along their line, the Boers opened up, and the Highlanders' massed ranks made them an easy target. With a determined charge, a few men from the Black Watch actually managed to break through the Boer trenches, but they were quickly killed or captured. Some of the others got tangled up in a wire fence in front of the trenches, and at first there was confusion, even panic, but then the Highlanders began taking cover behind rocks and anthills and tried to return fire, while the artillery attempted to support them. The storm that had delayed them on their march had given way to hot sunshine, and for hours it burned down, as the Highlanders stuck stoically to their task, pinned down without shade or water. Then at about 1pm, a group of Boers were spotted trying to work their way around the British right flank. Two companies were ordered to trickle back a few hundred yards to deal with the threat, but soon more and more men decided it would be a good idea to get in on the act, and before long, the Highlanders were in flight. Officers threatened to shoot those who did not stand their ground, but to little effect. It was another British humiliation.

Methuen had lost 902 dead and wounded, while Boer casualties were just 236. Wauchope's body was found 200 yards from the enemy trenches. The official Boer account of the battle said the bravery of the Highlanders was 'wonderful against the hail of Mauser bullets that met them', but the victors could afford to be magnanimous. From the British point of view, the enterprise had gone wrong right from the start. The artillery barrage had been aimed at the wrong target, and all it had achieved was to warn the enemy that an attack was imminent. Methuen put the failure down to Wauchope and bad luck, while the Highlanders blamed Methuen. A bitter poem by a Black Watch soldier asked:

> Why weren't we told of the trenches?
> Why weren't we told of the wire?
> Why were we marched up in column,
> May Tommy Atkins enquire…

It lacerated 'a drawing-room general's mistake' for which they had paid so dearly. Methuen believed his time was up, commenting: 'there must be a scapegoat, so I must bear my fate like a man, holding my tongue'. When he heard the news, Lansdowne did indeed call for Methuen's head, but once again Buller did not comply.

The Times recognised that things were looking very black. Magersfontein was 'the most serious event that the war has yet produced. British arms have received a severe check'. Following as close as it did to Stormberg, it had 'undoubtedly created a very grave situation.' The newspaper concluded that: 'The time has come for far greater efforts than have yet been made if the situation is to be retrieved and the war is to be carried to a successful conclusion.' While the journalist was writing his warning, Buller had already started firing his long-range naval guns in the direction of General Louis Botha's force of around 8,000 Boers at the village of Colenso on the Tugela River, which was blocking the way to Ladysmith. With 20,000 men under his command, Sir Redvers had been thinking about trying to cross upriver at Potgieters Drift to outflank the Boers, even though that would have taken him 15 miles away from the railway. Then he heard about the reverses at Stormberg and Magersfontein, while Milner was warning that there might be an uprising by Afrikaners in Cape Colony. Buller decided he would have to attack Colenso. He cabled Lansdowne that he fully expected 'to be successful' but added, 'probably at heavy cost'.

Shells from Buller's heavy guns had been screaming harmlessly over the Boers' heads, but they caused enough consternation among those on a hill called Hlangwane to make most of them abandon it. It overlooked the Boer positions and if the British could take it, it would be a wonderful place from which to mount a bombardment. Kruger was alarmed when the news reached him, and told Botha he must not give up the hill under any circumstances. On the night of 13 December the Boers held a council of war, and the general had to exercise not just his military, but also his diplomatic skills. Many officers were demanding that they should withdraw from the Tugela River altogether, so Botha came up with a compromise. They would abandon Hlangwane, but stick to their strong defensive triangular position with the Tugela River on two sides, and some kopjes on the third. The next morning, Botha flourished another inspiring message from Kruger: if they conceded Hlangwane, 'you give up the whole land to the enemy … fear not the enemy, but fear God…. If you give up position and surrender the country to England, where will you go then?' The council reversed its earlier decision and sent 800 men back to reoccupy the hill.

Oblivious to this drama in the enemy camp, Buller had decided against trying to take Hlangwane anyway, believing that it would have involved heavy fighting and that his troops would not be experienced enough to negotiate the thick scrub. His plan was to cross the river at two places he believed were fordable – the Old Wagon Drift and the smaller Bridle Drift, which was more than 3 miles to the west – though he realised Botha would probably site his strongest defences opposite them. Because of the number of points at which the river might be forded, Botha had had to form a very extended defensive line, but once again the Boers, or their conscripted African labourers, had constructed it with great skill, digging trenches in the tall grass along the river banks, camouflaging them with stones, and hiding the soil they had dug out. They had even made dummy trenches on the higher ground behind and armed them with dummy guns.

Buller set the attack for the morning of 15 December. Major-General Harry Hildyard's brigade was to lead the main assault, storming the Wagon Drift, while Major-General Fitzroy Hart's Irish Brigade would strike at the Bridle Drift; a detachment of artillery commanded by Colonel Charles Long would advance to support the action. Those naval guns left in the rear began firing again at 5.30am. There was no response from the Boers. Botha had ordered his men not to shoot until he gave the signal with a howitzer. Hildyard's brigade started to march towards the Wagon Drift, which was next to the only bridge the Boers had not destroyed. A mile ahead of them went Long's artillery: twelve field guns followed by six bigger naval guns. These were under the command of a Royal Navy lieutenant who protested to Long that they were getting too close to the Boer positions, but the colonel carried on and halted about 1,000 yards from the river to the east of the Wagon Drift. Botha had seen what was happening, and knew that if the enemy artillery opened up at this range, his lines could be smashed to smithereens. So, as Long's men began to prepare their guns for firing, the howitzer boomed out, and the Boers opened up on them with deadly Mauser fire.

Meanwhile, while it was still dark, Hart and his troops had marched off in close order towards the Bridle Drift, though some of his officers thought that keeping the men so tightly packed was asking for trouble. Patrols of Royal Dragoons, sent by Buller to protect Hart's left flank, had already been down to the river and seen large numbers of Boers on the other side. They sent off gallopers to warn him, but the major-general said he would ignore the Boers unless they attacked him in force and that he intended to cross by the Bridle Drift as ordered. At about 6.15am he came within sight of the river. It was more than 100 yards wide, swollen by recent rains. He saw that he was approaching a loop in the Tugela, which according to his map was to the east of the Bridle Drift, but his African guide, who spoke no English, told him to head even further east.

Hart could see the danger of going into the loop – where the enemy would be able to attack him from both sides – while the river blocked his advance, but for some reason, he was beginning to think the guide must be right, and the map wrong. Unfortunately, no further discussion was possible, because at that moment Hart's battalions were hit by artillery shells and Mauser fire, and the guide took to his heels. His interpreter, though, was made of sterner stuff, and told Hart that there was a ford by a kraal at the top of the loop. As the invisible enemy pummelled his force, the advance began to dissolve in confusion. The major-general could not be faulted for personal courage. As his men lay pinned down, he walked among them, shouting encouragement, but he could not get them moving. Lieutenant-Colonel Thomas Thackeray had led his troops to the west of the loop and got very close to the Bridle Drift, where the high banks offered some cover. They outnumbered the Boer defenders and might have been able to get across, but Hart ordered them back into the loop. Buller was standing behind the lines with his naval guns, which continued to pound what he still thought were the Boer positions on the hillsides beyond where they were actually dug in. Though they were now pouring rifle fire into the British ranks, their Mausers were smokeless and gave little clue as to their true whereabouts, but one thing the general could see was that Hart's Irish Brigade had gone off in the wrong direction, and he sent a galloper to warn them to keep out of the loop.

The general was also getting concerned about events by the Wagon Drift, where the main British attack was supposed to happen. He had ordered the artillery to stay well out of range of Boer rifle fire. Now he heard them burst into life, apparently very close to the river, and sent a staff officer to find out what was happening. The officer reported that they were under 'a little' rifle fire, but that they seemed 'quite comfortable'. The next thing he heard from the guns was – nothing – an ominous silence. He sent an officer to tell Hart to withdraw, then went down himself to see what had happened to the artillery.

Fortunately, the heavier naval guns assigned to Long had fallen about 600 yards behind his field guns, and they were at the limit of the effective range of enemy rifle fire. Their African drivers had run for it, but the gunners were able to cut their oxen teams free and begin firing. They suffered virtually no casualties, but Long's men were in the eye of the storm. They exhibited enormous courage, firing methodically in spite of the murderous attack under which they found themselves. Long was seriously wounded and his second-in-command was also hit, as were officers from both batteries. When about a third of the gunners had been killed or wounded, the acting commander ordered them to take shelter in two small dongas – dried-up stream beds – abandoning the guns and ammunition wagons while two officers rode off to seek help. They ran into Buller as he was on his way down to investigate. The two men were so dazed and shaken that Buller could barely understand their story, but he grasped the general idea, and rode on to tell Hildyard to call off the main attack, at least until Long had been rescued. Next, Buller ordered some of his reserves to provide covering fire for Hart, but almost as soon as they had begun, hundreds of stragglers and wounded men began to emerge in confusion from the loop, followed by the major-general. Meanwhile, Thackeray and his men had actually got to the end of the loop, and found the ford there, but the swirling waters made it impossible to cross. Eventually Buller's order to evacuate the loop reached the rest of the brigade, but it was not until late in the afternoon that many of them got back to camp.

There remained the problem of rescuing the guns. Buller sent Hildyard's men into Colenso village – one of the few places that offered any shelter – and they dug in behind walls to try to take on the Boers and draw their fire. The general, who had not been in battle for fourteen years, had by now been severely bruised in the ribs by a shell fragment. He managed to get some artillery horses to drag the naval guns back to a safer position, but the abandoned field guns were a much tougher proposition. When he reached the men in the larger donga, he asked for volunteers. A corporal and six gunners came forward, but that was not enough to make up two teams. So three staff officers also volunteered including Captain Walter Congreve and Lieutenant Freddy Roberts, Field-Marshal Lord Roberts' only son, aged twenty-seven. It was a half-mile race to the guns. Congreve and his horse were hit by Boer bullets several times, and they fell about 100 yards from their objective. Roberts had vanished, but the depleted teams managed to gallop back with two of the twelve guns. After the first expedition, the Boer fire got hotter still, and the next team was halted. Another attempt also failed. Finally, a last effort was mounted with three teams. One man was killed, a dozen horses were shot and no guns were rescued. After that, Buller gave the order to retire. By 3pm the Battle of Colenso was over. The British had lost 143 men killed and about 1,000 wounded or captured, as well as ten field guns, and they were not a step closer to Ladysmith. The Boers were said to have had only eight men killed. Congreve later found Roberts lying unconscious and seriously wounded.

In his first cable to London, Sir Redvers recognised that this was another 'serious reverse'. He was generous to Hart saying he had 'attacked with great gallantry', and praised the heroism of the attempts to save the guns. Of the artillery fiasco, he confined himself to reporting: 'it appears that Colonel Long, in his desire to be within effective range – advanced close to the river'.

The Times was now beginning to run out of gloomy superlatives: 'The serious repulse of Sir Redvers Buller on the Tugela, closely following on the terrible reverse experienced by the Highland Brigade at Magersfontein and the disaster to a portion of General Gatacre's command, has gravely compromised the military situation' it intoned. By midnight, Buller's frustrations had got the better of him, and he cabled Lansdowne in rather less restrained mode, saying he would have to 'let Ladysmith go', take up good defensive positions in Natal, and 'let time help us'. The next day, he sent a message by heliograph to Sir George White at Ladysmith asking how long he could hold out, and floating the possibility that he might have to expend as much ammunition as possible, and then make 'the best terms' he could.

Similar ideas had been floated by Milner. Let Ladysmith look after itself for the time being, and mount an offensive in the Orange Free State instead. Lansdowne, however, was now determined to remove Buller as commander-in-chief, and when the general's apparently defeatist messages were presented to the cabinet, they agreed he should be relegated to commander in Natal only. One of his last duties as commander-in-chief was to break the news to Lord Roberts of the death of his son, who had perished from his wounds. He drafted a cable that read: 'Your gallant son died today. Condolences. Buller.' The next day, 18 December, Buller got the news that he was being replaced as commander-in-chief by Roberts. Four officers were awarded the Victoria Cross for their part in trying to rescue the guns at Colenso, including Roberts and Congreve.

In the end, Britain deployed around half a million men in South Africa, while the Boers could muster no more than 90,000, and superior numbers and resources gradually began to turn the tide of war. Buller relieved Ladysmith in February 1900, and enjoyed a number of other successes before returning to Britain that November. The British took Bloemfontein and Pretoria, but even then the Boers fought a determined guerrilla war in which De la Rey played a leading role. Roberts' second-in-command, Lord Kitchener, retaliated by burning farms and herding civilians into concentration camps in which thousands died, until in May 1902, both the Orange Free State and the Transvaal made peace and once again became subject to Britain. On his return, Buller had received a rapturous reception from the public, but faced some fierce criticism in the press. When he tried to mount an ill-prepared public defence of his conduct, he was dismissed on half-pay for breaching king's regulations. Gatacre had suffered another reverse in April 1900, and Roberts relieved him of his command

and sent him home. Methuen had a number of successes in the guerrilla war, but in March 1902, his column was forced to surrender by De la Rey's guerrillas, and the baron, who had again been wounded, became the only British general to be captured by the Boers. After his release, he continued to serve in the army until 1919, and was credited with helping to mend relations between the Boers and the British in South Africa. Louis Botha, another champion of Boer–British reconciliation, became the first prime minister of the Union of South Africa.

17

Gallipoli, 1915

Conceived as a better alternative to the murderous stalemate of the Western Front, the attack on Turkey's Gallipoli peninsula was bedevilled by confused objectives, poor planning, and uninspired leadership. Soon it too turned into a bloody dead- lock. After eleven months it was abandoned, but not before 26,000 British soldiers had been killed.

Sir Maurice Hankey, secretary to the British government's War Council, believed the first few months of the First World War had revealed that on the Western Front 'any advance must be costly and slow. Days are required to capture a single line of trenches, the losses are very heavy, and as often as not the enemy recaptures his lost ground.' He concluded that: 'When viewed on a map, the total gains are almost negligible, and apparently incommensu- rate with the effort and loss of life.' Perhaps, there was another way, though. Could Germany be attacked 'most effectively … through her allies, and par- ticularly through Turkey'? Turkey, or more properly the Ottoman Empire, was known as the 'Sick Man of Europe'. Here was an idea to appeal to politi- cians shaken by the previously unimaginable carnage of the Western Front, and concerned that public opinion might soon demand a stop to it. The first lord of the Admiralty, Winston Churchill, in particular felt that there must be some better option than 'chewing barbed wire in Flanders' and that surely the Royal Navy could offer a way out. Despite a determined effort by Germany to build up its navy, Britannia still ruled the waves. She boasted twenty-four of the latest dreadnought battleships, outnumbering the enemy by almost two to one, and had forty older battleships against just a handful owned by the Germans.

Churchill saw an attack on Turkey as being a way of knocking away one of Germany's 'props', but those who urged concentration on the Western Front tended to describe other operations as 'sideshows', and derided them as a feature of 'cigar butt' strategy: the concept that politicians would stand around examining a map until one of them pointed his cigar butt and said: 'let's do something there'. The first lord of the Admiralty believed that if a few British warships could make it through the Dardanelles straits into the Sea of Marmara and threaten Constantinople, they would so intimidate the Turks that Britain would be able to 'dictate terms'. Once Turkey had been knocked out of the war, an invasion of Germany's other ally, Austria-Hungary, might be mounted through the Danube valley, though Churchill noted that an attack on the straits would be a 'very difficult operation requiring a large force'.

While these ideas were swirling around, in January 1915 Britain's ambassador in Russia told the Foreign Office that Nicholas II's forces were being hard pressed by the Turks in the Caucasus, and the Czar was asking whether Britain could mount some action in the eastern Mediterranean to relieve the pressure. Britain's War Council approved an attack on the Dardanelles by the navy alone, using superannuated battleships, due to be scrapped, which would not last five minutes against the Germans in the North Sea. Some admirals were very keen; others, like Sir Henry Jackson, were less so, but nobody said it was impossible or too dangerous. For the politicians, it looked like a pretty low-risk operation. The ships could have a go at blasting their way through to Constantinople. If they failed, they could just sail away again, and if it all worked out, it would not only damage Germany, but there was also a chance of some territorial benefit accruing to the British Empire.

There was a joker in the pack, though. The first sea lord, Lord Fisher, was an irascible and increasingly erratic septuagenarian, whom Churchill had brought out of retirement. Having approved the plan to use only old second-rate ships, he suddenly suggested that the world's most powerful battleship, HMS *Queen Elizabeth*, should tag along too, and what about persuading the Greeks to abandon their neutrality and throw in a huge army to mount a land attack? Now, like Topsy, the operation grew. Churchill told the commander, Vice-Admiral Sackville Carden, that he would get the *Queen Elizabeth* and a dreadnought cruiser, as well as his old ships, while the French also agreed to contribute a squadron of battleships, but as this fleet of sixty ships, including twenty-one modified trawlers for minesweeping, was being assembled, Fisher suddenly began voicing all kinds of fears. Eventually he told Churchill that Britain should be husbanding all her resources, and that included the old ships, for the only confrontation that really mattered – the one with Germany. Rather confusingly, he added that anyway if there was going to be an expedition to the Dardanelles, he was opposed to it unless the army was involved too. When Churchill suggested he should put his objections direct to the prime minister, Herbert Asquith, Fisher threw a wobbler and threatened to resign.

At the next War Council meeting, the first sea lord tried to walk out when discussion turned to the Dardanelles operation. By now, however, most of the other council members believed he was, to put it politely, a little eccentric, so the plans for the operation sailed serenely on. But Fisher's refrain was picked up by other navy top brass. Jackson said that 'strong military landing parties' would be required to knock out Turkish guns on shore, and that a naval bombardment alone was 'not recommended'. Soldiers would also have to occupy the Gallipoli peninsula on the western (European) side of the straits, otherwise even if warships made it through to the Sea of Marmara, it would be impossible for unarmoured supply ships to follow.

By February, doubts had begun to infect the War Council too. Asquith now wanted a 'fairly strong military force' sent, and on 16 February, the council decided that it should include 29th Division: the last uncommitted pre-war regular soldiers. It was not exactly clear, though, what the role of the troops would be. Were they to deal with any guns not destroyed by the navy, or to occupy the peninsula after the Turks had surrendered? If they were just for garrison duties, were precious regular soldiers really needed? In addition, all the plans focused on the European side, but the straits at their broadest were only about 3 miles wide, and no one seemed to worry about the Asian side where there were just as many Turkish guns. Anyway, the debate over troops all seemed a bit academic, as the naval bombardment was due to begin in three days' time, and none could be in place by then.

Two days after the War Council meeting, Churchill urged the secretary of state for war, Lord 'Your Country Needs You' Kitchener, to put 50,000 troops within reach of the Dardanelles to be ready if the Turks surrendered or if a revolution blew away the regime. Kitchener did not see why this force should require 29th Division, and offered mainly untested Australians and New Zealanders, but Churchill now maintained that it needed a 'stiffening of regulars'. The army, on the other hand, still believed the navy should be able to do the job more or less on its own. General Charles Calwell, director of military operations, thought only 'comparatively small landing parties of infantry and engineers' would be needed to complete the destruction of any Turkish defences that the ships had merely damaged.

When the War Council met again on 19 February, it was suddenly told about an analysis from 1906, which concluded that an exclusively naval operation against the straits would fail. They were probably not informed that the report also said that even a combined operation stood little chance. It was around 10 miles from the entrance of the Dardanelles to the Narrows, where the waterway was pinched in to a width of only about a mile. To get beyond the Narrows, the task force would have to run a gauntlet of more than 100 heavy and medium guns sited in forts on either side. There were also about 400 mines protected by eighty mobile guns, carefully sited behind ridges or in folds in the ground where shells arriving in a flat trajectory from naval guns were unlikely to hit them. To make things even harder for an invader, ships faced a 4 miles-per-hour current running against them in the straits, that got even stronger if the prevailing northerly wind was blowing. So how many shells would the navy need to eliminate these formidable shore defences, bearing in mind that guns fired from the moving platform of a ship tended to be less accurate than those fired from land? Admiral Jackson reckoned the answer was about 3,000, but an Admiralty committee that investigated the operation after the war would come to the conclusion that this was wildly optimistic, and the true figure would have been at least 20,000. For the moment, though, the more optimistic admirals thought none of this mattered, as the Turks' morale would quickly collapse once the Royal Navy opened up on them.

While confusion still reigned in the War Council, in the Dardanelles the shooting began that very day. It was not an auspicious start. One of the older ships broke down. Most of the shells missed, and by the end of the first day, not a single shore gun had been put out of action. For the next five days, the weather was too bad for any bombardments. Then on 25 February, the navy had a good day, hitting four Turkish guns. Over the next six days, Carden sent ashore demolition parties protected by marines, who proved far more successful than the warships, destroying a total of forty-eight guns. There was near euphoria back home. Even Fisher thought the Dardanelles operation was 'getting along nicely', and the War Council began to debate what terms the Turks should be offered when they capitulated, an event that would surely be the signal for the whole of the Balkans to join the

Allied side. Perhaps it was a good job they were feeling euphoric, for the nature of the enterprise had changed considerably. Far from being one from which Britain could just sail away if things did not work out, Churchill and Kitchener were now saying that if the navy could not do it, then the army must 'see the business through'.

On 4 March, more determined resistance from the Turks drove back a landing party, and the naval action became pretty low key. Every day, three or four ships would enter the straits, fire a few rounds and then retire into the Aegean. It is not clear why the attack was prosecuted with so little urgency, though Carden's number two, Vice-Admiral John de Robeck, apparently did not think much of the ships' crews, dismissing them as 'grandfathers'. Anyway, Churchill told Carden to hurry up and launch a major assault. That meant clearing the mines. The task force had no specialist minesweepers, so the job fell to the modified trawlers, manned by civilian crews. These vessels were barely capable of making 7 miles-per-hour, so were often virtually stationery against the current, and their naval commander had no experience of minesweeping. In seventeen attempts, they reached the minefield only twice, and managed to find just two mines. With the task force getting nowhere fast, a more determined effort was now set for 18 March.

By then, Kitchener had announced that he would now make 29th Division available as part of a force of 80,000 for the operation. General Sir Ian Hamilton, who had been his chief of staff in the Boer War, was chosen to lead it, though he knew little of the Dardanelles, the enemy or modern war. Now aged sixty-one, Hamilton realised this would be his last chance to lead troops in the field. Brave, and a fine sportsman, he also had a reputation for being witty, charming and rather sensitive. He liked poetry and art and had been bullied at school. Hamilton was used to taking orders from Kitchener, and now his instructions were that this was still essentially a naval operation and that the job of his men was to help the fleet penetrate the straits. Kitchener's parting words, however, left him in no doubt about how crucial the secretary for war thought the enterprise was: 'If the fleet gets through, Constantinople will fall of itself and you will have won, not a battle, but the war'. Unfortunately these rousing words were not accompanied by any intelligence on Turkish defences, or even any decent maps of the peninsula.

The battle plan for 18 March called for the warships to mount a concerted bombardment of the batteries protecting the minefields, while the trawlers nipped in and swept the mines. Two days before, Carden, who was nearly sixty, had collapsed under the strain of it all, leaving de Robeck in charge of Britain's biggest naval operation since Trafalgar. If anyone on the British side still believed that Turkey would have her neck rung like a chicken, it was quickly a case of 'some chicken ... some neck'. When de Robeck attacked, he got a bloody nose. Two British battleships and one French were sunk by mines and the Turks severely damaged three more ships, including the dreadnought cruiser HMS *Inflexible*. Just one Turkish heavy gun was destroyed, and no mines were swept. De Robeck immediately declared he was ready for another 'go', but London said no.

Hamilton had arrived at the Dardanelles the day before, and found himself 'most reluctantly driven to the conclusion that the Straits are not likely to be forced by battleships'. His troops, he thought, would have to 'open a passage for the Navy'. Back in Whitehall, Sir Maurice Hankey had just warned the prime minister that any military operation would be 'of the most formidable nature', and that unless it was meticulously prepared, there could be 'a serious disaster'. He was worried that 80,000 men might not be enough. On 23 March, de Robeck and Hamilton agreed to abandon the idea of a naval attack and prepare for the army to land, though Churchill made a last attempt to get the ships to have another go.

There had been no real discussion by the War Council of what had now become an invasion, and a very tricky one at that. The peninsula was about 50 miles long – 12 miles wide at its broadest point, and less than 4 miles wide at its narrowest – and yet it had five ranges of mountains. There were three defensive lines that had been built by the British and the French during the Crimean War when Turkey was the ally and Russia the enemy, which the Turks had taken over and strengthened. The combined Turkish forces on either side of the straits amounted to about 60,000 soldiers. They were of variable quality, but they had more battle experience than many of the Allied men they would face, and they were well dug in.

The commander of 29th Division, General Sir Aylmer Hunter-Weston, came up with a very bleak assessment. He pointed out that all the potential landing places were defended by trenches and machine-guns, and warned that so far during this war, 'none of the combatants has been successful in breaking quickly through even indifferent entrenchments'. If the operation had been 'carefully and secretly planned', it would 'almost certainly' have succeeded, but now he feared it no longer had a 'reasonable chance'. Hunter-Weston said if the expedition was recalled, it might cause 'much talk and some laughter' but it would not do 'irreparable harm to our cause'. On the other hand a landing that failed to secure a passage through the

Dardanelles for the navy would be 'a disaster to the Empire'. Hamilton was of a sunny disposition and notoriously uncomplaining, but ten days before the invasion was due to begin, he also began to agonise about the wire defences on the beaches, and suddenly asked for reinforcements. Perhaps he too was hoping Kitchener might call the whole thing off?

Hamilton's plan of attack involved landings on five beaches – S, V, W, X and Y – at Helles at the southern end of the peninsula, with another 10 miles further north on the Aegean side, at Z beach, which became known as Anzac, and was where mainly Australian and New Zealand troops landed. The navy would mount a feint attack much further up the peninsula, while the French would do the same on the Asian side. A formidable fleet of twenty-two warships and more than twenty support vessels would provide covering fire while the troops landed, but the number of shells they could use would be rationed, as the whole purpose of the land operation was to enable the fleet to get through to Constantinople, and they did not want to reach the Ottoman capital with their magazines empty. Unfortunately when 29th Division had left Britain for the Aegean island of Lemnos – the jumping-off point for Gallipoli – the ships had not been packed in a way that was suitable for landing on a hostile beach under heavy fire. The local harbour was too small for them to be repacked, so they had to go all the way back to Alexandria, causing a four-week delay. While they were away, the Turks scraped together every man they could find, plus supplies of ammunition, and shifted them to Gallipoli. Finally, at dawn on 25 April, the attack got underway.

The Australians and New Zealanders got ashore at Anzac beach, but were soon held up by thick scrub. At X beach, close to the tip of the Aegean side of the peninsula, the troops came across only a handful of Turks, and landed without any problems. Then they were not sure exactly what to do, but they moved inland and dug in. A couple of miles further up the coast at Y beach, the South Wales Borderers, along with men from the King's Own Scottish Borderers and two companies of Royal Marines stormed up the cliffs and found no enemy soldiers. By 7am the British were on the cliffs, awaiting the advance of the troops who had landed further south. Colonel Matthews of the Marines did not see a single Turkish soldier as he reconnoitred a couple of miles inland to the village of Krithia, which appeared deserted. By 3pm, with no sign of other British forces, Matthews withdrew his men from the higher ground they had reached inland, and moved back to the top of the cliff to entrench. Unfortunately, the ground was hard and matted with roots, and their heavy digging tools had been left on the beach, so they were not properly dug in when the Turks attacked an hour later. With the help of shells fired by one of the warships, Matthews' men drove them off. As soon as night fell, however, the Turks were back, and in the dark, the navy could not offer support. The battle raged all night, and the Turks suffered casualties of about 50 per cent, but the British lost perhaps a third of their force, and were badly shaken. During the night, some walking wounded got down to the beach and asked the navy to take them off, but before long they were joined by others who were not wounded. At first Matthews was too busy fighting off the Turks to notice, but eventually he saw that virtually his whole right flank had drifted away.

At S beach, at the tip of the peninsula on the straits side, another 750 men from the South Wales Borderers found themselves faced by just one platoon of Turks and also got ashore without difficulty. They seized a ridge and then waited for further orders. About a mile to the west, they could see the landing at V beach, by the village of Seddelbahr, was not going well, but they had no instructions to assist. The Irish troops landing there ran into formidable enemy defences, meeting a hail of rifle and machine-gun fire from trenches and an old fort. They were also held up by wire entanglements. Few of the Royal Dublin Fusiliers survived the first minute. Most did not even make it out of the boats, which 'drifted helplessly away with every man in them killed'. Those who got to the beach were pinned down, while those who reached the village were quickly overwhelmed by the defenders. As for the Royal Munster Fusiliers, they 'never wavered' said a captain, but the first forty-eight men to follow him were all cut down. The officer reckoned he lost 70 per cent of his company, but the Turks fought gallantly too, suffering heavy losses from 'hellish' fire from the supporting ships.

Hamilton was trying to keep tabs on the action from the *Queen Elizabeth* and Hunter-Weston from another ship, while a Roman Catholic chaplain, who landed with the men, got the view from beach level. He said they were packed 'like sardines' with bullets and shrapnel falling all around them. The narrow beach was a scene of 'indescribable confusion', with troops, mules and horses running in every direction. Almost immediately, he was hard at work: 'I had not one moment; one wounded and dying man following on after another. Just time, if a man was conscious, to hear his confession, and a muttered act of contrition, to give absolution, and the anointing, before a new man claimed attention.' The casualties had 'wounds of every description'. Often they were disfigured, with 'features blown away'. A dying nineteen-year-old moaned for his mother: 'Sights that at ordinary times would have unmanned anyone, were passed over with a business-like indifference.'

W beach also proved very sticky. There were only 200 Turks defending it, but it was narrow, overlooked by cliffs, and covered with wire. The naval bombardment had been ineffective, and the troops ran into heavy rifle and machine-gun fire, so it was only when reinforcements arrived that they were able to overcome determined resistance. The Lancashire Fusiliers won six Victoria Crosses that day. With more soldiers landing during the night, by the morning the invaders had taken control of Helles – the tip of the peninsula. The action had cost around 3,800 casualties, which was about a fifth of the total strength of 29th Division. The Turks had probably lost about 1,000.

On 28 April the invasion force began trying to move up the peninsula, attacking the village of Krithia. It was deserted no longer. In fact, it was full of Turks, some of them firing machine-guns from hidden nooks and crannies. Landing reserves and supplies had taken much longer than expected, and the British were short of ammunition. Those units that did make progress found themselves having to withdraw because of a lack of support, and by the end of the day all the troops were back at their starting positions, even though 29th Division had suffered another 2,000 casualties. As was generally the case in the First World War, defenders fared much better than attackers, and when the Turks tried a couple of night attacks, they in their turn were beaten off. For the British though, just sitting tight was not an option, so 6 May saw what became known as the Second Battle of Krithia. By 3pm, under heavy fire from hidden Turkish machine-guns, the British attack had ground to a halt. Another assault the following day met the same fate. The only reason the Gallipoli campaign had been launched was to try to outflank the deadlock of the Western Front, and now it too was turning into a stalemate, with the British Empire forces up against a Turkish trench system similar to what was found in Flanders.

The following week, there was worse news from the naval front. Under cover of fog, a Turkish destroyer torpedoed the older battleship *Goliath*, which sank in two minutes with the loss of 570 men. The Admiralty had already heard that German submarines were on their way to the Dardanelles so now they withdrew the *Queen Elizabeth* and a number of other ships. Perhaps it was just as well. The submarines did indeed arrive, and during three days in late May, they sank two more British ships. By then Fisher had finally resigned as first sea lord (and run off into hiding), after Churchill had dispatched two submarines to the eastern Mediterranean without consulting him, while the trials and tribulations of Gallipoli and the Western Front put an end to Britain's last Liberal government, as Asquith had to form a coalition with the Conservatives. Their price included the removal of Churchill from the Admiralty, though he kept his seat on the War Council, which was renamed the Dardanelles Committee.

Back at the front, the first week of June saw the third attempt to take Krithia. The Allies committed 24,000 troops, plus 7,000 reserves. When their artillery began its bombardment, a strong wind blew smoke and dust back into the eyes of their own troops, reducing visibility to a few yards. On the right, the French suffered 2,000 casualties in the first few minutes, and were quickly driven back. This allowed the Turks to rake the Royal Naval Division with fire so fierce that one battalion of 850 sustained 625 casualties. On the left, the Lancashire Fusiliers were cut down in a hail of bullets. The invaders had concentrated their heavy howitzer fire on the centre, and that was where most progress was made, with five lines of Turkish trenches captured, and some troops able to dig in just short of Krithia, but no reinforcements were sent to them, and at the end of the day, they had been driven back to just 500 yards in front of their starting position.

General Hunter-Weston had learned some lessons from these setbacks at Krithia. Working with the French commander, General Henri Gouraud, he agreed that in future instead of attacking on a broad front, they should pursue a 'bite and hold' approach, attacking only the length of trench that could be effectively bombarded by heavy howitzers and limiting advances to ground that could be covered by most of their artillery. The new strategy was tried by the French on 21 June with considerable success. Heavy losses were inflicted on the Turks and a number of trenches were captured. Hunter-Weston applied it on 12 July with more mixed results. The line advanced 500 yards. Casualties were heavy – perhaps 4,000, but the Turks probably suffered twice that number. At this point Hunter-Weston was taken ill, and would never return to Gallipoli. Nor would 'bite and hold'. The strategy was quietly abandoned. Perhaps it looked too much like what was happening on the Western Front, which was exactly what Gallipoli had been designed to avoid, or maybe someone wondered just how much 'biting and holding' would be needed before the army controlled the straits and the ships could get through.

Early in May, the French command in the Dardanelles had asked for reinforcements, and Churchill could not understand why Hamilton was not making similar requests. When the War Council took the initiative and decided to offer them, the general replied that lack of space and shortage of water might mean he could not accommodate any, and then, in the same breath, that if he got another four divisions, he might be able to advance 1,000 yards. His dispatches got more gloomy, bemoaning the burgeoning of barbed wire and lamenting that he was getting 'tied up in trench warfare as in France'. When he was sent not four, but five more divisions, however, the general seemed to brighten up, saying success was 'generally assured'. One thing Hamilton had been asking for was some dynamic new generals to inject life into the campaign. He rejected one candidate he was offered as being too fat to negotiate the trenches, and the man he ended up with was the lieutenant of the Tower of London, Sir Frederick Stopford, aged sixty-one and not very well, who had never commanded in wartime. Stopford's task would be to take Suvla Bay, 3 miles further up the coast from Anzac beach, and establish a base there. The bay was about 2 miles wide, with hills and ridges at a little distance from the beach. On 6 and 7 August, the forces at Helles tried to mount diversionary attacks. They were a disaster: 29th Division ran into the stiffest Turkish resistance yet, no ground was gained, there was no evidence that a single Turkish unit was prevented from moving north and another 3,000 casualties were suffered.

Meanwhile, the Suvla landing early on 7 August began badly. A navigational error by the navy saw some men dropped in the wrong place, while troop carriers got stuck on reefs hundreds of yards offshore. A sergeant from the Northumberland Fusiliers said it was all quiet until the ship's captain shouted: 'Cast off the lighters', then the Turks had let rip with artillery and rifle fire. Five minutes after the first lighter went out, it came back full of wounded men, and in no time the beach was covered with bodies. The troops of 11th Division landed without trouble, but then found that a little hill, Lala Bala, had strong defences and a small but determined garrison who killed or wounded 250 of the invaders, including most of the officers. Stopford's men managed to take the hill, and by 6am most of the Turkish strong points near the beach had been cleared, though the enemy still held much of the high ground further away. Then, for the next few hours, the attack stagnated. Brigadier William Sitwell, commander of 34 Brigade, had been shaken by the confusion of the landings. Many of his men were ill in the heat of the day, and, not knowing where the Turkish positions on the ridges were, he was afraid his flank might be vulnerable if he advanced. In fact, at this stage, there were few enemy soldiers in the area, and 31 and 33

Brigade were able to take Chocolate Hill, so that by the end of the day, the British were in control of the high ground closest to the beaches, and were able to start landing supplies without interference from Turkish infantry.

Stopford had sent a message to Hamilton saying he had not yet advanced much beyond the beach. It was nine hours before Hamilton replied, urging him to make progress before Turkish reserves arrived. Another sixteen hours passed before Stopford told him that the men were consolidating. He said they were like 'sucked oranges' and needed rest. General Frederick Hammersley, commander of 11th Division, did try to get things moving, but his brigadiers told him it was all very difficult: the men were tired, there was little water, the mules had not arrived, and they were short of guns. Hammersley gave way and agreed that there would be no further attack until 9 August. Still trying to crack the whip, Hamilton sent Stopford another message saying that aerial reconnaissance had revealed no Turks on the Anafarta Ridge to the north-east of the beach, so 'you will be able to gain early footing'. He also dispatched to Suvla his staff officer, Colonel Cecil Aspinall, who was greeted by the sight of men bathing and lying on the beach. An enemy officer watching the scene through his telescope thought it looked like 'a boy scouts' picnic'. Aspinall reported back to Hamilton that 'golden opportunities' were being lost. Meanwhile Hammersley and Stopford decided to mount an attack on the ridge at 5am the next day. Now Hamilton himself appeared, and demanded an immediate advance. Hammersley said it could not be done. By the time the brigades were ready it would be dark, and they would be moving into unknown territory. Hamilton finally managed to get the attack brought forward – by one hour – to 4am.

The enemy had made good use of the delay. General Liman von Sanders, a German seconded to the Turkish command, got two divisions sent to reinforce Suvla. The local commander, Feizi Bey, decided on a counter-attack at dawn on 9 August, but von Sanders wanted action more quickly, and removed him in favour of 34-year-old Mustapha Kemal, who as Kemal Ataturk would go on to become the first president of the Turkish Republic. Kemal, however, agreed with his predecessor, saying the men were too exhausted for anything else. Still, Turkish defence was stern enough, and when the British attacked, most were stopped in their tracks by a hail of gunfire. One group found a gap in enemy lines and nearly made it to the top of Anafarta Ridge, but they had no support and were driven back. Even if they had managed to go further, they might just have advanced into trouble.

Of four lighters transporting water, three had failed to make it ashore. Water, food and ammunition would all have been in desperately short supply for any units far from the beach. When Kemal launched his own attack, it fared no better, and soon he was ordering his men to dig in. Suvla had produced yet another stalemate.

To break it, Hamilton planned a new offensive for 21 August. Stopford advised strongly against, and was replaced by General Henry de Lisle. Once again most units gained no ground, and at least 10,000 more casualties were sustained. Some of the wounded were burned to death when they could not drag themselves away as artillery shells set fire to scrub. In fact, the Suvla operation had succeeded in its ostensible objective of establishing a major new supply base, and the Turks did not have sufficient artillery to drive the British out, but it was a cul-de-sac, not a springboard. Some had dismissed Gallipoli as a 'sideshow'. Suvla now looked like a sideshow to the sideshow.

When Hamilton asked London for another three divisions, he got a dusty response. Two huge offensives on the Western Front in the spring had proved fruitless at the cost of 250,000 casualties. Now the French wanted an autumn attack to drive the Germans from their soil. Churchill opposed it, saying it was unlikely to be successful and might cost another quarter of a million men. Kitchener sympathised with him, but replied that 'we had to make war as we must, not as we would like to'. In September, far from getting reinforcements, Hamilton had 25,000 of his troops removed. Only Churchill now argued in the Dardanelles Committee for sending more men. The leading conservative, Andrew Bonar Law, said any further commitment would be a 'useless sacrifice of life'. The committee also considered a report from the Australian journalist, Keith Murdoch, father of media mogul Rupert, who had visited the peninsula and said that Hamilton and his staff were regarded with 'contempt' by the troops and that 'sedition' was 'talked around every tin of bully beef'.

The army already had some idea of how low morale was from a committee of inquiry into a failed night attack at Helles in mid August. There should have been 100 men from the Highland Light Infantry involved, but because of sickness, only sixty were available. Many of these were exhausted after a long stint digging trenches, and most had been involved in a night attack in July when there were heavy casualties and no ground was gained. No written orders had been issued, and neither the senior officer who ordered the attack, nor his number two, were anywhere near the front when it was launched. The preliminary artillery bombardment missed the Turkish trenches by a considerable margin, the groups all set out at different times so that the Turks were able to concentrate their fire on each one in turn, and the men were so thinly spread that no one could see the soldier next to him. The attack just melted away. If an officer got anywhere near the Turkish lines, he found himself alone, because the men had drifted back to the trenches after going just a few yards. The inquiry put the blame squarely on the poor, bloody infantry. The operation had failed 'for one reason only, namely the misconduct of the men whose duty it was to carry out the attack....The cowardly behaviour of the men 1/6th Highland Light Infantry has brought great discredit on the regiment to which they belong and on the land of their birth.'

On 14 October, Hamilton lost his chance to win the war. He was recalled and replaced by Lieutenant-General Sir Charles Monro, who had been commanding the Third Army in France. His brief from Kitchener was to find whether there was any means of breaking the deadlock, or whether the troops would have to pull out – something that would be, the secretary for war repeatedly told the Dardanelles Committee, 'the most disastrous event in the history of the Empire'. By the time Monro arrived, however, the troops were under deadly attack from another enemy – disease. A few had perished before they even got to Gallipoli, like the poet Rupert Brooke, who died after a mosquito bite became infected. On the peninsula, no-man's-land between the trenches was covered with dead bodies decomposing under the hot sun. A second lieutenant in the Lancashire Fusiliers said there were a 'tremendous' number of flies: 'At night they lived on the dead and in the daytime they just buzzed around our trenches.' When the men wanted to eat, they had to wave their hands over the food 'and then bite suddenly, or a fly came with it. Any bit of uncovered food was blotted out of sight by flies in a couple of seconds.' Not surprisingly, dysentery was soon rife, and even those who did not catch it 'had very unpleasant tummy trouble and were constantly on the trot'. By October, the force was losing 5,000 men a week to disease. This put a huge strain on those still fit enough for duty. One private reported that they had to spend twenty-four hours in the firing line, then they got eight hours out of the line, followed by sixteen hours digging, then back into the front line – a maximum of eight hours' sleep in every forty-eight. No wonder, as he put it, many men 'broke down completely and had to be sent away'.

Monro told Kitchener that few of the troops were capable of sustained effort. The Turks held all the high ground, there were reports that heavy guns were going to be arriving from Germany, and he recommended a rapid exit, though he believed it would be a dangerous operation in which up to 40 per cent of the force might be killed or wounded. Having chosen their new general, the Dardanelles Committee – now re-renamed the War Committee – did not like his advice, so they sent out Kitchener himself to see if things were really as bad as Monro said. The first thing that struck him was the land itself. In the words of another army officer, it was 'almost indescribably difficult for military operations; it consists of a tangled mass of deep ravines with precipitous sides and choked with scrub'. Kitchener also came to the conclusion that if the Germans did arrive, it would be impossible to hold the British positions, but he thought Monro's assessment of the losses that evacuation might entail was too pessimistic.

By now, the Gallipoli operation had lost its most energetic advocate. Churchill had temporarily left politics to go and command a battalion on the Western Front and the War Committee received calls from assorted army top brass for the adventure to be abandoned. On 23 November the committee decided on evacuation 'notwithstanding the grave political disadvantages which may result', but Asquith insisted that any decision must be made by the full cabinet, where a number of noble lords objected. Fears surfaced that the badly-mauled Russians might make a separate peace with Germany, de Robeck popped up to say that the Turkish forts at the Narrows might be captured after all, and Kitchener opined that just four more divisions could enable a breakout from Suvla. Monro immediately poured cold water on these ideas. Four new divisions would cause impossible congestion, the weather was getting treacherous: gales in October had often stopped supplies arriving, then in November men drowned as heavy rain flooded the trenches, while others died of exposure in sleet and snow.

Finally, on 8 December, the cabinet decided to evacuate Suvla and Anzac, though Helles would be held for the moment, ostensibly to stop the enemy establishing a naval base there, but most believed it was just a face-saver. Anyway, while the government had been agonising, an unofficial retreat had already started, with generals at Gallipoli running down their stores and their garrisons, so by the time the government had made its mind up, there were only 80,000 men remaining. In the end, nothing became Gallipoli like the leaving of it. The evacuation was by far the most successful part of the operation. A meticulously planned campaign of deception concealed what was happening from the enemy, with dummy casualty clearing stations, noisy empty supply carts running back and forth every night, unmanned rifles firing automatically from empty trenches, and men in muffled boots marching silently to the shore. In January, the posturing over staying at Helles was abandoned, and the garrison was evacuated from there too. When Turkish patrols finally did creep forward, they found British positions deserted. The withdrawal had been carried out without any significant casualties, though plenty of supplies had had to be abandoned.

Overall, though, the operation had been a complete failure, and an appallingly costly one at that. Britain lost more than 26,000 killed in action, plus nearly 45,000 wounded. The Australians, New Zealanders and Indians suffered around 12,000 dead, the French about 8,000. Total Allied dead and wounded were more than 132,000. Turkish casualties may have been even higher. Among British troops, casualties from disease and sickness were about double the number sustained in battle. Of the infantry who fought at Gallipoli, a third would never appear in action again. Conceived as a way of getting around the stalemate of the Western Front, Gallipoli failed to shorten the war by a single day.

18

The Battle of the Somme, 1916

Every other disaster featured in this book was a defeat. The Somme was a victory, sort of. Although the British Army failed to achieve most of its objectives, it did push the Germans back, and the battle was seen by some as playing a crucial role in their final defeat two years later. Even if that is true, the astonishing scale of the British losses – nearly 20,000 killed on the first day alone – mean it is hard to describe the Somme as anything other than a disaster.

During the opening months of the First World War, the Germans had quickly grabbed the region of north-east France that held the country's most productive industries, as well as nearly all of Belgium. Then the conflict settled into the bloody stalemate Gallipoli was meant to circumvent, with an unbroken line of trenches running from the Channel to the Swiss border. During 1915, this front barely moved. Two big British offensives broke on the trenches, the barbed wire and the machine-gun nests. At Neuve-Chapelle in March, 11,000 were killed and wounded, while at Loos, in September, there were 61,000 casualties: in both cases for gains of less than 1,000 yards. One senior officer, General Sir Horace Smith-Dorrien, who we last met escaping from the Zulus at Isandlwana (see chapter fourteen), protested about the likely losses when told to mount a counter-attack, and was dismissed in short order. The French had lost even more heavily – 50,000 to edge the line forward 500 yards in Champagne, 60,000 at St Mihiel, 120,000 near Arras. On 6 December, the first military conference of all the Allies – Britain, France, Italy and Russia – was held at Chantilly, presided over by Marshal

Joseph Joffre, generalissimo of all French forces. It agreed that the British and French should mount a joint offensive on either side of the river Somme. This was an odd choice. There was no great strategic or military target to be won, and if the Germans were defeated, then they could easily fall back to a new defensive line, but the great plus for Joffre was that the Somme was where the trenches of the two Allied armies joined. He would be able to keep an eye on the British.

Less than two weeks later, 54-year-old General Sir Douglas Haig, a veteran of the Sudan and the Boer wars, took over as commander-in-chief of the British Expeditionary Force. Haig, a Scot who had once been turned down by the army's Camberley Staff College for failing his maths exam, was well connected at court. His wife was a maid of honour to Queen Victoria and Queen Alexandra, and he became a close friend of King George V. The army talent spotters first noticed him because of perceptive reports he wrote on French and German military manoeuvres. The new commander-in-chief had originally favoured a different plan – concentrating the attack further north, and then 'rolling up' the German line, while on 29 December, former prime minister Arthur Balfour, now first lord of the Admiralty, voiced his scepticism about the Somme offensive. The enemy had been hard at work making their defences 'impregnable', and Britain might lose huge num-bers of men – far more than the Germans sitting in their trenches – while making negligible gains. Secretary of state for war, Lord Kitchener imme-diately slapped him down. The Germans were occupying France's 'most valuable mining and manufacturing districts'. Besides, the British could not keep troops in the field indefinitely, and this represented the only chance of winning the war in 1916. If they failed to take it, Britain would run the risk of losing the conflict 'through exhaustion of our resources'. Balfour was not the only politician who was unconvinced, though, and at the War Committee on 13 January 1916, Minister of Munitions David Lloyd George reminded his colleagues what had happened to the British offensives of the previous year, and said 'we could not have another of the same sort'. He suggested delaying until the British were 'really strong enough'. The Welsh Wizard still wondered whether striking somewhere else might do the trick: Egypt? Mesopotamia? But the search for an alternative theatre had been dealt a formidable blow by the disaster at Gallipoli, and on 22 February, the committee endorsed the Somme offensive to be mounted in May or June.

The launch pad for the 'Big Push' would be the 14 miles of trenches to the north of the river held by the British, and the 8 miles to the south occupied by the French. Britain sent another 200,000 men across the Channel: regulars of the 29th Division who had survived Gallipoli, territorials, but mostly soldiers of Kitchener's new volunteer army, many of whom had joined up in local 'pals' battalions. While the Allies were preparing, the Germans launched a huge offensive against the great French fortress of Verdun, 150 miles to the south-east. Within a month, 90,000 French troops had been killed. There was widespread feeling in France that Britain was not taking her fair share of casualties, and at a conference on 28 March, French political and military leaders told Kitchener and Haig it was high time the British 'played their part'. The commander-in-chief still did not feel ready, complaining he did not yet have an army, only 'a collection of divisions untrained for the field' and there were worries on the French side too. In early May, even 'the Tiger' – leading politician Georges Clemenceau – was urging Haig to restrain Joffre. A week later, however, the War Committee was told that French losses at Verdun had mounted to 115,000, and that it was only a matter of time before the Germans broke through and hit the road to Paris.

Verdun simultaneously made an Anglo-French offensive more urgent and reduced France's potential contribution. On 19 May they cut the number of divisions they planned to make available from forty to twenty-five. Joffre wanted the offensive mounted on 1 July. Haig would have preferred 15 August, but when he mentioned the later date, Joffre shouted that the French Army would have ceased to exist by then, and the British commander fell into line. On 23 May, Winston Churchill, just back from commanding a battalion on the Western Front, told the House of Commons a few home truths about what it was really like and how, every day, thousands of British soldiers were 'knocked into bundles of bloody rags … and carried away to hasty graves or to field ambulances'. He warned against 'futile offensives'. Not for the last time, he was a voice in the wilderness. By the time he spoke, the commanders in France were working non-stop towards the assault, though the War Committee had still not endorsed the date. With barely a week to go, on 23 June, General Sir William Robertson, chief of the Imperial General Staff (CIGS) and the most senior military official in London, told the committee that on the Somme, Britain would have more men, but the Germans would have more guns. Balfour drily remarked that we seemed to have superiority 'except in the one thing that really mattered'. More members might have expressed scepticism if Robertson had told them that Britain's superiority in men was likely to melt away within days of the offensive being launched because of the number of troops the Germans held in reserve.

The artillery onslaught designed to soften up the Germans before the offensive began the next day. The previous year, along with the failure at Gallipoli, a scandal over a shortage of shells on the Western Front had helped bring down the Liberal government. Now there were plenty, and more than 1,500 guns were getting through nearly 1.75 million of them. Unfortunately, many were duds, and even those that did explode, instead of destroying barbed wire, trenches and dugouts, often managed only to churn up the ground, making it harder for infantry to advance. German dugouts in particular were hard to destroy, being up to 40 feet deep and reinforced with concrete. During brief pauses in the bombardment, British soldiers made raids across no-man's-land to investigate the effects and snatch German prisoners for interrogation. On two successive nights, it was reported that raids had failed 'owing to intense machine-gun and rifle fire'. This in itself might have been seen as a useful pointer to the effectiveness or otherwise of the barrage, but no alarm bells appear to have been rung, and some prisoners delivered reassuring messages of how the shelling was stopping food and water being delivered to the German front line, and of how morale was plummeting.

Meanwhile Haig warned his generals against caution. General Sir Henry Rawlinson, commander of the Fourth Army, planned to halt for an hour and consolidate when he had taken the last German line of defence. Instead, Haig, who had held his first commission in a cavalry regiment, told him to keep advancing, while the horse soldiers – virtually unused since the first month of the war – were instructed to be ready to pour through the gap the infantry was going to knock in the German lines. On 28 June Haig wrote to King George V, telling him he had been driving around behind the lines visiting troops, and that everywhere they were 'in great spirits'. The next day, a British raid produced a fine haul of forty-six prisoners but they reported that German morale was excellent, and that night, in another foray, out of forty-two men from the West Yorkshire Regiment, thirteen were killed and twelve wounded.

Still, this was no time for faint hearts. The day before the attack, Haig believed: 'Preparations were never so thorough, nor troops better trained.... With God's help, I feel hopeful.' The preparations included the digging of plenty of mass graves. The number of French divisions who would attack was now down to eight, along with nineteen British. Robertson told the

War Committee that the plan for day one was to push the front forward by 1½ miles. There were only six German divisions facing the British, and 'we could get on all right'. Back at the front, Rawlinson, usually a little more sceptical than Haig, felt 'pretty confident' of success, though 'only after heavy fighting', while a major in the Royal Sussex Regiment said the troops had 'a wonderful air of cheery expectancy'. Major-General Jackson told his men how important the operation was: 'Success will mean the shortening of the war, failure means the war prolonged indefinitely.' The Germans were 'outnumbered and out-gunned'. If every man was 'determined to get through', the enemy would go to pieces. The 7th Manchester Pals Battalion was simply instructed that the word 'retire' was 'absolutely forbidden'.

Early on Saturday 1 July the guns rained down another quarter of a million shells on enemy positions in a bombardment loud enough to be heard in London, 200 miles away. During the weeks leading up to the offensive, British sappers had been burrowing beneath the German lines planting huge explosive charges. Now seventeen of them were detonated, gouging huge craters out of the earth. One close to the village of Beaumont-Hamel killed dozens of Germans, but almost immediately survivors were dragging out machine-guns from dugouts that had survived and siting them on the edge of the craters that would soon become death traps for the advancing troops.

At 7.30am the whistle sounded, and the British went over the top. Most were from Kitchener's new battalions, and had never fought before. (Their creator would never know how they performed, for he had died less than a month before when his ship hit a mine off the Orkneys.) The biggest number of men came from the industrial north – first Yorkshire, then Lancashire, while the next biggest group were from Ireland, mainly Ulster. The soldiers were weighed down with 66 pounds of equipment – sandbags, groundsheets etc. – and those were the lucky ones. Others might carry up to 76 pounds with picks, shovels and trench ladders. Even the official historian recognised that this burden made it 'difficult to get out of a trench, impossible to move much quicker than a slow walk, or to rise and lie down quickly'. The objectives for Rawlinson's Fourth Army on that first day were a string of otherwise insignificant occupied French villages: Serre, Beaumont-Hamel, Thiepval, Pozières, Contalmaison, Montauban and the German strong points around them. Near Serre, according to one observer, the Accrington Pals were 'mown down like meadow grass'. It would become a familiar simile. One hundred German machine-guns had fired at them from armoured emplacements, and because the gap cut in the British barbed wire was too narrow, they were caught in a traffic jam, making a perfect target. At his headquarters 10 miles away, Haig was being told that his men had entered Serre and Thiepval and that 'everywhere' they had crossed the enemy's first line trenches, so that he confided to his diary that initial reports were 'most satisfactory'. Unfortunately, they were also quite untrue.

The innumerable shells had not done their job. Corporal Shaw of the Royal Welch Fusiliers said: 'they hadn't made any impact on those barbed wire entanglements. The result was we never got anywhere near the Germans'. His comrades 'were just simply slaughtered'. Even when progress was made, for example, to the south of Serre where the Essex Regiment managed to break through the first line of German defences, enemy artillery made it impossible to send reinforcements and gradually the Germans counter-attacked using craters made by the British bombardment, doggedly advancing from one to another, until they had forced the attackers back. It was a similar story at Ovillers and La Boisselle, where the Germans waited until the British were 200 yards away and then opened up with merciless machine-gun and artillery fire. About seventy of the attackers got into the German trench, but no reinforcements could be got to them and they were driven out by counter-attacks and forced to return to their own lines through the British dead and wounded littering the field. At Fricourt, the West Yorkshire Regiment overran the first German trench, but was then cut to pieces in the open ground between it and the second line. Within an hour and a half of setting off, half were dead. Many British reports noted the courage and tenacity with which the Germans fought.

The fog of war was much in evidence. Having reached the German trenches, the Seaforth Highlanders simultaneously received two messages: one saying hang on all costs and the other saying retire to your starting point. Having sustained heavy losses, they withdrew. In another sector, Irish troops took a German redoubt but then had to retreat when their own artillery started firing on them. To help the guns avoid shelling their own men as they advanced, British soldiers were given tin triangles that glinted in the sun to wear on their backs. The trouble was that they provided very helpful targets for the Germans when the soldiers tried to crawl back to their own lines. The 36th (Ulster) Division captured, and for a time held, a strong point named the Schwaben Redoubt, but they too were driven back. By the river Ancre, the ground was swampy and two-thirds of the Royal Inniskilling Fusiliers were killed or wounded before being driven back to their starting point. Altogether, 5,500 Ulstermen died, while four won Victoria Crosses.

Before the 16th Battalion of the Northumberland Fusiliers attacked Thiepval, their brigadier told them that it would literally be a walkover. They would not even need their rifles because the bombardment had been so devastating. The men advanced behind a ball punted by a talented footballer among them, but before they reached the German wire they were cut down by machine-gun fire. Footballs were also in evidence at Montauban. Captain Wilfred Nevill of the East Surrey Regiment dribbled them with his men towards the German lines. It was the last game he would ever play. This sector, at the southern end of the British line, saw the biggest advance. The artillery bombardment had been more successful, destroying wire, trenches and dugouts. The British captured well-fortified trenches and two redoubts, along with four guns and 500 prisoners. They held on against German counter-attacks, and then just after 10am, the Manchester Regiment and the Royal Scots Fusiliers entered the deserted, devastated village, even advancing beyond it to capture a brickworks where the Germans had been using chimneys as observation points. The cost had been terrible: seventy-six officers and 1,664 other ranks were killed. The Royal Scots Fusiliers were also in action at Contalmaison, to the north, where they advanced up to 1,000 yards for the loss of six officers and 327 men. In spite of losing almost all of its officers, XV Corps captured the village of Mametz. More than 150 men were killed by a single machine-gun nestling in the base of a crucifix. Nor were those who went over the top the only casualties. Haig had failed to inflict enough damage on German artillery, and opposite Beaumont-Hamel, a quarter of the troops being held in reserve were killed or wounded by enemy guns. At Loos the previous year, Rawlinson had complained that there were not enough guns to bombard German batteries, but at the Somme the position was even worse. Fewer than 180 tried to target enemy artillery, compared with more than 1,200 firing at barbed wire and trenches. The result was that more than 800 German guns survived the initial bombardment to rain shells on British troops.

South of the Somme, the French fared better. Their Sixth Army encountered less well-defended German positions and was able to push the enemy back along the whole 8-mile front. By the end of 1 July, the British Army had lost an incredible 19,240 men killed – the worst toll for a single day in its history, and the highest suffered by any army in the whole ghastly war – plus another 36,000 wounded. Of 143 battalions in action, thirty-two suffered more than

50 per cent casualties. Many troops in the second wave were unnerved by the number of wounded being carried back after the first attack. Albert, the nearest major town to the front, saw casualties brought in by wheelbarrow, stretcher and cart. Once their wounds had been dressed, they were laid on the ground to wait to be evacuated. The overwhelming numbers meant that those not expected to survive had to be left to one side. 'It was hard to ignore their cries for help' said one man working there, 'but we had to concentrate on those who might live'. Others who had been wounded still lay screaming and crying for help in no-man's-land because German sniper and machine-gun fire made it too dangerous to try to rescue them.

Haig was philosophical. The record casualty figures could not be 'considered severe in view of the numbers engaged, and the length of front attacked'. It had been 'a day of ups and downs', but with an attack of this magnitude, 'varying fortunes must be expected', and overall the situation was 'much more favourable than when we started today'. Rawlinson conceded that casualties had been 'heavy', but consoled himself with the thought that there were 'plenty of fresh divisions behind'. The attack had had one beneficial effect however: the Germans were forced to withdraw sixty guns and 20,000 troops from Verdun in order to strengthen their forces on the Somme, and the British commander would be told by his government's representative with the French High Command that our ally was 'pleased' with his efforts, and that they had kept the French in the war.

The next day, Haig visited two casualty clearing stations, and found the wounded 'in wonderful good spirits'. He wanted to mount further attacks, but General Sir Hubert Gough reported that the trenches held by his VII Corps were so clogged with dead and wounded that it would take days to clear them, and assaults in most sectors had to be put off until 3 July. The men went over the top again, but once more they failed to achieve their objectives. The French continued to do better, and by the following day had broken through on a 6-mile front, but ominously the commander of the German Second Army, General Fritz von Below, ordered that all lost ground must be 'attacked and wrested back from the enemy'. He forbade 'the voluntary relinquishing of positions... The enemy must be made to pick his way forward over corpses.' Haig, however, was convinced that the Germans were being worn down and ordered his generals 'to continue the operations relentlessly and allow the Enemy no respite'. They mounted the first night attack of the battle, with inexperienced troops who did not know the terrain, and the Germans beat them off, inflicting heavy casualties. The only success was the capture of Bernafay Wood. Meanwhile, a new hazard was appearing on the battlefield. Heavy rain had turned much of the ground into cloying mud, with some trenches and shell-holes becoming impassable. On 6 July La Boisselle was captured, but the following day the bloody round of attack and counter-attack continued as the British took Contalmaison, only to lose it again that evening. On 8 July they took most of Trones Wood, but again a German counter-attack forced them out.

After a week of throwing themselves against the German lines, the best the British had been able to manage was to drive the enemy back less than 2 miles, and this only in a few places. Haig wrote to his wife to tell her the battle was 'developing slowly but steadily in our favour. In another fortnight, with Divine Help, I hope that some decisive results may be obtained. In the meantime, we must be patient and determined.' On 10 July, the British finally captured Contalmaison, now a pulverised ruin, 2,000 yards from the starting point nine days earlier. Two days later, they tried using some new poison gas, but German shells sent it up in flames, killing many on the British side. That same day, however, the French got what they wanted. The final German attack against Verdun failed.

The Holy Grail for Haig was for the infantry to make a big enough gap in the German trenches for the cavalry to pour through into 'the open country beyond the enemy's prepared lines of defence'. It would be the breakthrough for which the Allies had waited two long years. On 14 July, Bastille Day, Rawlinson launched 48,000 men at the enemy trenches after a massive bombardment. Caught by surprise, the Germans fell back, but when Rawlinson ordered his cavalry to take High Wood, the ground was too slippery for the horses. They managed to hang on in the wood through the night, but they had to withdraw the next day. Overall though, the British had managed to take more than 4 miles of the German second line. Haig was elated, telling his wife the enemy were 'very much disorganised and rattled'. For those trying to dodge the bullets in no-man's-land, it did not always feel that way. An attack on Pozières on 17 July was driven off by such intense machine-gun fire that a further one planned for the next day was cancelled. Haig proclaimed himself 'dissatisfied', but he gained encouragement at the end of the month, when some captured enemy officers expressed the view that Germany was 'beaten'. On the other hand, a young infantryman named George Leigh-Mallory, who would disappear climbing Mount Everest in 1924, told his parents: 'the German war machine must be far from run down if he can put up the fight he has done'.

Since early July the wounded had been arriving in London. The writer Vera Brittain, who was working as a nurse, later recalled 'the immense convoys which came without cessation for about a fortnight'. By the end of the month, Robertson was telling Haig the politicians were 'beginning to get a little uneasy' about the casualty figures, and asking 'whether a loss of say 300,000 men will lead to some really great results'. If not, they were saying, 'we ought to be content with something less than we are now doing'. They were also 'enquiring why we are fighting and the French are not'. Haig insisted that the attack must go on because 'in another six weeks, the Enemy should be hard put to find men'.

Churchill was less easily satisfied than his former colleagues, and sent the War Committee a sober assessment of the true state of affairs: 'We have not conquered in a month's fighting as much ground as we were expected to gain in the first two hours.' Even where Haig had managed to advance, it was on too narrow a front to be turned into a real breakthrough, and when the Germans had been driven back, they had simply constructed more formidable defences from which they could pour lethal artillery fire on any British offensive. What if Haig's plan finally succeeded and the British took Péronne or Bapaume, what good would it do? None of the objectives were of any 'strategic or political consequence'. Any element of surprise had been lost long ago, and the British were just 'using up division after division'. Churchill was wasting his paper and ink. Robertson dismissed the criticisms: the British had lost 'only' 18,000 men during the last week, which was much lower than the 56,000 on the first day. The Somme had stopped German attacks on Verdun, and prevented the Kaiser helping Austria against Russia. He also made the extraordinary claim – on the basis of no apparent evidence – that German losses were 1.25 million against total Allied casualties of 160,000. No one at the War Committee seems to have queried these figures.

Reality threatened to put in an appearance on 2 August, when Haig told his commanders that the Germans had 'recovered to a great extent from the disorganisation' inflicted on them in early July. German positions must in future be assaulted only from promising starting points, and should not be attacked 'without careful and methodical' preparation. The very next day, though, a poorly prepared last-minute attack on Guillemont ran into a hail of machine-gun fire. The men went forward three times, and three times they were driven back. Half the officers were killed, and ninety-six out of 600 men. On 5 August the War Committee got the benefit of Haig's reply to Churchill's criticisms. The troops were in 'excellent heart' and 'under no circumstances must we relax our effort'. What was needed was 'a vigorous offensive well into the autumn', which would be excellent preparation for a 'further campaign' next year. The committee pledged its full support. It was to be business as usual on the Somme. Now Haig had a plan to capture a ridge at Pozières as a prelude to a general advance northwards, while Gough had another go at Thiepval. A week after the War Committee dismissed Churchill's worries, the general had lunch with King George V and the French president, Raymond Poincaré, who was 'most anxious' that there should be a 'decisive advance' before Christmas to stop the French and British people 'grumbling'. Haig replied that if they had good weather 'much will be done' by then.

The latest attempt to capture Thiepval also came to nothing, and Haig complained that the men had been in the line for so long, they 'had lost most of their dash'. When the Germans tried to launch an offensive in Leuze Wood, they came on as bravely as the British, and met the same fate, as they were cut down by machine-guns. On the Somme, attack was decidedly not the best form of defence. As Corporal Shaw of the Royal Welch Fusiliers put it: 'When they were counter-attacking, they were mown down, just the same as we were, and yet they were urged on by their officers just the same as our officers were urging us on.' On 18 August it must have been hard to hear the discussions at the War Committee because of the din from goal posts being moved. This time when Balfour asked Robertson about how many men the Germans had lost, Robertson 'did not really know', though his 'impression' was that they were losing 'as many and more than we were'. With thousands of glum British heroes being sped up the line to death each week, Balfour suggested striking somewhere else at a 'thinner' German line. Robertson simply replied that this 'could not be done', but now rather than holding out the hope of a major breakthrough on the Somme, he said it would be enough 'if we only held the Germans' to allow the Russian armies in the east to 'get on' against them. Far from 'getting on', by the following week, the Russians were begging for another big attack on the Somme to take the pressure off them. In fact, in the east, things were going from bad to worse. Romania joined the Allies, and was immediately set upon by Germany, Austria and Bulgaria. Now she too was pleading for help, and the War Committee agreed that putting more men through the Somme mincer was the best way to do it.

September began with small successes. The Germans were finally driven from Guillemont, where three Victoria Crosses were won, but the

Schwaben Redoubt stubbornly refused to be captured. The commanders decided that the infantry were to blame. General Sir Claud Jacob complained of their lack of 'martial qualities' while General Gough thought they were showing 'poor spirit'. Haig too was furious: 'the units did not really attack', and the proof was that total losses 'were under 1,000.' He noted that the men had previously exhibited 'slackness' in their, presumably unenthusiastic, saluting of him as he drove through the village where they were billeted. On 9 September, the 16th Division liberated the village of Ginchy, or rather what had once been Ginchy before it was shattered beyond recognition. The cost was 240 officers – more than half – and 4,090 other ranks out of 10,400. Presumably Haig thought these kinds of casualty figures were more like it. What was it the secretary to the War Council, Sir Maurice Hankey, had written about the Western Front before Gallipoli? 'Any advance must be costly and slow… When viewed on a map, the total gains are almost negligible, and apparently incommensurate with the effort and loss of life.'

Back on 29 July, Haig had been promising that the Germans would run out of men within six weeks. Well, six weeks had come and gone. Now he declared that the next British offensive on 15 September would bring the 'crisis' of the battle. It could be the moment when the cavalry finally broke through. Back in London, pessimism appeared to be taking over the War Committee, though not enough to persuade them to end the battle, or even to mount a serious examination of what was being achieved at what cost. Asquith warned, rather superfluously, that advances might be 'slow work'. Would there be a breakthrough by Christmas? He did not think so. The foreign secretary, Sir Edward Grey, said the campaign must continue, even though he did not know what it would 'lead to', while Robertson added helpfully that there was 'nothing else to be done'.

Ever since the start of the battle, Haig had been crying out for deliveries of Britain's new secret weapon, the tank. Now, finally, he had eighteen to deploy in an attack on Leuze Wood, though some voices urged him to hold them back until he could use them in greater numbers. Of the tanks in action on 15 September, ten were hit, and nine broke down, but in some places, they helped the troops advance 2,000 yards – the best result since day one – taking four lines of trenches and three heavily fortified villages. There were reports of some Germans being so overawed that they immediately put their hands up. The prime minister's son, Raymond Asquith, a lieutenant in the Guards, was killed that day, while a future prime minister, Harold Macmillan, was badly wounded but survived after lying all day in a shell-hole which was twice blown in on him by the monstrous anger of the guns. Eleven days later, the tanks also played a part in an action near Gueudecourt where 500 German prisoners were captured for the loss of just five British soldiers, and in the taking, at last, of Thiepval. On 27 September Haig noted that casualties in the 'heavy fighting' of the previous two days had been as few as 8,000 – a figure he thought was 'very remarkable' and a sign that the Germans were 'not fighting so well'. Although two more attempts to take the Schwaben Redoubt failed, the British captured as much ground between 15 and 30 September as in the whole of the campaign up to that point.

The success inspired Haig to develop a 'Grand Design' for October. The Fourth and Reserve armies would first take Bapaume, and then advance a further 15 miles to Cambrai. This would entail capturing the new defensive line that the Germans had built along the Le Transloy Ridge. Why all this should suddenly be possible when an advance of only 5 miles had been achieved in three months was not altogether clear. Anyway, the 'design' turned out to be rather less than 'grand'. The first day of the offensive – 1 October – was fine, but the German machine-gun fire was lethal, and little progress was made. The next day it poured down, making it very hard to move artillery and reducing the effectiveness of the bombardment. On 3 October, two companies from the Duke of Wellington's Regiment waded through 100 yards of mud towards the German lines, but when they got as far as the barbed wire, they were cut down. For the next two days, the rain was so hard that it was impossible to mount any assaults, and the Germans used the respite to strengthen their defences. At least Haig's spirits were not dampened. He wrote to the king on 5 October to tell him that the offensive had been 'highly satisfactory'. The Germans were now 'much less capable', and sometimes abandoned their trenches at the first sight of the British infantry, who were 'almost twice as efficient as they were'.

On 7 October, Rawlinson's Fourth Army mounted an attack on the Transloy Line. Hampered by the cloying mud, they were beaten back. Commander of XIV Corps Lieutenant-General the Earl of Cavan, who had been involved in the assault, questioned whether the continued offensives were worth the losses they brought, and on 8 October Haig himself had to warn General Gough to hold back his best drill sergeants from assaults as the army could not afford to lose any more. This concern did not, however, provoke any broader questions about British strategy, and the next day the commander-in-chief was telling the War Committee that the attacks must go on 'without intermission'. While the carnage continued, the Viscountess D'Abernon, a famous socialite and beauty who had trained as a nurse to help the wounded, became one of the very few women to visit the front line. She was horrified by 'the wickedness and waste of life, the lack of any definite objective commensurate with all this destruction, desolation and human suffering'. At a casualty clearing station, she noted that the officers were 'almost without exception … mere boys'. This was the picture of life on the Western Front that the newspapers did not report. Instead, as Corporal Diffey of the Royal Welch Fusiliers put it, they 'wrote of tremendous victories and killing Germans as a sport… We could laugh aloud at these reports, plagued by lice and living among the debris of war.'

A further attack by Cavan's men on the Transloy Line on 12 October, was, Haig had to concede, 'not altogether a success'. The Germans had adopted the simple tactic of pulling their machine-guns half a mile back so they dodged the artillery bombardment, but still took a terrible toll of the advancing troops. At Gueudecourt, the British also tried a new tactic: the creeping artillery barrage, with the shells meant to keep falling ahead of the infantry as they advanced. This too turned out to be not altogether a success, as synchronising the movement of the troops and the aiming of the shells proved too difficult, and a tenth of the attackers were killed by their own guns. One of those who died that day was 2nd Lieutenant Donald Hankey, the son of Sir Maurice Hankey. The grand design of a breakthrough to Cambrai had failed. Rawlinson complained that the bad weather had slowed the attack down and given the Germans 'a breather'. In contrast with Haig's upbeat assessments, he considered the enemy artillery was 'better organised, and his infantry is fighting with greater tenacity'. Back on 1 July, each British battalion had 1,000 men, but now few could muster more than 400, and many of these were not fully trained. Some guns were too badly worn to be accurate, the aircraft which had helped them to target German defences could no longer see the enemy because of deteriorating weather, while at ground level, the rain and mud 'were so bad as to make mere existence a real trial of body and spirit' according to the official history.

So, time to call a halt? Or at least a pause to take stock? Certainly not. The 18 October saw another assault on Le Transloy, and three days later an attack by 48,000 men on two lines of trenches. Haig was still confident that he could push the Germans back to Bapaume, which obstinately remained 3 miles behind their lines. On 23 October he met Joffre and they agreed to 'continue to press' the Germans throughout the winter. The trouble was that even when the British did make an advance, as they did on 28 October, it was becoming a nightmare to keep them supplied. Packhorses got hopelessly bogged down in the mud and it would take a man carrying a load twenty-four hours to do a round trip to the new front line, during which time he would often be under fire. Finally, on 3 November, Lloyd George, who had replaced Kitchener as secretary of state for war, began to raise doubts, telling the War Committee that: 'At no point had the Allies achieved a definite, clear success', that the Germans had 'recovered the initiative' and that Haig's 'policy of attrition' was inflicting bigger losses on the British than on the enemy. It was like a light going on. The committee declared that if the offensive was continued into the following year, it 'was not likely to lead to decisive results', while the losses would be out of proportion to any gains made. Then they made the familiar call for action in 'another theatre'.

The next day, another attack on Le Transloy was beaten off, and Haig got a letter from Cavan complaining that his men were completely exhausted and that all his officers agreed that these were the worst conditions they had ever seen. One British soldier spoke of having hardly any sleep for five days and nights. He had been 'longing to be hit' so that he would just have a chance to rest, and eventually he got his wish. Many of the wounded died because of the time they were left lying in no-man's-land. Years later a private in the Royal Fusiliers spoke of hearing their moans from the trenches: 'but you couldn't go out to help them. There were rats feeding on their flesh.' Nothing daunted, Haig started planning yet another offensive. With a big conference of all the Allied commanders due to be held on 15 November, he sent his chief of staff, Lieutenant-General Sir Launcelot Kiggell to see Gough. Gough was so astonished at what Kiggell said that he got his own staff officer to write down his words. The fact was, explained Kiggell, that Britain's position would be 'somewhat strengthened' if Gough's Fifth Army could 'win some success' before the meeting. He had 'no desire to pressure Gough into an action where the prospect of success was not sufficiently good to justify the risk' but just 'a tactical success' would be very welcome. Gough said the best he could manage was an advance of 1,000 yards, and set a date of 13 November. Many of the 40,000 men involved would be setting off from exactly the same position as their ill-fated predecessors of 1 July. Among the objectives were Beaumont-Hamel and Serre, which were supposed to have been captured on that very first day. The attack took place in dense fog, and some British troops ran past German positions without noticing them, then found themselves fired on from the rear. Others got stuck in the mud and were shot down as they tried to move. The troops attacking Serre found the bodies of comrades killed on 1 July. A few managed to get into the village but were driven back. The north bank of the river Ancre became a killing ground as German machine-guns took a terrible toll. An officer in the Royal Naval Division said that at first there were 'hundreds' on either side of him, but as they advanced further, he was left almost alone. By the end of the day, 5,000 German prisoners had been taken, including some who had been caught by surprise and were not even dressed, but none of the objectives were captured.

The battle resumed next day, and at last Beaumont-Hamel was captured, so Haig had a 'success' to parade at his conference, but the fiercest fighting of this phase of the conflict was around the German stronghold of Butte-de-Warlencourt, a low hill that was the last natural obstacle before Bapaume. It was said to have been taken and re-taken seventeen times. On the night of 18 November, the British Army managed to advance 1,000 yards along the river Ancre through falling snow and thick mist. A Canadian officer wrote later that he saw men fall dead from exhaustion in their efforts to get out of the mud. It 'appeared to be a cruel useless sacrifice of life', when it should have been clear 'to the very stupidest brain that no success could possibly result'. It proved to be the final action, and on 19 November the weather finally put an end to the Battle of the Somme.

For all Haig's promises that the big breakthrough was just around the corner, in fact the biggest advance managed by the Allies at any point was less than 6 miles. Bapaume should have been captured during the first days of the offensive. Instead it remained 3 miles out of reach. No gap had been created through which the cavalry could race. No French town had been liberated. No German supply or communication lines had been disrupted. Even Haig now had to admit that: 'The Enemy's power had not yet been broken nor is it yet possible to form an estimate of the time the war may last.' The price had been more than 400,000 British and British Empire casualties – including nearly 100,000 killed – and 200,000 French killed and wounded. More than half of all British casualties were inflicted by artillery and nearly 40 per cent by machine-guns. The Germans too suffered grievous losses: perhaps 450,000. One German soldier wrote of a whole battalion being reduced to 'a handful of half-mad wretched creatures, worn out in body and mind' and a dispatch runner named Adolf Hitler, who was wounded in the battle, would later describe the Somme as 'more like hell than war'. Haig's offensive did force the Germans to withdraw troops from Verdun, but the scale of the losses, compared with the tiny gains, make it hard to describe as anything other than a disaster.

In a battle where the most striking feature was the extraordinary courage of the individual soldiers, who went over the top time and time again to face a very high probability of death or serious injury, with only the slimmest possible chance of making a significant gain, more than sixty British soldiers were executed for cowardice or desertion. One was Private Henry Farr who refused to go into the front line on 16 September. He had spent two years at the front and had only recently been released from hospital for shell shock. That did not save him. Ninety years later, he and 300 other men executed during the First World War would be officially pardoned by the British government. Barely two months after the Battle of the Somme ended, the Germans began to slip quietly away from the positions they had so stalwartly defended at such cost to the British, pulling back to a new and much more formidable line of defence – the Hindenburg Line – up to 35 miles to the rear. On 25 February, the British took Butte-de-Warlencourt without a fight, and then Bapaume, but when the Germans launched their major offensive in March 1918, they retook the whole of the Somme battlefield in just a few weeks, and until they finally agreed to an armistice in November 1918, they continued to be a formidable adversary. Haig remained commander-in-chief for the rest of the war, and at the end of it, he was awarded an earldom and £100,000, the equivalent of perhaps £3 million today.

19

The Road to Dunkirk, 1940

The 'Dunkirk spirit' is a phrase that has passed into the language to describe a British determination to do one's best however grim the situation, and certainly the evacuation of more than 300,000 Allied soldiers from the French port under fire during the Second World War was a great achievement. The campaign that led up to it, however, was one in which the cream of the British Army suffered one of the most comprehensive defeats in its history.

Twenty-three years after the Battle of the Somme, the British Expeditionary Force was back in France, and this time Adolf Hitler was not an obscure corporal but the Führer of the German nation. Britain declared war on Germany on 3 September 1939, and within a day the first members of the BEF were starting their journey to France. By the end of the month, there were more than 150,000 British troops across the Channel. France was generally regarded as the greatest military power in Europe, but her terrible losses in the First World War meant that she had 300,000 fewer men with which to confront the Germans than she had in 1914. Since then, the French had built an elaborate chain of fortifications known as the Maginot Line, which ran along their border with Germany and was defended by forty-one divisions. They had only thirty-nine guarding the longer Franco-Belgian frontier, even though this had been the route of the German invasion of 1914.

If that were to happen again, the Allies were determined that this time the enemy would not be allowed to seize France's key industrial region just over the Belgian border. Once they had taken it, it took years to eject them, so now the idea was to confront the invader in Belgium. Unfortunately, the plan was pretty theoretical. Until 1936, Belgium had been France's ally, but it then withdrew into neutrality. The French and British commanders had had no meetings with their opposite numbers in Belgium. There had been no joint exercises. No fronts had been allocated to the different commands, there were no supply or ammunition dumps for the Allied armies and there were no pre-prepared defensive positions. Indeed the Belgians even sent troops to their border with France to resist any incursion by the Allies. Churchill would complain later that Belgium's lack of co-operation had prevented the British Army from establishing 'a strong defensive position'.

The original plan from the German High Command did indeed envisage an attack on France through the Low Countries. It was not particularly ambitious. The Germans would drive a wedge between the BEF and the French and advance to the Somme, taking over some important air bases. The trouble was that it was essentially the plan that had failed in 1914, when initial gains petered out into a war of attrition that Germany eventually lost. Buoyed up by his dramatic victory in Poland, Hitler started looking for something a bit more exciting, and General Erich von Manstein provided it. One army group – B – would indeed attack in the north as the Allies were expecting, but further south, Army Group A would be stuffed with armoured panzer divisions. While the Allied armies moved forward to confront the threat from Army Group B, Army Group A would nip in behind them, cutting them off in the rear. Before it could do that, it would have to thread its way through the narrow, twisting lanes of the Ardennes Forest and fight its way across the river Meuse, but then it would be in glorious open country, and its tanks could race on to Paris or the Channel ports. It was an audacious scheme. The Allies actually had about 500 more tanks than the Germans and some French tanks were more powerful, while the French alone had more aircraft than the enemy, even leaving aside the additional contribution made by the RAF.

The German invasion of France has come to be seen as a textbook example of *Blitzkrieg* – lightning war – but in fact it took a long time to get going. By the beginning of May 1940, the offensive had been postponed more than twenty times during the 'phoney war', and the BEF had more than 300,000 men across the water. Much of their training had been devoted to practising bayonet charges and digging trenches. The force had plenty of vehicles, but many had not been built for military use and were in a poor state of repair. According to General Bernard 'Monty' Montgomery, then commander of the BEF's 3rd Division, this led to French roads being 'strewn with broken-down vehicles'. In Montgomery's view, the British Army was quite unprepared for war, particularly because of its shortage of anti-tank and anti-aircraft guns. When the secretary of state for war, Leslie Hore-Belisha, who gave us the Belisha Beacon, also expressed misgivings, he was quickly shifted to another job. The force's commander was Viscount Gort of Limerick, who had proved himself to be a soldier of great bravery in the First World War, winning the Distinguished Service Order (DSO), the Military Cross, the Victoria Cross and being mentioned in dispatches eight times. He had been appointed to lead the BEF over the heads of several other senior generals, though he was described by a fellow officer as 'a simple straightforward, but not very clever man', who, unlike General Gordon, believed very strongly that orders must be obeyed. The British government made it clear that he would be taking his orders from the French, but which French? The commander-in-chief was 68-year-old General Maurice Gamelin, while beneath him was the operational commander of the armies in northern France, General Alphonse Georges. Georges and Gamelin had separate headquarters more than 30 miles apart, and were not on very good terms. Georges, meanwhile, delegated much of his authority to General Gaston Billotte, who commanded the army in the north-east, where most of the BEF was stationed. The French command structure was regarded as slow, rigid and cumbersome. Gamelin reckoned it took him forty-eight hours to get an order to the front. Still, in the first week of May, the French did not feel that there was any call for concern. Gamelin restored normal leave arrangements for the army, and any commanders expressing concern about shortages of weapons were told by General Billotte not to worry, because 'nothing will happen before 1941'.

In Britain, however, a political crisis was brewing. On Friday 10 May, the day before the Whit bank holiday weekend, amid growing criticism over his apparently lethargic conduct of the war, the prime minister, Neville Chamberlain, resigned, and was succeeded by Winston Churchill. That very day, without any niceties like declarations of war, the Germans attacked the Netherlands, Belgium and Luxembourg. They quickly neutralised the supposedly impregnable Belgian fortress of Eben Emael by audaciously landing soldiers on its roof in gliders and getting them to thrust explosives down its air shafts. According to the Franco-British plan, Allied forces should now move up to a defensive line inside Belgium along the Meuse and Dyle rivers, but hours after the Germans had crossed their border, the Belgian ambassador in London made a diplomatic protest about the British Army crossing his country's southern frontier without an official invitation. Indeed, one of Montgomery's units was denied admittance because the frontier guard said it did not have proper documentation. That was sorted out when a British truck crashed through the barrier, and the men moved forward, but then when they reached the position they had been allotted, they were blocked by Belgian forces. In spite of these difficulties, however, as the Germans expected, the French and British armies did advance to meet the invasion force. The Luftwaffe even reined back its aerial attacks to make it easier for them. Further south, the French believed the Ardennes was impassable for armoured divisions, and Allied air reconnaissance failed to spot German panzer units backed up in a 100-mile traffic queue behind the frontier. In keeping with the Allies' policy of avoiding anything that might 'provoke' Germany, French bombers had been confining themselves to dropping nothing more deadly than leaflets. On his return from one mission, a pilot did report a huge convoy apparently heading for the Ardennes, but no one took any notice even when other fliers said they had seen the same.

Invading through the Ardennes was a gamble. Its tight little lanes ran between steep slopes, through dense woods and over hump-backed bridges, and just a single large vehicle breaking down could have brought the invasion to a halt. While the vehicles negotiated the roads, the infantry marched over fields and on woodland paths. The first Germans to cross the Luxembourg border came in cars dressed as tourists. The border police just waved them through. They were actually soldiers specially trained to spot and disconnect any explosive devices designed to sabotage bridges, and engineers who could remove obstacles. In fact, they found nothing to hamper them until they reached the Belgian border where there were roadblocks and minefields that they worked all night to clear. By the morning of 11 May, German panzers commanded by General Heinz Guderian were already advancing across the southern tip of Belgium towards France. French and Belgian forces tried, but failed, to hold them up. As German columns moved through Luxembourg, the RAF asked for permission to bomb them from the French High Command. When no permission was forthcoming, they did it anyway, but the Fairey Battles they used were slow and underpowered. Even though the thirty-two bombers faced little more than small arms fire, thirteen were lost and only one returned undamaged, while the impact on the Germans was 'negligible' according to the official history. On 12 May, six Fairey Battles attacked bridges now held by the Germans on the Albert Canal, and managed to knock a section out of one them, but not a single aircraft returned. One RAF survivor was told by the German who captured him: 'You British are mad. We capture the bridge early Friday morning. You give us all Friday and Saturday to get our flak guns in circles all round the bridge, and then on Sunday, when all is ready, you come along.'

When the French command heard that German tanks were rolling through the Ardennes, they thought at first that it must be a small diversionary attack, and refused to put up any barriers in case it obstructed their own cavalry. Once again, the RAF tried an attack with Fairey Battles, and once again it was a disaster, with only one aircraft out of eight returning. Eventually, Gamelin decided that he had better do something, so he ordered eleven French divisions to move to the sector, and gave them top priority on the railways, which meant the first troops should arrive by 14 May, with the whole force in position by 21 May. That, he reasoned, should be plenty of time, as the enemy would have to halt and re-group at the river Meuse before attempting to cross it. As might have been expected, the German panzers did get themselves into a terrible traffic jam for a time, but the Allies squandered another chance to inflict serious damage on them from the air.

Halting and re-grouping at the Meuse, or anywhere else, was the last thing on Guderian's mind. Each of his divisions carried its own ammunition, food and fuel, though in order to conserve supplies, they would often just help themselves at petrol stations. They also had a pool of mechanics that would do running repairs, commandeer civilian trucks or just raid them for spare parts. His force raced through villages as fast as they could go towards the Meuse, the crossing of which he saw as his greatest challenge. Also heading for the river, further north, was another panzer force commanded by General Erwin Rommel. By dawn on Monday 13 May, brushing aside some half-hearted opposition, a group of his men had managed to cross via a narrow weir. The French troops in this sector were not as strong as they seemed. They were reservists, thinly spread, short of anti-tank and anti-aircraft guns, and some had marched for 75 miles before going into action. Once they were on the west bank of the Meuse, Rommel's men, though equipped with only small arms, managed to see off a force of French tanks sent to attack them. Under constant fire and using a cable ferry, rafts and a pontoon bridge, by the following morning they had got fifteen tanks across the river. Guderian also crossed on 13 May. While the Luftwaffe attacked French soldiers, French fighters stayed on the ground, awaiting orders. The next day, British and French bombers tried to destroy a German pontoon bridge at Glaire, but by then the Germans had well-sited anti-aircraft guns and the attack was beaten off with heavy losses.

Further north the same day, the BEF in Belgium started to experience its first real German attacks, though they were nothing like what its French allies had been suffering. British soldiers had been given a 22-mile stretch of the river Dyle to hold. Early that morning near the village of Gastuche, the Germans managed to scramble across a lock and wipe out a position held by the Durham Light Infantry. Meanwhile, RAF losses were mounting alarmingly – twenty-nine bombers on 12 May alone – meaning that there were just seventy-two left out of the 135 it had across the Channel when the invasion had begun just two days earlier. Even more worrying than the loss of aircraft was the loss of experienced pilots. Sir Cyril Newall, chief of the Air Staff, warned that this could not go on: 'If we expend all our effort in the early stage of the battle, we shall not be able to operate effectively when the really critical phase comes.'

But who was to say things were not already 'critical'? Ignoring the French forces left to his rear, Rommel raced on. His modus operandi was to motor along, 'guns blazing'. As his men approached woods and villages they would shoot at them as a way of finding out whether any enemy forces were present. Civilians lay 'huddled in ditches' with 'their faces distorted in terror'. The general's philosophy was that 'the day goes to the side that is the first to plaster its opponent with fire'. If the precise position of enemy forces was not known, 'fire must simply be sprayed over enemy-held territory'. The Germans also had ways of terrifying enemy troops. Their Stuka dive bombers were fitted with wailing sirens, and often kept making their passes long after they had run out of bombs in order to maintain the effect. One BEF officer described the impact of an attack that killed no one and left just ten men wounded. The soldiers, he said, were 'absolutely shattered'. They 'sat about in a complete daze, and one had to almost kick them to get them moving'. On the other hand, the Stukas were vulnerable, as a French unit of Curtiss Hawk 75 fighters – by no means the best machines in the air force – showed when it came upon a dozen of them flying close to Sedan and shot them all down without losing a single aircraft. Over the next couple of days, many French soldiers fought bravely to try to halt the German headlong advance, but to little avail, while some commanders were feeding falsely optimistic reports to Gamelin. One told him that a counter-attack on the morning of 14 May had 'sealed off' a German breach in the French front line at Sedan. It had not, and now, scarcely pausing for breath, Guderian's tanks were rushing hell for leather towards the Channel. For its part, after further heavy losses, the RAF decided that Fairey Battles could no longer be used for daylight raids.

The next morning, Churchill was awoken by a telephone call from the French prime minister, Paul Reynaud, telling him: 'We are beaten. We have lost the battle.' He seemed more on the ball than the French High Command who still appeared to be inhabiting a parallel universe where, although the Germans had crossed the Meuse and were streaming westwards, they were being 'held'. On the very day that Reynaud called Churchill, Gamelin claimed to detect 'a lessening of enemy action', and said the front was 're-establishing itself'. In fact, that day one German panzer division advanced 40 miles and crashed through the 2nd French Armoured Division while it was still forming up. In the north, even though her army was virtually intact, the Netherlands surrendered. Lord Gort's liaison officer, Major Osmund Archdale, also seemed to be getting a truer picture than the French commander-in-chief. He said French officers were beginning to crack. They had tears rolling down their faces. When Gamelin finally told the French foreign minister, Edouard Daladier, the true extent of the German breakthrough, he refused to believe it, exclaiming that it was 'impossible'.

On 16 May, Churchill flew to Paris. Reynaud, a pugnacious man, was doing his best. Sixteen French generals had been dismissed for failing in their duty. Those still in their jobs gave orders that soldiers who surrendered strongholds too hurriedly should be fired on, but by now the gap in the French defences was 40 miles wide. As it advanced, German Army Group A began cutting the BEF and the French armies fighting in the north off from their supplies of food, fuel and ammunition. Britain's best soldiers, with the army's most modern equipment, could soon find themselves at Hitler's mercy. In Paris, Churchill saw panic. He was told that the Nazis would be arriving in a couple of days and the Foreign Ministry was burning documents. When he asked Gamelin where his strategic reserve was, he was told: 'There is none.' When he wanted to know when the general was going to counter-attack, the response was a shrug: 'Inferiority of numbers, inferiority of equipment, inferiority of method.' This was not strictly true. As we have seen, the French actually had more aircraft than the Germans, but only a third of them were at the front and they failed to co-ordinate air and ground operations in the way the enemy did. The French had more tanks, but they were scattered thinly through the army, while the Germans concentrated theirs at critical points. They also had plenty of anti-tank guns, but too many lay in store. Meanwhile, in the north, Billotte, alarmed at the prospect of the Allies being cut off in their rear, had to order the British and French troops who had just advanced into Belgium to retreat as quickly as they could. Gort pulled back to a new line on the Escaut.

The following day, Colonel Charles de Gaulle, with a scratch armoured force, made repeated brave attempts to halt the German dash for the Channel, but failed, and by its end, Guderian was 70 miles beyond Sedan. In the north, Brussels fell to the Germans. Now Reynaud sacked the 68-year-old Gamelin and replaced him with 73-year-old General Maxime Weygand, while he appointed as vice-premier 84-year-old Marshal Philippe Pétain, a hero of the First World War. Weygand was in Beirut when he was appointed. His first act was to cancel a counter-attack planned by Gamelin, and then it took him until the evening of 19 May to get to Paris. When Reynaud suggested a briefing that night, the new commander said tomorrow would be fine. In the meantime, Gort had already received from Billotte an echo of Gamelin's despairing words to Churchill. There were 'no reserves, no plan, and little hope!' and he was 'exhausted'. The revamping of the French command did not bother Guderian. He just ploughed on regardless, crossing the Somme near Péronne and traversing in minutes areas that had been fought over for months, at the cost of tens of thousands of lives in the First World War. This was another huge gamble. His thinly stretched forces would be immensely vulnerable if the Allies could mount a full-scale counter-attack.

But none came. The German general's 2nd Panzer Division raced into Albert and captured a British artillery battery that was drawn up on the barracks square, equipped with only training ammunition. Before nightfall, he had reached Abbeville and then Noyelles on the coast, after advancing 200 miles in ten days. Now the RAF withdrew its remaining operational aircraft from France. Of 261 fighters that had gone out, only sixty-six returned; seventy-five had been destroyed in combat, while another 120 that were damaged but repairable, were abandoned. Things had been hotting up on the ground too. When 1st Battalion, the Tyneside Scottish Regiment were sent to defend a stretch of the Canal du Nord, they discovered that it was dry, and would be a doddle for German armour to cross. After blowing up an important bridge, they were ordered to move on to the village of Saulty, but on the way they were ambushed by German infantry and tanks. All but eight of the battalion's 450 men were killed or captured. That evening, Gort warned the War Office that the BEF might have to be evacuated.

It so happened that Weygand had decided to go on a fact-finding mission to Abbeville on 20 May, but he had to abandon the journey halfway through when he found out that the town had already fallen. So he would fly to Béthune instead, and meet Billotte. No joy there either. The French had had to abandon the airfield. So what about Calais? King Leopold of Belgium got there, but Gort was incommunicado because he was moving his headquarters, and by the time he arrived, Weygand had left for Paris. One of the problems the BEF faced was the misleading and generally over-optimistic information about the overall state of the battle. On 20 May, the 7th Battalion, the Queen's Own Royal West Kent Regiment, had taken up a position to the east of Albert. Its commanding officer, Lieutenant-Colonel Basil Clay, had been given the reassuring news that the situation had 'materially improved', and the nearest panzers were miles away. That turned out to be not quite right. Almost immediately, Clay and his men found themselves machine-gunned by enemy aircraft. Then German tanks were upon them. They fought bravely, but with the exception of about seventy who managed to escape, almost all of them were killed, wounded or captured, including Clay himself. Among the other troops in the area were the 5th Battalion, the Buffs, who had moved into the eerily deserted town of Doullens, south-west of Arras, empty apart from a few remaining civilians packing up for a rapid departure. They were supposed to defend 6 miles of the road to Arras, but they had no artillery, no anti-tank guns, and no support on their left flank. Thanks to a warning from two officers who had managed to get away from Albert, the Buffs were ready when the Germans attacked. Not that it made much difference to the outcome. Only about eighty out of 605 men managed to come through the battle.

Some units of the BEF were known rather disparagingly as 'digging battalions'. They were essentially labourers in uniform, and were poorly armed and not properly trained for combat, but now as the situation grew more desperate, they sometimes found themselves in the front line. One unit was put into position close to Amiens, again on the assumption that there were no German forces in the vicinity. When enemy tanks appeared over the brow of a hill, some of the 'diggers' were reduced to charging them with bayonets. Not surprisingly, they were soon overrun. On 20 May, General Sir Edmund 'Tiny' Ironside, chief of the Imperial General Staff, turned up at the front. The Allies agreed on a plan for the French V Corps to counter-attack the Germans in the Cambrai area the next day, while the BEF targeted them to the south of Arras, but unfortunately Billotte was 'in a proper dither', and it needed strong words from Weygand to keep him on the straight and narrow. That afternoon, the project took a bit of a knock with the news that the Germans had now taken Cambrai, though it was held by only a weak advance guard. A little later, Gort saw a copy of the French written order, which said the attack would happen 'on or after May 21'. After he complained, a corrected order was sent to the commander of V Corps, General René Altmayer, making it clear that the attack must take place the next day, but Altmayer did not receive the order until 2.30pm on the 21 May, and then he broke down saying his men were too tired to fight and that he was prepared to take responsibility for disobeying an order. Ironside's comment on what he had seen across the Channel ran: 'Situation desperate. God help the BEF. Brought to this state by the incompetence of the French command.'

The war ended on 21 May for General Billotte when he was killed in a road accident. Gort, meanwhile, had decided to press his attack whatever the French did. His chief of staff, General Henry Pownall, saw this as something approaching the last shot in the locker. If it did not work, he observed in his diary, the BEF might be '*foutu*' – finished. Gort had managed to scrape together a force of garrison troops and territorials, plus some field artillery and seventy-four tanks. Most were Matilda Mark Is, capable of only 8 miles an hour, but there were sixteen of the faster and more formidable Mark IIs. They would be up against two of Rommel's panzer divisions and the motorised SS Totenkopf Division. Plenty of factors were not in the British force's favour. Some of the tanks had had to travel 120 miles on their own tracks, there was no proper radio contact between units, and the promised air support failed to arrive. The 7th Battalion, the Royal Tank Regiment (RTR), were not deterred, and attacked the village of Wailly, terrorising the German infantry holding it and putting many to flight. Rommel's artillery told him they were too far away from the British tanks to have any effect, but, running from gun to gun, the general told them to fire anyway, and managed to put some of the leading British tanks out of action; in turn, the RTR nearly killed Rommel, shooting his aide dead just a few yards from him. A group of seven Matilda IIs bypassed Wailly and headed for Mercatel. Oil leaks as well as problems with engines and tracks knocked out three of them before the fighting started, and two more were soon disabled in action, but the other two ran on for miles, shooting up German soldiers and trucks as well as knocking out at least five tanks, but eventually they were both hit and their crews captured.

By the time 7 RTR was ordered to retreat, they had lost all their Mark IIs and nearly half of their Mark Is, and their commanding officer had been killed. The 4th Battalion of the RTR also went on a rampage, setting fire to about forty German vehicles, but it too met fierce resistance and lost two-thirds of the thirty-five tanks it started with. During the battle, the SS Totenkopf Division had panicked and beaten a hasty retreat when they saw German tanks ablaze. It was the most significant challenge that the invaders had faced. They had lost more than 370 killed, wounded or captured and the German command had been worried that the offensive might drive a wedge between its armour and the infantry advancing behind. The British counter-attack had certainly rocked the enemy back on his heels for a moment, but only for a moment. In spite of the bravery of the men who prosecuted it, it failed to achieve any of its objectives, and it had not been big enough to make any real dent in the Germans' overall fighting capacity. Besides, the loss of so many British tanks meant that there was no possibility of repeating it. The following day the French finally launched their counter -attack towards Cambrai. It started well, but then it too was driven back.

As the Allied front fell apart, more British troops were still being dispatched to France. On the day the French counter-attack fizzled out, 1,500 Irish and Welsh Guards arrived at Boulogne. At the harbour, they had to fix bayonets to fight their way through a crowd of civilians trying desperately to get away, and there seemed to be plenty of confusion among the French forces. At first they had been planning to hold out in the port's citadel with its thick medieval walls until reinforcements arrived, but then the naval officer in charge decided to evacuate the garrison, and began spiking the guns. When two sailors queried the order, however, he stopped. Even with the arrival of the Guards, there were not enough men to defend Boulogne properly, and there were only eight guns. The Germans were expected to attack from the south, and the approach to the town was supposed to be defended by a French force at Nesles-Neufchâtel, but the trains carrying it had been delayed, so all that stood in the enemy's way was another scratch force made up of a few gun crews, supplemented by headquarters staff, drivers and telephonists. They fought with great courage, but they were only able to hold up the panzers for a couple of hours, and when German tanks entered Boulogne, the guards marched back to the harbour to be evacuated. One of the British 'digging' units – Pioneers' 5 Group – built a barricade of cars, lorries and furniture from bombed-out houses, along with all manner of other objects. They then set fire to it as German tanks approached, which gave them just enough breathing space to join the Guards at the harbour.

More British reinforcements were sent to Calais. It was done in such secrecy that the territorials of the Queen Victoria's Rifles did not know where they were going, and the 3rd Battalion of the Royal Tank Regiment arrived without their tanks. They found the city on fire and ran into a group of dejected Allied soldiers hoping to get away. While the RTR men waited for their tanks, they were sent to take shelter in the sand dunes to try to avoid attack from German aircraft. At first their commanding officer, Lieutenant-Colonel Reggie Keller, was told to proceed to Boulogne, but by the time the tanks had been unloaded, he received another order directing him to St Omer, about 20 miles inland, instead. He sent out a small advance party to try to locate the general headquarters to clarify which instruction he should follow, but they could not find it. Eventually, 'against my better judgment', as he put it, Keller set off for St Omer, but soon ran into a German armoured column which knocked out seven of his tanks. During the middle of the battle, he got a call from Brigadier Claude Nicholson, the new commander of all British troops in Calais, telling him to take all his remaining tanks back there. The following day, 23 May, the War Office dispatched two more battalions – regulars from the Rifle Brigade and the King's Royal Rifle Corps. Nicholson hoped to station them along Calais' battlements to form an inner line of defence. As the new men arrived, the first thing they saw was a long line of corpses and an even longer line of wounded men at the Gare Maritime. That night, German panzers tried to take Calais, but withdrew when they met heavy gunfire. The next morning, Nicholson sent out patrols, but they could not force a way through German anti-tank guns and the brigadier concluded that he was surrounded. He received a telegram from the War Office, saying that 'in principle' it had decided to evacuate the British garrison.

By this time, ill feeling between the French and British commands was growing, and when the local commander in Calais got wind of the planned British evacuation in the early hours of 24 May, he protested. As day broke, French coastal guns had begun shelling German positions, but then, in an eerie re-run of Boulogne, at about 11am, they spiked all but one of their guns, and the gunners were ordered to get down to the harbour and leave on French ships that were waiting for them. Meanwhile, the Germans launched a fierce attack, and Nicholson realised he would have to withdraw to an inner perimeter by the sea. With a British evacuation apparently planned, he ordered Keller to burn his remaining tanks. In the harbour, the Germans sank a British destroyer and severely damaged another two, while one naval commander sent a message to Dover saying the situation was 'desperate unless reinforcements arrive forthwith'. While the battle raged, 2nd Lieutenant Hugo Ironside, an RTR intelligence officer, picked up a telephone ringing in the citadel, one of the last Allied strongholds, to find his distant cousin, CIGS Sir Edmund Ironside, on the line. Sir Edmund was terribly sorry, but the evacuation had been cancelled. Calais must fight to the finish. Please pass on the news to Nicholson. The War Office confirmed the change of plan to the brigadier. He was under the orders of General Marie-Bertrand-Alfred Fagalde, who commanded all troops in the Channel ports. Fagalde had not ordered an evacuation, and Nicholson must obey him 'for the sake of Allied solidarity'. Nicholson halted Keller's work of destruction, and managed to save a few light tanks, then he withdrew his soldiers to their inner perimeter and told them to fight to the last man and the last round. An uplifting message came from Anthony Eden, the secretary of state for war: 'The eyes of the Empire are upon the defence of Calais.'

Nicholson obeyed his new orders to the letter, turning down two German invitations to surrender. On 25 May, the enemy unleashed a fearful artillery barrage. The brigadier scraped together his remaining armour for a counter-attack, but before he could mount it, the Germans had broken through the British line. Now BEF soldiers had to fight a guerrilla war from street to street and building to building, as they were driven back towards the sea. That evening, British destroyers appeared for a time in the harbour and shelled German positions, but once they had withdrawn, the Luftwaffe began dropping incendiary bombs on the citadel. By midday on 26 May, Allied troops were exhausted and running out of water, and white handkerchiefs began to appear at the windows. At 4pm, the commander of the King's Royal Rifle Corps, who were still fighting in the Old Town, told his troops that now it was every man for himself. Some of the remaining British soldiers in the citadel were planning to lie low and then try and escape after dark, until a French naval officer came running in shouting: 'Gentlemen, the French commander has surrendered.' In spite of the order from London that there should be no evacuation, a flotilla of about fifteen yachts and trawlers had crossed the Channel, and managed to pick up around 440 English and French soldiers. Nicholson would die a prisoner of war.

The bad news was piling up for Lord Gort at his headquarters near Lille. Not only had Calais fallen, but the Belgians too seemed to be on the point of capitulating, which would open up a 20-mile gap on his left flank. According to General Pownall, his chief of staff, the BEF's commander went off to sit on his own for a while. When he came back, he gave the instruction for two divisions to be removed from the south and sent over to General Alan Brooke on the British left. This went against the orders Gort was getting from the French and from London, and meant the end of any real hope of a counter-attack southwards, but it also meant that the BEF had some chance of mounting a fighting withdrawal to the Channel. It was a brave decision, but it left Gort's army fighting a grim rear-guard action. Reality would now be brought brutally home to the politicians in London thanks to a visit to the general by Lieutenant-General Sir John Dill, vice-chief of the Imperial General Staff. After hearing his report, Eden sent the BEF a new message. There was no prospect of the French being able to mount an assault from the Somme that was formidable enough to cut through the Germans, so the 'safety of the BEF' was now the 'predominant consideration'. The 'only course' might be for the force to fight its way back to the Channel for evacuation. They would be informing Reynaud shortly, but in the meantime Gort must not discuss this with the French or the Belgians. In reply, the general warned that most of the BEF and its equipment 'will inevitably be lost even in best of circumstances'. It would be a dreadful blow. The BEF included virtually the whole of Britain's regular peacetime army. Without them, who would train the hundreds of thousands of new recruits the country was going to need to prosecute the war?

When Churchill met Reynaud, the French prime minister said he could now put only fifty divisions in the field, against Germany's 150. Although France was bound by treaty not to surrender without British agreement, many of Churchill's colleagues thought she might do it anyway. Things were so grim that the foreign secretary, Lord Halifax, had put out tentative peace feelers to Hitler via Mussolini. Eden told Gort he was now 'authorised to operate towards coast forthwith in conjunction with French and Belgian armies'. The next day, however, King Leopold of Belgium asked the Germans for a ceasefire. Gort's decision to reinforce Brooke had been vindicated. The troops he had sent had arrived before the enemy could exploit the gaps left by the Belgian surrender. Now the key task for the BEF was to establish a corridor along which Allied troops could funnel to the Channel, but there were not enough men to hold the whole line, so it was a case of selecting and fortifying key points. The Royal Norfolks, now severely understrength and worn out, were allocated a section of canal close to the village of Le Paradis, and strengthened the position as best they could. They kept being told that the French were about to mount a counter-attack, but none seemed to materialise. Instead there was a determined German assault with infantry, tanks and artillery. The Norfolks asked brigade headquarters for support from British guns, but the reply was that they had no ammunition. When the Norfolks ran out of ammunition themselves, they surrendered. Ninety-seven of the soldiers at Le Paradis who gave themselves up to the enemy, including the commanding officer, were murdered by members of the SS Totenkopf Division. The commander of one of the SS companies involved in the massacre would be convicted of murder and hanged in 1949.

The 2nd Cameronians were one of the regiments deployed to defend the almost dried-up Ypres–Comines canal. They were attacked by three German divisions, and lost seven out of ten of their officers, as well as 128 men. Other units holding the line, like men from the Grenadier Guards and the Royal Warwickshire Regiment, also suffered heavy losses. The town of Wormhout, about 10 miles south of Dunkirk, was being held by the 8th Battalion of the Worcestershire Regiment and the 2nd Battalion of the Royal Warwickshires, with some machine-gunners and a battery of anti-tank guns. The Warwickshires had arrived only the day before, believing that they had been taken out of the line to rest, but in no time they were being bombed by German aircraft. The troops were ordered to hold the town 'at all costs to the last man and the last round' so that 'a vitally important operation may take place'. The first German ground troops rolled up in lorries. They were halted by a roadblock, and fanned out over the fields. Next the tanks joined in, but British anti-tank fire knocked out four of them. As his men began to run out of ammunition, Major Philip Hicks of the Royal Warwickshires eventually told them to run for it. Once again the SS murdered prisoners: up to ninety of them. This time it was the SS Liebstandarte Adolf Hitler Regiment. They lined some up outside a building and machine-gunned them, while others they herded into a barn, and then threw grenades in after them.

By the time the prisoners at Le Paradis and Wormhout had been massacred, the evacuation of the BEF was underway. Weygand had still not sanctioned the operation, so Dill, now promoted to chief of the Imperial General Staff, asked Eden to make it clear to Gort that he was no longer bound by French orders. Eden told the BEF commander: 'Your sole task now is to evacuate to England the maximum of your force possible.' The rest, as they say, is history. Gort had warned that, at the very best, most of the BEF's men and equipment would be lost, and Churchill braced the House of Commons for 'hard and heavy tidings'. There were estimates that perhaps only 45,000 soldiers might be rescued. In the end, as at Gallipoli, by far the most successful part of the whole operation was its abandonment. In a masterpiece of courage and improvisation, the Royal Navy, supported by the French Navy and civilian craft of all descriptions from both countries, managed to remove 198,000 British and 140,000 French and Belgian troops from the beach at Dunkirk, right under the noses of the Germans, while 30,000 French soldiers, many of whom could not be rescued, fought a final brave rear-guard action.

For reasons that are still disputed, Hitler had called a stop to Guderian's rampage on 24 May when Dunkirk appeared to stand at his mercy, and by the time the general was allowed to move again three days later, the British had managed to strengthen their defences. Then almost immediately, the Führer ordered the panzers to move south to prepare for the conquest of the rest of France. This halt was crucial to the success of the evacuation. Was Hitler concerned because in some parts of his force, half of the tanks were now out of action? Had Gort's raid near Arras shaken the Germans enough to make them a little more careful about keeping adequate reserves? Did Hitler believe that at some point, the French – supposedly Europe's greatest military power – must have a serious counter-attack in them? Or was he convinced by Göring's boast that the Luftwaffe could destroy the Allied forces on Dunkirk's exposed beaches without any help from the army? Anyway, the result was the escape of the BEF.

On 4 June, after the rescue was completed, Churchill reminded the House of Commons that although Dunkirk had been a 'miracle of deliverance…. Wars are not won by evacuations'. Indeed, the previous few weeks had been a 'colossal military disaster'. Britain had lost more than 11,000 soldiers killed, another 14,000 wounded and 41,000 more captured or missing: a total loss of more than 66,000. Of nearly 2,800 guns that the BEF had taken to France, only about 300 were salvaged. About 64,000 vehicles out of 68,600 were lost, and in the evacuation six Royal Navy destroyers were sunk and nineteen damaged, as well as 140 other craft. The French lost 90,000 killed and 200,000 wounded, the Belgians had 23,000 casualties, and the Dutch just short of 10,000. German losses were 27,000 killed and 111,000 wounded.

After Dunkirk, Reynaud wanted to carry on the fight, but Weygand and Pétain would not support him, and on 16 June he resigned. Pétain took over, and asked Hitler for an armistice that same day. On 22 June, France surrendered. After returning to Britain, Gort, without whom Hitler might have been holding 200,000 British prisoners of war, was never again appointed to command an army in the field, but he was made a field marshal, and, as governor of Malta, played a vital role in the island's heroic defence against the attacks of the Axis powers. Weygand became defence minister in Vichy France, but he proved a stickler for seeing that the armistice terms were not overstepped, objecting for example to German attempts to establish supply routes for Rommel's Afrika Korps through French African territory. The Germans arrested him in 1941, and he remained in custody for the rest of the war. After the liberation, the French put him on trial for collaboration, but he was acquitted. Both Gamelin and Reynaud were imprisoned until Germany's defeat, but Reynaud went on to be a minister in two more French governments. Guderian tried to use his *Blitzkrieg* tactics again in the vast wastes of the Soviet Union, but with much less success, and was relieved of his command for allowing his troops to retreat. Back in Germany, he was appointed chief of the army's general staff, but was sacked again in 1945 for manoeuvring to persuade Hitler to surrender. Rommel went on to command the Afrika Korps, and met with great initial success, being made a field marshal at the age of fifty, but Montgomery finally defeated him at El Alamein. He also played a leading role in the defence of German-occupied France after D-Day, but began to turn against Hitler when he felt the war was being lost. In October 1944 he took cyanide rather than be put on trial for treason.

20

The Fall of Singapore, 1942

For Churchill, it was 'the worst disaster and largest capitulation in British history'. The supposedly impregnable fortress of Singapore fell to the Japanese just a week after their first troops came ashore. A heavily outnumbered invasion force routed the British and British Empire troops, no fewer than 85,000 of whom surrendered.

When Britain's alliance with Japan broke down in the 1920s, the government decided to turn the island of Singapore into one of the great fortresses of the British Empire. About the size of the Isle of Wight, it stood right at the end of the peninsula of Malaya, in those days a British colony, and was linked to it by a 1,000-yard causeway. The then vast sum of £60 million was spent equipping it with a naval base to the east of the causeway, plus a dockyard, barracks and communications centre. Singapore's huge guns pointed seawards to deal with any naval attack, and to its north lay 200 miles of jungle. From here the Royal Navy could control the Indian Ocean.

In late 1941, tension was mounting in the Pacific, and at 3.45pm on the afternoon of 7 December, RAF Hudson bombers spotted Japanese warships off the east coast of Thailand, to the north of Malaya. Because of an eighteen-hour time difference, in Hawaii it was still night-time, and the Japanese had not yet attacked Pearl Harbor, but now they fired on the Hudsons. In the event of the Empire of the Rising Sun being about to invade Malaya, Britain had a plan. 'Operation Matador' involved moving troops across the border into neutral Thailand and being ready to attack the enemy as they tried to land on its beaches, but in London, the war cabinet already had quite enough on its plate with the war against Germany, and the military in the Far East had been under strict instructions to avoid hostilities with Japan. Two days before, however, the government had authorised the Far East commander-in-chief, Air Chief Marshal Sir Robert Brooke-Popham, who was sixty-three and about to leave the job, to put Matador into operation if he was convinced the Japanese were moving against Thailand. Brooke-Popham put all troops on alert, but hesitated to light the blue touch paper. Suppose the Japanese ships were just a 'demonstration against Thailand', and he violated Thai neutrality and started a war with Japan that perhaps the Americans would sit out? If it really was an invasion fleet, there was still a problem. Matador was supposed to be implemented twenty-four hours before the start of an enemy landing, 'and this', according to Brooke-Popham, 'was most unlikely to be available should the ships seen turn out to be part of a Japanese expedition'.

In the space of a few hours, early on 8 December everything became much clearer. The Japanese attacked Pearl Harbor, shelled coastal defences at Kota Bharu in eastern Malaya, and bombed Singapore City, killing about sixty people. The city's lights blazed helpfully throughout the raid because no one could find the man with the key that would turn them off. At Kota Bharu, the sea was rough, but Japanese troops fought their way ashore that afternoon. When they were confronted with barbed wire on the beach, even though they were under heavy fire, they had burrowed under it with bayonets and spoons. The Royal Australian Air Force managed to sink some landing craft, but were impressed at the coolness with which the enemy fired back at them with their rifles. Four aircraft were lost while low cloud allowed the Japanese warships and cruisers to slip safely away. In Singapore, 400 miles to the south, the authorities were undismayed. The RAF believed, wrongly, that the Japanese had been driven off the beaches and it also seemed that their warships had been withdrawn, but Lieutenant-General Arthur Percival, who was in charge of the island's defence, warned that 'the first round does not necessarily decide the contest'. In fact, the landing at Kota Bharu was just a diversion. The main Japanese invasion force was coming ashore across the border in Thailand. A few days before, a British spy in the country had discovered that neglected airstrips around Singora and Patani had been mysteriously cleared of undergrowth, while drums of aviation fuel had been hidden nearby. Now British reconnaissance aircraft saw Japanese fighters parked on them.

In September 1940, Churchill had dismissed the prospect of a Japanese attack on Singapore from Malaya as 'remote' because if they tried it, their 'plight ... cut off from home while installing themselves in the swamps of the jungles' would be 'forlorn'. Anyway, they 'would never attempt a siege of Singapore with a hostile, superior American fleet in the Pacific'. That little problem, of course, had just been dealt with at Pearl Harbor, and in reality, Singapore was extremely vulnerable. Local commanders reckoned they needed more than 550 aircraft, but there were only just over 150. Churchill had said that 'the prime defence of Singapore is the Fleet', and yet the chiefs of staff reckoned that it would take 180 days to get it there. In 1941, Sir John Dill, chief of the Imperial General Staff, suggested postponing the North African offensive to allow more troops to be sent to Singapore. Churchill said no, though he allowed the battleship HMS *Prince of Wales*, which had helped sink the *Bismarck*, and the cruiser HMS *Repulse* to go and provide a 'vague menace'. The odd voice had been raised to express scepticism about how much of a 'fortress' Singapore was. In May 1938, Major-General Sir William Dobbie, general officer commanding, Malaya, said that an attack from the north was 'the greatest potential danger.... The jungle is not in most places impassable for infantry' while a colonel in the Argyll and Sutherland Highlanders said the Japanese would be able to use tanks there. When he gave his troops thorough training in jungle warfare, most other officers thought he was a bit odd. In August 1941, Brigadier Ivan Simson had arrived in Singapore as chief engineer, and proposed a major upgrade of its defences, but Percival rejected his plan on the grounds that it would be 'bad for morale – for both troops and civilians'. Percival was a survivor of the Battle of the Somme, and had been seriously wounded in the attack on the Schwaben Redoubt. 'A very brave and gallant officer', he won the MC, the DSO and the *Croix de Guerre*, but he had no experience of a top command in wartime, and no experience of combat at all since 1922. Alfred Duff Cooper, Churchill's special emissary to the Far East, warned his boss that the lieutenant-general was not a leader. Sir Henry Pownall, formerly Lord Gort's chief of staff in France and now Brooke-Popham's successor as commander-in-chief, Far East, thought him 'uninspiring ... and rather gloomy', while the senior Australian commander in Singapore, Lieutenant-General Gordon Bennett, conceded that he was 'brainy', but also regarded him as 'weak and hesitant'.

The question of whether Singapore was a great stronghold or a sitting duck was now about to be put to the test. Over Thailand, RAF Blenheim bombers tried to attack the newly arrived Japanese but were beaten off by their formidable Zero fighters. The British flew back to Alor Star in north-west Malaya to refuel, but as soon as they landed, Japanese bombers hit the airfield, destroying eight out of ten Blenheims and setting fire to buildings and fuel dumps. In spite of heavy monsoon rain, the Japanese also attacked six more airfields, reducing the number of operational British aircraft available in Malaya from 110 to 50. For Percival, the enemy's aerial prowess was 'an unpleasant surprise'. By dusk on 8 December, because of the threat from Japanese troops, the Australians were evacuating Kota Bharu airfield. They were supposed to destroy the five airworthy aircraft still left on the ground, but when they had dealt with two, the ground crews complained they were coming under fire, and got out. The next morning, Kuantan airfield, to the south, was also abandoned, under the mistaken belief that the Japanese were landing nearby. Bombs were not destroyed as they should have been, and some of the 600 personnel fleeing stopped buses at gunpoint, forced off the passengers, then took them over. Aircraft from RAF Butterworth, opposite Penang Island and nearer to the Japanese, managed to bomb them at Singora, but at the cost of three more Blenheims. Squadron Leader Arthur Scarf, who had battled against a swarm of Japanese fighters to get through to his target, and paid with his life, was posthumously awarded the Victoria Cross.

Percival did order some British troops across the Thai border. Men from the Punjab Regiment managed to blow up a column of Japanese tanks and infantry and destroy three bridges, but an attempt by another force to grab a crucial stretch of road known as 'the Ledge' failed. On 2 December, HMS *Prince of Wales* and HMS *Repulse*, now the heart of the rather grandly titled 'Far Eastern Fleet', had arrived in Singapore. There should also have been an aircraft carrier but she had scraped her bottom in Jamaica. Before he left London, Air Chief Marshal Sir Arthur 'Bomber' Harris had told the task force's commander Rear-Admiral Sir Tom Phillips: 'don't get out from under your air cover. If you do, you've had it'. Now Phillips was keen to use his powerful ships to disrupt the Japanese landings in Thailand, so on the evening of 8 December they set sail along with four destroyers. When they were at sea, the air force told them it would be impossible to provide cover over Singora because of the loss of the north Malayan airfields. Drizzle and low cloud shielded the ships on 9 December, and Phillips was also confident that his radar-controlled anti-aircraft guns would keep them well protected. In the evening, as the skies began to clear and Japanese aircraft shadowed them, the admiral decided to call off the mission and head south. Then he got word about the enemy landings in Malaya, and, as that was on his way back, he decided he must do what he could to hinder them. In that area, 453 fighter squadron, based in Singapore, could have given air cover, but Phillips did not tell them where he was going. Just after 11am on the morning of 10 December, the Japanese aircraft struck. HMS *Repulse* managed to shoot two down, and the crew cheered 'with more abandon than any football crowd'. Then a torpedo hit her and she sank. HMS *Prince of Wales* may have destroyed one more enemy aircraft as she was repeatedly bombed. It seems to have taken half an hour before the ships sent out a signal to say they were under attack, and another half hour for this to reach the air force operations room. Just as the battleship was sinking, Buffalo fighters from 453 squadron did arrive, but by then there was no Japanese aircraft to be seen. The enemy had allowed the British destroyers to pick up more than 2,080 survivors from the nearly 2,300 men aboard the two vessels, though Phillips went down with his ship. HMS *Repulse's* commander, Captain William Tennant, conceded the attacks were 'without doubt magnificently carried out'. At first, Churchill could not believe the vessels had been lost. In all the war, with its many dreadful setbacks, he said: 'I never received a more direct shock.... As I turned over and twisted in bed the full horror of the news sank in upon me.' It meant that in the whole of the Indian and Pacific oceans, the Allies had no capital ships except the American survivors of Pearl Harbor: 'Over all this vast expanse of waters Japan was supreme.'

Developments on land were not quite so calamitous, but they were bad enough. The next airfield to be abandoned was Butterworth, and Air Vice-Marshal Sir Paul Maltby admitted that some of the RAF and RAAF personnel getting out 'did not behave at all steadily'. Then came Sungei Patani, where large stocks of fuel were left for the enemy. After a couple of days' fighting, Japanese aircraft outnumbered the defending forces by two to one. Penang, off Malaya's west coast, was another island that was supposed to be a 'fortress'. It was an important port, and plenty of ammunition was stored there, but it was still waiting for anti-aircraft guns to be delivered. For three days from 10 December, the Japanese bombed and strafed it, setting the main town of Georgetown alight and killing and injuring 2,000 people. They also made another landing on the east coast about 30 miles south of Kota Bharu. Another two airfields were abandoned before the runways could be blown up, and Brigadier Billy Key, defending the central northern state of Kelantan, had to pull his troops back 140 miles down a railway, pursued by enemy soldiers and bombed from the air the whole way. The Japanese now started to bring their tanks into play. The British side had none, and many of the Punjabis and Gurkhas trying to hold a key road junction at Jitra in the north-west had never even seen one, but they fought bravely and threw back the enemy several times. In the end, though, they had to withdraw. The troops were exhausted, and guns, ammunition and vehicles were abandoned. In fact, only a staunch rear-guard action by the Gurkhas prevented the retreat turning into a rout, and all this the invader had achieved in spite of being seriously outnumbered. A Japanese journalist wrote that the British were 'like little spiders routed by mosquitoes'. As stragglers from Jitra headed south, enemy snipers disguised in Malayan dress mingled among them and then ducked into the jungle to fire on them. A crossroads at Gurun, about 30 miles to the south, had been selected as the next place for the retreating forces to hold, but planned defences had not been built because the War Office was not prepared to pay high enough wages to local people. When they got there, the soldiers found themselves bombed from the air, and, to their astonishment, attacked by tanks. They thought enough bridges had been destroyed to hold up enemy armour. Now they had to pull back another 20 miles.

Percival had originally intended to reinforce Penang and defend it to the death, but on 14 December, he decided it could no longer be held. Everything that might be useful to the enemy was supposed to be destroyed, but some of those responsible for sabotage had decided discretion was the better part of valour, so the Japanese were able to take over the radio station and use it to pump out an undiluted diet of anti-British propaganda. They quickly made capital out of the fact that only Europeans were being evacuated from the island, with the local Asian population being left to its own devices. In western Malaya, the defenders did fight some skilful delaying actions, and made the Japanese pay heavily for their gains, and on Boxing Day, there was an orderly evacuation of Ipoh, with stores either removed or destroyed. Percival paid tribute to local civilians who had stayed at their posts until the bitter end, noting that 'Chinese and Eurasian girl operators of the telephone exchange' kept working in the midst of enemy bombs until they were ordered to leave. This contrasted with the view the authorities in Singapore itself took of local people, where there were many summary executions of alleged fifth columnists supposedly working for the enemy. In one case, putting out newly washed sarongs on a bush to dry was deemed to be a signal to Japanese bombers. On New Year's Day, 1942, at the market town of Kampar to the south of Ipoh, the Leicesters and East Surreys fought bravely and doggedly hand-to-hand against attacks made 'with all the well-known bravery and disregard of danger of the Japanese soldier' as Percival put it. Then when ground was lost, the Sikhs launched a ferocious charge through mortar and machine-gun fire to regain it. The battle, said Percival, proved 'that our trained troops, whether they were British or Indian, were superior man for man to the Japanese troops'. But with the enemy ruthlessly exploiting their total command of the sea, and making new landings 30 miles further south and more, Kampar had to be given up on 3 January.

About 40 miles south of the town, on the Slim River, the Hyderabads kept having their position encircled by Japanese troops who sneaked along old, disused roads off the main highway, while the 2nd Argylls were taken completely by surprise when enemy tanks appeared among them. British sappers had been supposed to destroy a crucial road bridge over the river, but a Japanese raiding party got there first and was able to hold it. In fact, the mobility of the Japanese was catching the defenders on the hop everywhere. Lieutenant-Colonel Spencer Chapman watched in awe as they poured along the roads 'on bicycles in parties of 40 or 50 ... travelling as light as they possibly could.... All this was in very marked contrast to our own first-line soldiers' who were 'equipped like Christmas trees', with packs, heavy boots and even great coats 'so that they could hardly walk, much less fight'. By now, said Percival, his troops were suffering from 'utter weariness'. They had been on the move ever since the Japanese had arrived, with little rest, while the enemy's complete supremacy by air and sea was leading to 'a general sense of futility'. Lieutenant-General Bennett, on the other hand, blamed the constant reverses on a lack of 'aggressive spirit' among unit commanders.

Singapore's first reinforcements had arrived on 3 January from the 45th Indian Infantry Brigade. Most had enlisted only a few months earlier and had never fought before. Percival described them as 'very young, unseasoned and under-trained'. Such training as they had undergone had been for fighting in the very different conditions of the Middle East. On 7 January, Percival's superior, General Sir Archibald Wavell, the supreme commander in the region, made a fleeting visit to the front line. He was dismayed at the poor state of the troops, and ordered a further withdrawal. Percival drew up plans to stop the Japanese taking the Malayan capital, Kuala Lumpur, and keep them off the airfields nearest to Singapore for at least a couple of weeks to enable further reinforcements to be brought in, but the Japanese continued to pour their own reinforcements in through the Malayan ports they had captured. On 9 January, they overran the town of Kuala Selangor, about 30 miles from the capital. The following day, the 28th Indian Brigade fell back under heavy artillery and air attack, intending to regroup at Serandah village, 15 miles north of the capital, but they found it was already in Japanese hands and had to fight their way through it. On 11 January, Kuala Lumpur was abandoned. By now Singapore itself was being bombed almost every day, and the inadequacy of its radar defences and anti-aircraft guns was being cruelly demonstrated.

The new arrivals of the 45th Indian Brigade were put under Lieutenant-General Bennett with his Australians to protect a line to the south of Kuala Lumpur, which ran from the central mountain chain to the Malacca Straits. On 14 January the 27th Australian Brigade mounted a clever ambush at a bridge near Gemas, but by the next day, Japanese sappers had repaired it and their aircraft were dive-bombing Australian positions. Meanwhile, 40 miles to the south, the enemy were bombing the seaport of Muar, held by the raw troops of the 45th, and on 15 January, the crack Japanese 5th Guards Regiment completely overran them, killing nearly all of their officers, while other Japanese soldiers landed at Batu Pahat, 25 miles further down the west coast. Singapore's second instalment of reinforcements had arrived on 13 January: the 53rd Brigade Group were British territorials who had been on their way to the Middle East when they were diverted. They had been at sea for three months. Few had ever been abroad before, and none had any jungle training. Now they too were about to get a baptism of fire, as they were moved up to join Bennett's force. At this point, the most advanced Japanese forces were hundreds of miles from their bases, and a determined counter-attack might have caused them real trouble. So the 45th were ordered to re-take Muar in a three-pronged attack, but one prong stumbled straight into a Japanese ambush, and the offensive was cancelled. Instead, the Japanese mounted a fierce counter-attack of their own on Bakri where most of the 45th was based. Percival admitted that the inexperienced Indians were virtually helpless: 'they did not even know how to take cover'. It looked as though all British forces in the area might soon be surrounded, and Bennett ordered a withdrawal along the road to Yong Peng, but once again the Japanese had got there first, having driven out the 53rd after a fierce fight. The British had no wireless to tell headquarters what had happened. As Indians and Australians poured south, they were attacked by tanks, artillery and low-flying aircraft and suffered heavy casualties. Eventually

Lieutenant-Colonel Charles Anderson ordered his men to leave behind all their guns, vehicles and equipment and try to escape through the jungle. Out of 4,000, only about 900 got through. Those wounded who had been left behind were murdered by the Japanese in cold blood, while about 200 Australian and Indian prisoners were beheaded by troops commanded by Lieutenant-General Takuma Nishimura near Parit Sulong.

Churchill was now getting alarmed at the speed with which the Japanese were careering down the peninsula, and cabled Wavell on 15 January to ask what defences existed on the landward side of Singapore if British forces should be pushed out of Malaya. 'Little or nothing' was Wavell's reply, 'until quite recently all plans were based on repulsing seaborne attacks on the Island and holding land attack ... farther north'. Churchill exploded. He was 'staggered'. It was 'incredible' that the 'fortress' could do no better than this. On 20 January, he set out a ten-point plan, including strong points for artillery, mining and booby-trapping, to be carried out by mobilising the entire male population of the island. He added the message: 'I expect every inch of ground to de defended ... and no question of surrender to be entertained until after protracted fighting among the ruins of Singapore City.' However, the prime minister's words were not quite as clear-cut as they seemed, because the next day, he was writing to the chiefs of staff: 'Obviously nothing should distract us from the Battle of Singapore, but should Singapore fall quick transference of forces to Burma might be possible.' Wavell responded that if the south of Malaya fell, Singapore could not be held for long and wondered whether reinforcements currently on their way should be diverted to Burma. When the Australian prime minister, John Curtin, heard about this, it was his turn to be enraged. Such a move would be an 'inexcusable betrayal'. The Australians had been assured that Singapore was being made 'impregnable'. Accordingly, on 23 January, yet more reinforcements arrived, though these included some Australian troops who had received virtually no training – 'recruited on a Friday and put on a boat for Malaya the following week', in Bennett's words.

Wavell may have said that Singapore's days were numbered once Malaya fell, but by 19 January, he was already telling Percival to draw up a plan for a retreat from the mainland and the continuance of resistance on the island. There was still the occasional minor success for the British side, like a determined Sikh bayonet charge that drove the Japanese from Kluang airfield on 23 January with heavy losses. Three days later, however, the Japanese made a major new landing well down the east coast at Endau, about 70 miles from Singapore, and although an Australian battalion mounted a successful ambush, by 27 January, Percival was telling Wavell that the situation was 'very critical'. He had just nine fighters left in Malaya, and, with his commander's approval, he decided to withdraw all forces to Singapore on the night of 30 January. Even that did not go according to plan. The 22nd Indian Brigade was short of ammunition and completely isolated. It had no radios and the telegraph line had been destroyed. Its commander, Brigadier George Painter, ordered the men to try to get back through the jungle, where malaria, dysentery and other diseases took their toll. Painter was among those eventually captured, and only about 100 managed to make their way to Singapore.

Once the last retreating troops were across, the causeway was blown up, leaving a gap 70-feet wide. The drawbridge was up at the island fortress! Its population of half a million was now doubled by refugees from the mainland. The main city and the last remaining airfield, Kallang, were at the far southern end. The other three had been abandoned because of Japanese bombing. The coastline was 70 miles long, and proper beach defences such as pill-boxes, mines, barbed wire, and anti-boat and anti-tank obstacles were to be found only on the eastern side. Getting local people to work on additional defences had proved impossible with Japanese bombs constantly crashing down. Singapore's huge guns were designed to repel an enemy approaching from the east, and some could fire in that direction alone, while even those that could be swung around were equipped only with armour-piercing shells, which were effective against ships, but much less so against infantry. Percival had about 85,000 men, but these included 15,000 administrative staff and non-combatants, and many of the others were not really first-line combat troops. The floating dock had already been scuttled and its staff evacuated to Ceylon. There was supposed to be a month's supply of food, but ammunition was having to be rationed, and morale was plummeting alarmingly. As another lot of reinforcements arrived on 5 February, one of its transports, the *Empress of Asia*, was sunk by dive-bombers. Most of the men on board were rescued, but nearly all their weapons and equipment went to the bottom.

Three days later the Japanese mounted a ferocious bombardment, and just before 11pm that night, the first invaders came ashore. Some arrived in landing craft, but others swam across the ½-mile wide straits. They attacked along a 9-mile front on the north and west shores, and because their shells had knocked out the field telephone system, the artillery got no orders to fire until the Japanese had a firm footing. The invaders did take some heavy losses, but within the hour they were sufficiently well established to start ferrying artillery, tanks and ammunition across from the mainland. By the next morning, they had 23,000 troops on the island. It was just like Malaya all over again. The Australians in the west were quickly forced onto the defensive, but when they tried to withdraw to prepared positions in the village of Ama Keng, they found the enemy had already occupied it. That night, Percival had to throw in the last of his reserves, and the last aircraft left the island because Kallang was now too dangerous to use. Meanwhile, the Japanese were making fresh landings. Australian sappers detailed to blow up an oil depot, opened the taps first, so that when they detonated the charge, it sent a wall of flame into the swamps where the Japanese were hiding, killing many of them. The invaders were surprised that Percival had not used this tactic more often. Soon the defenders were forced to abandon the causeway. They might have blown a hole in it, but at low tide, the missing section was only 4 feet below the water, and men could easily wade across.

Confusion began to take over. Percival had drawn up a contingency plan to withdraw all forces to a small perimeter around Singapore City, but Brigadier Harold Taylor on the west of the island took it as an order to be implemented immediately, and started to pull his troops back. The Japanese poured into the gap. Other commanders made the same mistake, and soon the withdrawal was out of control. At this point Wavell made a further brief appearance to deliver another invigorating message: surrender was out of the question. Churchill wrote to Wavell that night:

> It was reported to Cabinet by the CIGS that Percival has over 100,000 men [this figure was too high, but the defenders did outnumber the 35,000 Japanese on the island by more than two to one].... It is doubtful whether the Japanese have as many in the whole Malay Peninsula.... In these circumstances the defenders must greatly outnumber Japanese forces who have crossed the straits, and in a well-contested battle they should destroy them. There must at this stage be no thought of saving the troops or sparing the population. The battle must be fought to the bitter end.

Wavell sent a gloomy reply: things were 'not going well'. The Japanese were 'getting on much more rapidly than they should' while British morale was 'not good' and some soldiers had an 'inferiority complex which bold and skilful Japanese tactics and their command of the air have caused'. As 10 February ended, Japanese tanks smashed their way through Hyderabadi troops around Bukit Panjang village. In view of the brutality the Japanese had shown in the other territories that they had conquered, a major preoccupation now was to evacuate the many female nurses still in Singapore. On 11 February about 2,000 got away on the *Empire Star* in spite of attacks by Japanese aircraft, but many evacuees drowned when another ship was sunk, and at Radji beach, a Japanese patrol found thirty-four nurses and patients waiting to leave, and slaughtered them.

The Japanese had allocated 100 days to take Malaya and Singapore. By 12 February, they had used up only sixty-seven, and already the British were dismantling the radio station and burning the banknotes. The city was full of armed deserters who lurked in cellars, prowled the city in search of loot, or tried to fight their way aboard any ship that was leaving. A number of food depots were now behind Japanese lines, and there was only a week's supply left, while water was desperately short because Japanese bombing had damaged so many water mains. The streets were blocked by bomb craters, disabled vehicles, collapsed buildings and dead bodies. Bennett and other commanders advised an early surrender, but Percival said they must fight on, and Wavell cabled his agreement: 'You must continue to inflict maximum damage on enemy for as long as possible by house-to-house fighting if necessary.' By this stage, one RAF officer described Percival as being in 'a state of dither. He appeared utterly broken.' On 14 February, the enemy entered the Alexandra Military Hospital. They claimed they had been fired on, and bayoneted medical officers, orderlies and patients, including one on an operating table. The next morning, they shot another 200; that day became known as 'Black Sunday'. There was only twenty-four hours' water supply left and ammunition had almost run out. Percival called his commanders together, and said it would have to be counter-attack or capitulation. A new telegram arrived from Wavell with more inspiring words, but a let-out clause: when Percival was 'fully satisfied' that he was no longer able 'to inflict loss and damage to enemy' then he had 'discretion to cease resistance'. In fact, an organised counter-attack might still have met with some success, for the Japanese were dangerously short of supplies, but the commanders agreed that none was possible, and immediately sent a delegation to discuss surrender. The next day Percival signed the capitulation at the Ford Motor Works on the outskirts of the city, and 85,000 British and British Empire soldiers became prisoners of war. Some of the reinforcements who arrived on 5 February had never even fired a shot.

The Japanese lost little more than 3,500 men in the conquest of Malaya and Singapore, the greatest city in South East Asia, and were astonished at how overwhelming their victory was. General Tomoyuki Yamashita had been confident enough to commit only 35,000 of his troops to the attack on the island, leaving a similar number behind in Malaya. During the whole campaign, British forces could not boast of a single significant success, and the spectacle of their relentless flight before the foe was a blow to Britain's prestige in the region from which it would never recover. One of the reasons for Percival's surrender was to spare the civilian population from the kind of atrocities that followed other Japanese conquests, but the fall of Singapore was followed by the murder of perhaps 50,000 ethnic Chinese in the city. After the war, General Yamashita was executed for war crimes in the Philippines and Lieutenant-General Nishimura for the massacre at Parit Sulong. Thousands of the Indian soldiers taken into captivity changed sides and fought in Japan's 'Indian National Army', but many others – including the Gurkhas – refused to a man, even in the face of threats and torture. Of the other prisoners taken at Singapore, at least 10,000 died of disease or were worked to death. Percival himself spent the rest of the war in a variety of Japanese camps. Maltreated and malnourished, he was freed in time to be present at Japan's formal surrender in September 1945. On his return to Britain, he was not awarded the customary knighthood for soldiers of his rank. He became president of the Far Eastern Prisoners of War Association and campaigned hard for them to be compensated by the Japanese, but could never live down his role in the loss of Singapore. Brooke-Popham, who had retired and left the island on 27 December 1941, had been pencilled in for a baronetcy, but this honour too became a casualty of the military disaster. The official Australian history of the war, however, asserted that the real blame lay much further up the chain of command, pointing to the Japanese 'monopoly of tanks', the lack of aircraft and the inexperience of many of the troops.

Bibliography

Asher, M., *Khartoum. The Ultimate Imperial Adventure*. (Viking, 2005, London).

Calvocoressi, P., Wint, G., and Pritchard, J., *Total War. The Causes and Courses of the Second World War, vol 2*. (Penguin, 1989, London).

David, S., *Zulu, The Heroism and Tragedy of the Zulu War of 1879*. (Penguin, 2005, London).

Deighton, L., *Blitzkrieg. From the Rise of Hitler to the Fall of Dunkirk*. (Castle Books, 2000, Edison, N.J).

Ensor, R.C.K., *England 1870–1914*. (Oxford University Press, 1949, London).

Gardiner, J. and Wenborn, N., *The History Today Companion to British History*. (Collins & Brown, 1995, London).

Gilbert, M., *Somme. The Heroism and Horror of War*. (John Murray, 2006, London).

Hibbert, C., *Redcoats and Rebels. The War for America 1770–81*. (Grafton, 1993, London).

Key, R., *The Most Distressful Country*. (Quartet, 1976, London).

Lloyd, A., *The Hundred Years War*. (Book Club Associates, 1977, London).

Macdonald, L., *1914–18. Voices and Images of the Great War*. (Penguin, 1991, London).

McLynn, F., *1066. The Year of the Three Battles*. (Jonathan Cape, 1998, London).

Meyer, K. and Brysac, S., *Tournament of Shadows. The Great Game and the Race for Empire in Asia*. (Abacus, 1999, London).

Morris, J., *Heaven's Command. An Imperial Progress*. (Penguin, 1973, Harmondsworth).

Ogg, D., *England in the reign of Charles II*. (Oxford University Press, 1963, London).

Owen, F., *The Fall of Singapore*. (Penguin, 2001, London).

Pakenham, T., *The Boer War. Illustrated Edition*. (Weidenfeld and Nicolson, 1993, London).

Pakenham, T., *The Year of Liberty. The Story of the Great Irish Rebellion of 1798*. (Weidenfeld & Nicolson, 1998, London).

Pakenham, T., *The Scramble for Africa. 1876–1912*. (Abacus, 1992, London).

Pearson, M., *Those Damned Rebels. The American Revolution as seen Through British Eyes*. (Da Capo Press, 1972, United States).

Pepys, S., *The Diary of Samuel Pepys, (3vs v2)*. (Dent, 1982, London).

Perry, J.M., *Arrogant Armies. Great Military Disasters and the Generals Behind Them*. (John Wiley & Sons, 1996, New York).

Bibliography

Ponting, C., *The Crimean War. The Truth Behind the Myth*. (Pimlico, 2004, London).

Prebble, J., *The Lion in the North. A Personal View of Scotland's History*. (Penguin, 1981, London).

Prior, R., *Gallipoli. The End of the Myth*. (Yale University Press, 2009, New Haven and London).

Remini, R. V., *The Battle of New Orleans. Andrew Jackson and America's First Military Victory*. (Penguin, 2001, London).

Ross, C., *The Wars of the Roses. A Concise History*. (Thames and Hudson, 1976, London).

Royle, T., *Crimea. The Great Crimean War 1854–56*. (Little, Brown and Co., 1999, London).

Salway, P., *Roman Britain*. (Oxford University Press, 1981, Oxford).

Sebag-Montefiore, H., *Dunkirk. Fight to the Last Man*. (Viking, 2006, London).

Seward, D., *The Hundred Years War. The English in France 1337–1453*. (Constable, 1978, London).

Smith, C., *Singapore Burning. Heroism and Surrender in World War II*. (Viking, 2005, London).

Smurthwaite, D., *The Complete Guide to the Battlefields of Britain*. (Mermaid, 1993, London).

Stenton, F. M., *Anglo-Saxon England*. (Oxford University Press, 1971, London).

Steven Watson, J., *The Reign of George III. 1760–1815*. (Oxford University Press, 1960, London).

Tanner, S., *Afghanistan. A Military History from Alexander the Great to the Fall of the Taliban*. (Da Capo Press, 2002, Cambridge, Ma.).

Taylor, A.J.P., *The First World War. An Illustrated History*. (Penguin, 1966, London).

Taylor, A.J.P., *The Second World War. An Illustrated History*. (Penguin, 1976, Harmondsworth).

Williams, B., *The Whig Supremacy. 1714–60*. (Oxford University Press, 1960, Oxford).

Woodham-Smith, C., *The Reason Why*. (Penguin, 1958, London).

Wright, E (ed)., *The Fire of Liberty*. (Hamish Hamilton, 1984, London).

Index

Index

Index

Index